Passage Through Abortion

Mary K. Zimmerman

foreword by
Harold Finestone

The Praeger Special Studies program, through a selective worldwide distribution network, makes available to the academic, government, and business communities significant and timely research in U.S. and international economic, social, and political issues.

Passage Through Abortion

The Personal and Social Reality of Women's Experiences

PRAEGER SPECIAL STUDIES IN U.S. ECONOMIC, SOCIAL, AND POLITICAL ISSUES

Praeger Publishers   New York   London

Library of Congress Cataloging in Publication Data

Zimmerman, Mary K
    Passage through abortion.

    (Praeger special studies in U.S. economic, social,
and political issues)
    Bibliography: p.
    Includes index.
    1. Abortion—United States.   2. Pregnancy, Unwanted—
United States.   3. Abortion—United States—Biography.
I. Title.
HQ767.5.U5Z55   1977   301   77-12742
ISBN 0-03-029816-4

The author gratefully acknowledges permission to reprint the following
material: Figure 1.1 reprinted with permission from *Family Planning Perspectives*, September/October 1975; Table 1.1 reprinted with permission from
the Center for Disease Control: Abortion Surveillance, 1975; Figure 1.2 reprinted with permission from the Center for Disease Control: Abortion Surveillance, 1975; portions of Table 3.5 reprinted with permission from the
Center for Disease Control: Abortion Surveillance, 1975; portions of Table 4.3
published by permission of Transaction, Inc. from Trans-Action, Vol. 3,
#6, Copyright © 1966 by Transaction, Inc.; portions of Table 4.3 reprinted
with permission from *Family Planning Perspectives*, May/June 1976, and Dr.
William Arney.

PRAEGER SPECIAL STUDIES
200 Park Avenue, New York, N.Y., 10017, U.S.A.

Published in the United States of America in 1977
by Praeger Publishers,
A Division of Holt, Rinehart and Winston, CBS, Inc.

789   038   987654321

Printed in the United States of America

To my parents, John and Gwendolyn,
and to my husband, Burton.

In bringing to light many aspects of the abortion experience, a contingency forced upon millions of women by unwanted pregnancy, Mary Zimmerman's analysis is assisted by the nature of her methodological stance. She relies almost exclusively upon the perspective of her subjects. The possible traps of subjectivism and personal bias are checked on her part by careful preparation for the interviews, self-discipline in conducting them, and presentation in tabular or quantitative form of the evidence bearing upon all key points in the analysis.

The author's attention to the network of personal relationships within which her interviewees were involved, and which comprised the immediate context for the experience of abortion, does not preclude her being concerned with the broader sociological implications of her findings. At least two such implications may be noted.

First, following the lead of Durkheim's analysis of suicide, she finds that abortion, too, is not solely a private or an interpersonal matter. It involves not only "significant others," but also norms, "generalized others," or "collective representations," whose group reference far transcends the subjects' immediate social circle. These norms are in the domain of the "community" and "society."

Secondly, she finds that social change such as is involved in the legalizations of abortion exacts severe personal costs from the women she studied. The legitimizing of abortion, followed by the provision of institutional settings where abortions are routinely obtainable—although not uniformly available—has not been accompanied by parallel changes in the moral definitions of abortion. Among many, abortion continues to be viewed as an immoral act. For the individuals involved in this study, the author indicates that the guilt feelings which result from the discrepancy between what is legally permissible and moral belief is the price which they must pay. She suggests that their modes of dealing with such guilt are rather fragile and ultimately experienced as unsatisfactory.

It is through such findings and their interpretation that the author endeavors to fulfill her objective of analyzing abortion as an experience whose understanding necessarily involves the laws, the institutions, and the moral beliefs prevalent in our society, as well as the personal relationships of the women who make this choice. In recent years, women have won new freedoms over the disposition of their lives, but at the same time they have paid for these gains by having to confront unprecedented moral dilemmas and vulnerabilities. Their experience teaches us all the lesson that social change in important spheres of living requires moral change and that such change takes its toll from those most directly affected. That her findings attain such import is a tribute to the skill and devoted care with which the author undertook this study of the abortion experience.

ACKNOWLEDGMENTS

This project began in 1973, the same year the United States Supreme Court reached its controversial decision on abortion. It was transported nearly halfway across the country before its completion. During the more than three years and across the many miles, there have been many persons to whom I am deeply indebted. They encouraged me and sustained me in what, at some points along the way, I felt certain was a fruitless effort.

Foremost among these persons is my research adviser, Harold Finestone, whose sensitive knowledge of social theory and refreshing, consistent approach to methodology have been a source of inspiration throughout the course of my work. I am also very grateful to Richard Hall, Theodor Litman, David Cooperman, and Beulah Compton for their suggestions and encouragement. Very special thanks must go to my friend and colleague, Wynona S. Hartley. Her enthusiastic support and understanding have fortified me at many times during this project.

I owe a great debt to the various health care organizations who cooperated so generously with me at all stages of the research. Specific individuals cannot be named, but without their voluntary efforts this study could never have been done.

Thanks should also go to the University of Minnesota Graduate School for providing me with a research grant in the initial stages of the study. As the research progressed, Mary Kovac provided invaluable help in transcribing interview tapes and in typing the manuscript. Finally, I would like to thank a most exacting editor, my mother, Gwendolyn Smith Zimmerman, for devoting her skills to the final manuscript.

Among all these people, those named and those unnamed, the one who has given and endured continuously has been my husband, Burton Halpert. My final thanks is to him.

CONTENTS

LIST OF TABLES AND FIGURES

1

ABORTION
IN PERSPECTIVE

INTRODUCTION

Since the late 1960s abortion has shifted position from an illicit, clandestine activity to one which is legal and open. It has moved from being a verbal taboo to being a frequent topic of conversation. It has become visible, no longer hidden. While this transition has been uneven across the various segments of American society and has emerged out of bitter and emotional controversy, it has been indeed dramatic. And, despite the fact that abortion continues to evoke controversy, the changes persist.

Rapid social transitions leave a wake of confusion in norms and values. In the case of abortion, this process is further compounded by the peculiar ambiguity which historically has accompanied abortion. Specifically, the dominant pattern has been one of ambivalence and lack of clarity between societal standards and societal practices. In antiquity abortion was subject to some debate at the moral and philosophical level, but in practice it was generally approved of and allowed to occur openly. Later, when Christian morality arose proscribing abortion, the societal atmosphere remained one of tolerance; for the most part, the issue was avoided and the practice allowed to continue unrestricted. Only in the last 150 years have societies intervened and restricted abortion in a major way. Even so, it seems that the practice has continued on with much the same frequency as before.

The coexistence of opposite and conflicting feelings about abortion is centuries old. The disjunctures between public policy, private morality, and individual behavior which make up this heritage are sharpened, however, in the current American abortion scene. On the one hand, the legality of abortion renders it acceptable and appropriate behavior. On the other hand, public moral sentiment—partly reflecting the years of severe restriction—tends to cast abortion (under most circumstances) as inappropriate behavior. The continuing controversy over abortion increases the uncertainty. Hence, the ambiguities of the past are still present today, intensified rather than diminished by recent changes.

While a substantial amount of writing and research has been done on the broad social trends related to abortion, very little has been done focusing on the actual *experience* of having an abortion. Where women undergoing abortion have been studied, the emphasis has been limited to the woman's mental condition—to determining either the presence or absence of individual pathology. The social characteristics of abortion experience have been ignored. Virtually nothing is known about how women pass through the various phases of an abortion: what they think, what they do, whom they talk to, how people treat them—in other words, what social patterns characterize the abortion process and what qualities of experience underlie these patterns.

The late C. Wright Mills, an ardent critic of modern social science, challenged sociologists "to understand the larger historical scene in terms of its meaning for the inner life and external career of a variety of individuals," (Mills 1959, p. 5). His view was that, before one can grasp the significance of large-scale social developments, one must have explored them in terms of the individuals involved and their social situations. The study that this book presents is a detailed account of Mills' directive. It is devoted to a description and analysis of the actual abortion passages of a group of typical women from a midwestern community. (In this book, the term "passage" refers to a progression, or course, of events.) The aim is to capture the qualities and patterns of abortion experience. The ultimate goal is to better understand the "real" significance of the changing status of abortion in contemporary society.

We begin our task in this chapter by outlining the current abortion scene in terms of its broad dimensions—social, political, and demographic trends. This view is presented to provide perspective, a background against which we can explore the central concern of this book. First, however, let us consider our research problem in more specific detail.

THE NATURE OF ABORTION EXPERIENCE

The mental and behavioral aspects of abortion have been studied up to now almost exclusively from a clinical rather than a social scientific viewpoint, with the consequence that emphasis has been placed on psychiatric disorder rather than on social roles, relationships, and interaction patterns. There has been little consideration of women's social worlds. Instead, when reactions to abortion have been observed, they have been interpreted as reflections of an underlying (permanently established) personality structure, or as the outward manifestation of various (inevitable) psychosexual processes. Women's reactions have been assumed to emanate from deeply internal or internalized patterns. The evidence that social action is largely a product of the situational demands and constraints of the present, mediated but not determined by what has occurred previously, has been completely ignored.

Until the late 1960s the overwhelming conclusion drawn from clinical research was that abortion constitutes a severe psychological trauma for normal women and is likely to increase the pathology of already disturbed women (see Chapter 2). Stimulated by the social changes of the last decade, however, recent and more systematic research has been conducted showing that abortion is *not* severely traumatic (see Chapter 2). One study, for example, compared abortion to childbirth and found abortion to be *less* harmful psychologically (Athanasiou et al. 1973). At present the evidence is clearly weighted against the trauma theory.

Beyond the issue of long-lasting emotional scars, disagreement still exists in both lay and clinical communities over the degree to which abortion disrupts women's lives on a short-term basis. Some believe that, while it may not always produce long-term psychological disorder, abortion still causes considerable upheaval in terms of emotional stress, confusion, ambivalence, and general social and mental disruption (see Chapter 2). Others deny that most women experience abortion with much interruption of their normal, everyday social patterns. They argue that women who choose to have an abortion are those for whom it presents few problems (see, for example, Rosen and Martindale 1975). Partly because of self-selection, according to this view, abortion is experienced relatively smoothly—for the most part, not very differently from any other minor medical procedure. It is not a pleasant event, but neither is it an extremely disruptive one. In sum, the disagreement boils down to whether or not abortion presents women with a major crisis.

Perhaps because the "abortion as crisis" view has been frequently aligned with the antiabortion movement, and the "abortion as harmless" view has been used by those who favor abortion, this disagreement has tended to be seen as an either/or issue. That is, either abortion is viewed as a crisis or not; either it constitutes a major disruption or it does not. The fact that abortion experience cannot be viewed so uniformly becomes clear when one compares the following two statements. (The quotations that appear in this book from the interviews with the women subjects frequently include in parentheses the interviewer's questions. Following each quotation, also in parentheses, is the subject's identification number.)

> I felt toward it like I had decided I had to have surgery. . . . (How about the day of the abortion?) I was pretty nervous, pretty apprehensive, but then I was nervous when I went in for my gall bladder. . . . Actually, really I enjoyed it. It was pleasant. I enjoyed the whole thing. . . . (5)

I really don't remember anything. All I remember is lots of pain. . . .
(Can you remember anything about the day of the abortion?) Just
pain. My mom and dad took me up. Like, I almost freaked out. I
tried—I wanted to talk to Dad so bad, but I couldn't. It was already
started and he [the doctor] couldn't quit . . . there is no way I could
go through that again. (18)

Abortion, like other social experiences, is enacted and reacted to variably.

A few social scientists are exceptions to this "either/or" trend, having
studied abortion experience and found differential patterns (see Chapter 2).
They define these patterns narrowly, however, in terms of psychological states
such as guilt, stress, and anxiety, reminiscent of clinical research. The authors of
these studies then try to explain the variation in terms of deeply internalized
attitudinal and belief differences thought to be associated with various religious
groups, social classes, or social roles. Like clinical researchers, these social scientists have neglected the important impact of women's immediate social
worlds—their social positions, degree of integration into social life, and relationships with others.

This study approaches abortion experience from the standpoint of crisis or
degree of disruption and focuses on immediate social factors in the women's
lives. The remainder of this section examines the theoretical linkages between
these two elements.

Thomas (Volkhart 1951) views the experiences of everyday life as a series
of situations. Persons are seen as continually passing through situation after
situation. Each situation and the person's own role in it must be defined so that
the person can act and can pass on to the next situation. In order to make sense
of each new situation, persons construct "schemes" or sets of parameters en-
compassing "normal" situations and behavior. All experience encountered which
falls within these parameters can easily be made sense of. The parameters demarcate standard elements so that upon entering a new situation the person
identifies the elements in that situation which are similar to those of previously
experienced situations. She or he is thereby able to render the new one under-
standable.

When the new situation is within the normal range, the process of defining
occurs in a taken-for-granted way. In situations where the elements fall outside
the parameters of normality, however, the person has to stop and take stock of
the situation and her role in it and must construct a definition in order to act:

. . . social situations never spontaneously repeat themselves, every
situation is more or less new. . . . The individual does not find
passively ready situations exactly similar to certain past situations.
. . . The individual in order to control social reality for his needs,
must develop . . . general schemes of situations. . . . Of course, every
important and unexpected change in the conditions of life results . . .

> in a disorganization of activity. As long as he can, he still applies the old schemes . . . but, as soon as the results of his activity become unsuccessful even in his own eyes, he is entirely lost; the situation becomes for him completely vague and undetermined. (Thomas in Volkhart 1951, p. 158–60)

Situations which are not immediately sensible—for which existing "schemes" do not work—we designate as problematic situations. Following Strauss (1959) we can further suggest that such problematic situations, in contrast to routine ones, put the individual's identity in question and may result in a major redefinition which Strauss calls a "turning point."

The women in this study who experienced abortion were certainly confronted with a "problematic" situation. It was problematic in the sense that, for them, pregnancy constituted, to use Thomas's words, an "important and unexpected change in the conditions of life." Unplanned pregnancy calls for a new "scheme" or definition of the situation. An orientation toward resolving the pregnancy through abortion increases the problematic nature of the situation—hence, the difficulty of coming to terms with it—because abortion involves the implications of deviance and stigma. In such cases, according to Thomas, the person is confused and "is ready to accept any definition that is suggested to him" (Volkhart 1951, p. 160).

Implicit in Thomas's analysis of new and problematic situations and how persons come to terms with them is the importance of other persons. Interactionist theory emphasizes the importance of others in all human interaction (Mead 1934; Blumer 1969). According to this view, because humans can think and can construct symbols, they attribute all the objects of their world with meaning. This symbolic meaning is not the product of one individual, however, but rather emerges out of joint and reciprocal interaction among individuals. In other words, the meaning of objects is negotiated and constructed socially.

Objects include not only physical entities but social entities as well. Abortion, therefore, can be considered as a social object—an object with social meaning. Following interactionist theory, the symbolic meaning of abortion for the woman—the definition of a "problematic situation" in Thomas's view—is a product of the woman's interaction with others. Hence, it is important for this study to examine carefully with whom the woman interacts and the nature of that interaction.

In addition to the specific nature and qualities of social relationships, a person's overall integration into society is also important in routinizing a problematic situation. Durkheim (1951) was central in pointing out the shielding effect upon the individual of being closely bonded to others in social group affiliations:

> There is, in short, in a cohesive and animated society a constant interchange of ideas and feelings from all to each and each to all,

something like a mutual moral support, which instead of throwing the individual on his own resources, leads him to share in the collective energy and supports his own when exhausted . . . he needs others. Because he is a more complex being, he can maintain his equilibrium only by finding more points of support outside himself. (Durkheim 1951, pp. 210, 214)

Well-integrated social groups give persons insulation, protecting them from potentially disruptive experiences. Thus, being closely affiliated with others in well-defined social roles having some degree of continuity (what we shall later refer to as "affiliation") is another important factor to be examined in this study.

These theoretical ideas form the research perspective of this study. To summarize, abortion and the pregnancy it terminates constitute a new and problematic situation for the women involved. This situation is particularly problematic because implications of deviance for the women are evoked. Women must construct meaning for their situations to make sense of them, reducing the problematic aspects so that they may move on to new experiences. Since meaning is established through interaction with others, and because of the protecting and smoothing effect of social involvement, the women's social participation and social relationships are of central concern.

Let us now move on to consider the major social trends which serve as the backdrop for the study.

ABORTION IN HISTORY: A TRADITION OF AMBIGUITY

Induced abortion appears to be as old as civilization itself.* Anthropologists suggest that it is a universal feature of all societies, having held an important role in the limitation of births for all groups. In preliterate societies it was the chief "preventive" method. Early documentation for this claim is sparse, but evidence does exist. The earliest reference to an abortion-producing agent occurs in an ancient Chinese medical work dated approximately 2700 B.C. Old Testament Jews were evidently familiar with abortion, as it is mentioned in their writings. Mention is also found in the laws of ancient Mesopotamia.

---

*Material for the first part of this section is drawn from Aptekar (1931), Devereaux (1955), Himes (1963), Bates and Zawadzki (1964), and Schwartz (1968). Material for the latter portion dealing with the United States comes from Kimmey (1973) and Sarvis and Rodman (1973).

The frequency of occurrence is difficult to estimate for early societies, but most writers conclude that abortion was relatively common. There is sound evidence of its prevalence in ancient Greece and Rome. In Greece, abortions were commonplace and institutionalized to the extent that a group of midwives performed them as an explicit part of their duties. While there were some ancient Greeks who wanted abortion prohibited, others including Plato and Aristotle encouraged it as a method of maintaining desired family size. For this purpose, abortion was recommended as a matter of public policy. In Rome, abortion appears to have been enacted freely until the decline of the Empire. At that time, it was forbidden on the grounds that it deprived the Roman husband of his offspring.

The evidence suggests that abortion was treated casually until the emergence of Christianity. While there were probably few societies which gave it totally unqualified approval, the practice was nevertheless allowed to continue openly and without intervention. It would appear that abortion in pre-Christian times was not considered particularly reprehensible.

There were two times prior to the emergence of Christianity when abortion was notably opposed—by the Hebrews during Old Testament times and again by the Romans in the later stages of the Empire. Modern writers point out that these were also periods of great concern for the survival and expansion of these societies. They argue that antiabortion sentiment emerged out of practical rather than purely moral concerns. Specifically, stands against abortion were taken in order to help increase the birth rate.

A similar argument has been offered to account for the position taken by early Christians. With the rise of Christianity came the origin of the view that abortion is deeply immoral. The Christian attitude held that once a woman is pregnant it is by the will of God, and nothing should be done to interfere, regardless of the circumstances. It may well be, as some have suggested, that the desire to increase Christian populations was behind this view. Whatever the source, it constituted a marked departure from previous definitions of abortion. It is true that early Jewish teachings had discouraged abortion except in cases of danger to the mother's health, but the Christian view was much more intense in its prohibition.

The Christians' concern with abortion also involved the issues surrounding the point at which life begins. The conclusion they reached in this matter was that the fetus possesses a soul from the moment of conception and, hence, constitutes "life" in the fullest sense. With this belief, the notion of abortion as crime was established—a view which was unknown in previous times.

The criminal nature of abortion was further accentuated in the Middle Ages when abortion was explicitly equated with murder. An official statement to this effect was made at the Diet of Worms in 1521. During this same period, however, there is evidence that abortions continued to be performed frequently, particularly within European aristocratic circles. In 1650, the Dean of the

Faculty of Medicine in Paris wrote of the large group of abortionists who were constantly busy destroying the evidence of the sexual activities of the French nobility.

Generally speaking, a hiatus between religious teaching and public practices with respect to abortion has continued from early Christian times into the present within Western societies. The place of abortion in the Orient has not been as well reported. It is known, however, that abortion was practiced; and the general assumption is that it was not considered as reprehensible an act as it was in the West.

Keeping our attention on the West, we come to a major turning point which occurred in the nineteenth century.

In the United States, as in Europe, abortion was not regulated significantly by the state until the 1800s. The first restrictive abortion statute was passed by the British Parliament in 1803. This law made the abortion of a "quick" fetus (where there was recognizable movement of the fetus *in utero*) a capital offense. Before quickening, abortion was treated as a lesser offense. Prior to this statute England had gone by a common-law ruling that a woman had the right to terminate a pregnancy at any time.

The first United States law was passed by the state of Connecticut in 1821. It paralleled the English law, forbidding abortions in all cases after quickening. The death penalty was *not* imposed. The second United States law was embodied in the New York Revised Statutes of 1829. This law differed significantly from the first in that it provided a therapeutic exception: abortion was permitted if necessary to save the potential mother's life. It also considered abortion *before* quickening to be a crime, although a lesser one. It was this second law which served as a model for most abortion laws passed subsequently by the other states. Later in the nineteenth century, the quickening distinction disappeared and penalties increased. Until 1967 almost all state laws limited abortions to those necessary to preserve the life of the pregnant woman. A few states also allowed the health of the woman as an acceptable therapeutic indicator.

There is an ongoing debate among scholars as to the original intent of the early United States laws (Sarvis and Rodman 1973). Some argue that these laws were designed to protect the life of the unborn—a moral rationale. Others, however, argue that the initial intent was primarily practical and medical in nature—specifically, to protect women from the surgical dangers of abortion. In 1958, the New Jersey Supreme Court said of that state's law (patterned on the New York model), "The design of the statute was not to prevent the procuring of abortions so much as to guard the health and life of the mother against the consequences of such attempts" (Kimmey 1973, p. 49).

It would appear that the strong moral connotations later attributed to restrictive abortion laws were absent at the laws' inception.* Thus, through

---

*A similar observation has been made in the case of narcotics laws (Duster 1970).

most of the nineteenth century, American women lived with less moral and legal restriction than in more recent times.

The frequency of abortions in the United States during the nineteenth and early twentieth centuries can only be estimated from physicians' reports. In his 1910 book on abortion, Taussig presents his own investigations and those of his colleagues, concluding that approximately 25 percent of all pregnancies were terminated by induced abortion. He goes on to add, "No doubt the actual number is even considerably higher than this" (Taussig 1910, p. 5). Within the two decades that followed, other studies suggested that the number of induced abortions in the United States ranged somewhere between one-half million and two million (Villard 1926; Spengler 1931). The number of live births numbered 2,113,000 in 1931.* Taking the midpoint of the abortion estimate, the ratio of abortions to live births would have been roughly 1 to 2.

Looking back over the history of abortion in society, two features appear with some regularity.

The first is the vagueness and lack of consensus in cultural standards defining the place of abortion. No society has been entirely successful in establishing abortion as either unequivocally right or unequivocally wrong. In most cases, the appropriateness of abortion has remained vague. Even when, for example, abortion was outlawed in the United States, it was never clear whether this prohibition was intended for medical safety or moral condemnation. Symptomatic of the confusion surrounding the abortion issue has been the overwhelming tendency to avoid the issue as much as possible.

A second relatively persistent feature has been the substantial frequency with which abortions have been performed. Rather than reflecting "the moral decay of modern society," as is so often suggested, substantial numbers of abortions probably have characterized most societies throughout history. Technology and organizational patterns have changed, but women have always had the desire to restrict births. The persistent frequency of abortion is testimony to the inability of any society to successfully stop them.

In summary, normative ambivalence and vagueness, along with a relatively high frequency of occurrence, have characterized abortion historically, creating a sense of cultural ambiguity. As we shall see in the next section, ambiguity continues to characterize present times.

RECENT CHANGES IN THE STATUS OF ABORTION

The recent emergence of abortion as a public issue in the United States and the resulting societal changes can be best understood by using the concept

---

*Statistical Abstracts of the United States, no. 55. Washington: United States Printing Office, 1933: 83.

of legitimation. Legitimation refers to a process of justification (acceptance)—a process whereby an act becomes institutionalized and established as a regular and proper part of the social order.* To analyze the particular case of abortion, legitimation can be differentiated in terms of three types, or levels: symbolic legitimacy, institutional legitimacy, and moral legitimacy.

Symbolic legitimacy (Gusfield 1967) occurs with the public pronouncement by agents of legal-governmental authority that an action or event is acceptable. *Institutional legitimacy*† comes about when the action is incorporated openly into the mainstream of the established institutional structure of society. *Moral legitimacy* exists to the degree that societal members' attitudes confirm the propriety and acceptability of the action in question.

In 1966 abortion was not legitimate at any of these three levels. With respect to symbolic legitimacy, the laws and public behavior of legal-governmental agents condemned abortion. No state allowed abortion except under the most restrictive circumstances. Many states made absolutely no exceptions. At the level of institutional legitimacy, abortion generally was excluded from established institutional settings. Professional medical participation was difficult unless the abortion was somehow disguised. In accordance with legal therapeutic exceptions, some hospitals did perform a small number of abortions each year. The restrictions, however, were severe and the approval process often too lengthy for an abortion to be managed within a medically safe time frame. In the years before 1967, not even 1 percent of all the actual abortions estimated to have occurred were performed legally in appropriate medical surroundings.**

At the third level, moral legitimacy, there was very little public opinion support for abortion in the 1960s. Attitude surveys showed that the majority of Americans considered abortion to be wrong (Blake 1973). This notion of immorality was infused with the shady, back-alley context in which abortion was typically cast. It was an evil, seldom discussed. In the words of one young woman interviewed for this study:

> In our life we were raised up with this thing of abortion being a butcher with a big knife, you know. And, you're going to come out and bleed to death. Abortion became a dirty word. It really did. You know, people—when you say "abortion"—they just kind of shudder. (31)

---

*The idea of legitimation as justification can be found in the writings of Max Weber (see H. Gerth and C. W. Mills, eds. "Politics as a Vocation," *From Max Weber*. New York: Oxford University Press, 1946, p. 78).

†This type of legitimacy is somewhat similar to what Gusfield (1967) refers to as instrumental legitimacy.

**This figure was reached based on 8,000 legal (hospital) abortions in 1966 (Lader 1973) and 1 million total abortions estimated yearly for the same period (see Chapter 2).

Since the late 1960s, abortion has been shifting from this predominantly illegitimate status toward a more legitimate one. The seeds of transition began to germinate on all three levels in the early 1960s. Long before that, however, in the 1920s and 1930s, the issue of fertility control was a very important one in the United States. It is interesting that while there was a significant birth control movement during that time, abortion was generally opposed. Later, during the 1940s and 1950s, through the vehicle of several conferences, health care professionals began to voice concern about the prevalence of illegal abortion. Recommendations designed to lower the incidence of illegal abortion resulted from these endeavors, but virtually no social action did. Finally, in 1962, a dramatic event succeeded in bringing the abortion issue to the attention of the public.

An Arizona woman, Mrs. Sherri Finkbine, had taken the drug thalidomide very early in pregnancy (see Finkbine 1967). Subsequently, she learned of the drug's ability to produce severe deformities in the fetus. She and her husband then arranged for a therapeutic abortion at a local hospital. She also contacted the local newspaper in order to warn others of the danger of the drug. Public reaction to her case was intense and divided. Because of the publicity, medical personnel became afraid of criminal prosecution and refused to permit the abortion. An appeal to the Arizona State Supreme Court failed.

The event became a national controversy—for many, a national scandal. It also was a cause around which new pressure for reform of abortion laws was rallied. The issues evoked by Mrs. Finkbine's situation were intensified over the next few years by the outbreak in 1964 of rubella epidemics. Fear of a deformed or severely damaged baby caused thousands of women to seek abortion. Some succeeded, but many others were denied. As a result of these epidemics and the Finkbine case, the justice of restrictive abortion laws began to be questioned at the public level.*

Observers cite these developments as the beginning of recent changes in the status of abortion in the United States. They also point out, however, the contribution of other intersecting societal trends of the 1960s. Kimmey (1973) notes that both the civil rights movement and the growing openness about human sexuality contributed to the growth of abortion reform. Sarvis and Rodman (1973) add to this the contributing force of the reemerging women's movement, the start of interest in a consumer approach to health care delivery, and the growing alarm over rapidly increasing world population. According to Russell and Jackson (1973), two other factors helped bring the issue of abortion into sharper focus: documentation of criminal abortion as the leading single

---

*Mrs. Finkbine eventually secured a therapeutic abortion in Sweden. The fetus was found to be grossly deformed.

cause of maternal mortality in the United States and the rising illegitimate pregnancy rate.

At the same time the abortion debate was kindled, in 1962, the American Law Institute revised its Model Penal Code. The issue of abortion was included. The revised code stated, "A licensed physician is justified in terminating a pregnancy if he believes there is substantial risk that continuance of the pregnancy would gravely impair the physical or mental health of the mother or that the child would be born with grave physical or mental defect, or that the pregnancy resulted from rape, incest, or other felonious intercourse" (American Law Institute 1962, p. 189). This statement was timely in that it appeared just at the time when many reform groups were organizing. It was adopted by many of these groups as a specific aim for early action to change long-standing, restrictive state laws.

The abortion movement of the 1960s pressed for institutional as well as legal change.

Symbolic legitimation began to occur with the changing of state laws. This process began in 1967 and culminated in the United States Supreme Court decisions of 1973*, which nullified those restrictive laws still in existence. By 1969 nine states had reformed their laws; by 1972 that number had risen to 17 (Smith, Kahan, and Burr 1974). The Court's decisions removed the ability of states to restrict abortion during the first trimester of pregnancy, leaving the abortion decision to the pregnant woman and her physician. The Court further determined that states could regulate the abortion procedure in the second trimester only in ways reasonably related to maternal health. Finally, the states were given the right to restrict abortion in the final trimester except when it might be necessary to preserve the life or health of the potential mother.

Institutional legitimation began in the mid-1960s and is still far from complete. In the early stages, abortion reform groups had to work within a strictly illegal framework. The first step taken was to provide counseling and referral services. While they could not provide women with legitimate, professional care, they could attempt to channel women to the safest, most economical abortions available. They could also attempt to avoid as much as possible approximating the stereotypic abortion situations which horrified most women.

As soon as the first states began to reform old laws, reform groups were able to expand and improve their services, referring thousands of women to areas of the country where legal, high-quality medical facilities were available.

Davis (1973) has studied this early phase of institutional legitimation in the state of Michigan. She points out the key role played by the clergy in this

---

*Doe v. Bolton, 410 U.S., 179 (1973); Roe v. Wade, 410 U.S. 113 (1973).

process: "Under the impetus of the abortion reform movement, a variety of legitimating groups—counseling clergy, cooperating physicians, public health groups, and women's liberation counselors—came together under the clergy mantle to promote abortion services" (Davis 1973, p. 262). What eventually emerged by the latter 1960s was a new alternative health delivery system, a network of services encouraging "openness and rational discussion" and discouraging the existent economic and social barriers to abortion. As Davis puts it, "The abortion event . . . [was] altered from a clandestine act to a 'maturing,' sobering, or even emancipating experience within a rhetoric of respectable medicine or mental health care" (Davis 1973, p. 263).

Thus, even before the 1973 Supreme Court decisions, abortion was already being brought closer to mainstream medical practice. These efforts were expanded considerably with the Court's decision so that today most abortions are performed either in hospitals or in specialized, freestanding clinics. This stands in significant contrast to the mid-1960s when hospitals handled barely one in every hundred abortions and when legitimate medical clinics for abortions were unthinkable.

While most abortions have been brought into the context of legitimate medicine, it must be noted that there is still substantial resistance by the health care establishment. A report issued by the Alan Guttmacher Institute (1975) found that by early 1974 only 24 percent of all non-Catholic hospitals in the United States had performed any abortions. Only 15 percent of all public hospitals had done so. The report concluded, "The [Supreme] Court's decisions had little impact on U.S. hospitals. . . . The principal impact was on the 158 nonhospital clinics that were providing more than half of all U.S. abortions by the first quarter of 1974" (pp. 228-29).

Resistance was also evidenced in the report's findings that abortion services were highly concentrated geographically, and the availability and accessibility of abortion services remained very uneven. This geographical variability is illustrated in Figure 1.1, which shows the percentage of estimated need for abortion services being met in each state.

Research also indicates that the farther a woman has to travel to obtain an abortion, the less likely she is to obtain one (Shelton, Brann, and Schultz 1976). These findings corroborate the Guttmacher Institute report which estimated that between 30 and 50 percent of those women who sought an abortion during 1974 were unable to obtain one. It should be pointed out that many of these women were poor, no doubt reflecting the low percentage of public hospitals which perform abortions.

Institutional legitimation has been only partially achieved. When one considers the percentage of abortions now performed in established medical settings, legitimation appears considerable. When, on the other hand, one considers the resistance of many hospitals and the uneven availability of abortion services, then the incompleteness of the legitimation process is much clearer.

FIGURE 1.1

Percentage of Estimated Need for Abortion Services Being Met,
by State, 1973

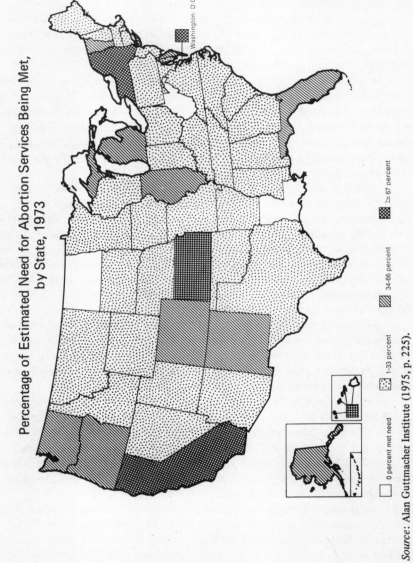

Washington, D.C.

0 percent met need   1-33 percent   34-66 percent   ≧ 67 percent

Source: Alan Guttmacher Institute (1975, p. 225).

Finally, let us turn to the level of moral legitimation.

Public attitudes do not necessarily follow changes in the social structure of a society—at least not directly nor immediately. Certainly, while public acceptance of abortion in the U.S. has increased since the 1960s, these changes do not nearly approximate the dramatic shift in legitimation on the two levels already discussed. While the majority of Americans do approve abortion under very restrictive circumstances (danger to the life of the prospective mother, the possibility of fetal damage, etc.), still less than half of the population approve of abortion in other cases (see Table 4.3). And, as Rossi (1966) has pointed out, it is these other cases which typify most actual abortion situations.

There is also some reason to suspect that moral legitimation of abortion may be even less than most opinion data indicate. This suspicion has to do with the wording of many survey questions (Moore 1973; Blake 1973). Many people believe that abortion should be legal and available for others, yet, at the same time, they do not personally believe that abortion is morally acceptable. Hence, the questions "Do you think abortion should be legal?" and "Do you think abortion is an acceptable thing to do?" may well get opposite responses from the same person. Many researchers assume that in asking the former question they are getting an indication of the latter. This is not a valid assumption. If, by moral legitimacy, we mean the personal beliefs of people about the morality and acceptability of abortion, then probably at least two-thirds of our population disapprove of or at least seriously question abortion.

Carefully considering the three levels of legitimacy in terms of the change in each since the late 1960s, we reach the conclusion that abortion is not yet fully legitimized. Specifically, while abortion is legal and to a great degree located within the confines of legitimate medical activity (though not within the mainstream of traditional hospital care), from the standpoint of societal members abortion is not a moral act. The ambiguity which has characterized the relationship between abortion and society throughout the past is still present today. As in the past, this ambiguity exists along with the substantial frequency with which abortions are enacted.

ABORTION TODAY: DEMOGRAPHIC TRENDS ⅄

In 1975 approximately 885,000 legal abortions were performed in the United States (Center for Disease Control 1977). A complete picture of abortion frequency must also include the number of illegal abortions still being performed. Noting how difficult this figure is to estimate, Tietze (1974) suggested a probable range the low point of which is 300,000. Cates and Rochat (1976) suggest a much lower number. Regardless of the exact number of illegal abortions, the overall number of abortions currently being performed yearly in the United States is at least one million, possibly greater. It is important to note that

TABLE 1.1

Percentage Distribution of U.S. Abortion Clients by Selected Characteristics, 1975

Characteristic	Distribution*
Residence:	
Abortion in-state	89.2
Abortion out-of-state	10.8
Age:	
≤19	33.1
20−24	31.9
≥25	35.0
Race:	
White	67.8
Black and others	32.2
Marital status:	
Married	26.1
Unmarried	73.9
Number of living children:	
0	47.0
1	20.2
2	15.5
3	8.7
4	4.4
≥5	4.2
Type of procedure:	
Curettage:	91.0
Suction	82.6
Sharp	8.4
Intrauterine instillation	6.2
Hysterotomy/Hysterectomy	0.4
Other	2.4
Weeks of gestation:	
≤8	44.6
9−10	28.4
11−12	14.9
13−15	5.0
16−20	6.1
≥21	1.0

*Excludes unknowns.
Source: Center for Disease Control: Abortion Surveillance, 1977.

FIGURE 1.2

Age-Specific Legal Abortion Ratios, United States, 1973–1975

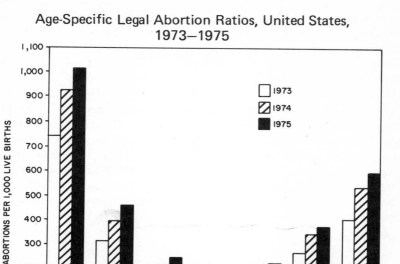

Source: Center for Disease Control: Abortion Surveillance, 1975.

this figure does not necessarily indicate an increase. Before legalization, rough estimates frequently were at one million or more; in fact, some estimates in the 1930s, cited previously, ranged as high as two million per year. Above all, it is clear from these numbers that abortion is a frequent event, much more frequent than is typically recognized.

Another way of illustrating the frequency of abortion is to use an abortion ratio, a comparison for a given year of the number of abortions for each 1,000 live births. For 1975, the abortion ratio was 282 (Center for Disease Control 1977), approximately one abortion for every three live births if we include illegal abortions.*

---

*Previously, we estimated that the abortion ratio for 1931 could have been as high as 500. This is further support for the view that the frequency of abortions has *not* increased in recent years.

A third way to look at abortion frequency is to consider the number of abortions in a given year for every 1,000 females of childbearing age (15-44) in the United States. In 1975, the rate was 18 (Center for Disease Control 1977).

As well as being frequent, abortion is widespread across all sociodemographic categories (see Table 1.1). It is engaged in by women at all stages of the childbearing years, by women in all types of male partner relationships, and by women with diverse socioeconomic and cultural backgrounds.

As indicated by Table 1.1, abortion most typically occurs in women who are under 25, white, and single. While the modal type appears to be the young, college-age woman, it is important to look within each life-cycle category in order to get a complete picture. Despite the frequency in absolute numbers for these women, the ratio of abortions to live births is lowest for them. This ratio is highest, on the other hand, for women 15 and younger and for women 40 and older (see Figure 1.2). Hence, although women at the youngest and oldest ranges appear in small absolute numbers, *among* them abortion is much more frequently chosen than among other age groups.

2

SOCIAL AND PSYCHOLOGICAL
STUDIES OF ABORTION

INTRODUCTION

The literature pertaining to social and psychological aspects of abortion experience is composed of research from three major fields: sociology, social psychology, and psychiatric medicine. For the following review, this literature has been organized in two sections. The first section considers studies by medical researchers. The second section discusses sociological and social-psychological research.

MEDICAL LITERATURE

Within the field of medicine, sociologically and psychologically oriented research on abortion stems from a view of abortion as a mental health problem. Studies are primarily psychiatric in nature and, therefore, are concerned with patient pathology—the identification of personality characteristics in women which are either antecedent causes or else aftereffects of abortion experience. Medical researchers have also looked at the attitudes and behavior of health care personnel involved with abortion procedures and patients. This latter group of studies is considered first.

Health Care Providers and Abortion

Recent studies of hospital personnel show physicians' attitudes toward abortion generally to be favorable (Wolf, Sasaki, and Cushner 1971; Mascovich et al. 1973), increasingly so when compared to past research (Sherwin and Over-street 1966). Studies of nurses indicate less favorable attitudes (Zahourek 1971; Bourne 1972); however, nurses' disapproval of abortion depends on the reason given for the abortion—more favorable attitudes are expressed when the abortion is performed as a result of rape, incest, or danger to the life or health of the woman—as well as on the type of training program the nurse has come from (Rosen et al. 1974).

Several studies of health care personnel lend support to Marder's (1970) observations of staff resistance to abortion expressed in terms of negative feelings, behavior, and even overt hostility. The possibility that such feelings may underlie more favorable, superficial attitudes has been explored primarily in studies of nurses. The assumption appears to be that nurses are the most likely candidates for such feelings because they have more direct involvement with patients and also because, since most nurses are women, they are considered likely to be particularly sensitive to abortion situations. Char and McDermott (1972) as well as Kane et al. (1973a) report strong negative reactions among nurses. Char and McDermott refer to this reaction as an "identity crisis." Kane's study as well as research by Mascovich et al. (1973) suggest a similar reaction on the part of physicians, although perhaps to a lesser degree. Harper, Marcom, and Wall (1972) go a step further by asking if the reported "identity crises" in nurses have a resulting impact on abortion patients. They find that in hospitals where nurses are less favorable toward abortion, abortion patients are less satisfied with the quality of their care after release than are patients in hospitals with a more favorable staff.

Psychiatric Studies of Abortion Patients

As we shall soon see, the psychiatric literature on abortion patients is abundant. Much of this literature, however, has to be considered with caution because it is plagued by the interrelated problems of: (1) a limited research methodology and (2) the intrusion of ideological bias—bias reflecting the re-searcher's views on the morality of abortion as well as on the proper role of women in society.

Methodological Problems

An important methodological problem of many psychiatric studies (par-ticularly those done before the late 1960s) is unrepresentative study populations. Studies were frequently limited to one hospital or one medical practice, in-creasing the likelihood of certain groups—for example, certain racial, religious, or income groups—being present and others excluded. Adequate descriptions of study populations were seldom given, making assessment of this factor difficult.

Perhaps a more fundamental source of bias, rarely acknowledged even by critics, is the fact that the women studied were for the most part seeking therapeutic abortion in a context where, otherwise, abortion was illegal. As pointed out in the last chapter, only about 1 percent of all abortions during the illegal period were in-hospital, "therapeutic" abortions; the majority of abortions were performed illegally. The women studied in hospitals constituted a very small proportion of all women having abortions; yet research findings were not qualified in this respect and generally were assumed to hold for all women.

Compounding this problem, therapeutic abortion was restricted by law to women defined as either physically or mentally unfit to bear a child. Psychological disturbance, therefore, was "built in" to the study groups. What is not known is how many women were merely "presenting" themselves in this way in order to get approval for an abortion.

Ideological Bias

The ideological bias of much of the psychiatric literature can be traced to the influence of Freud (Hall and Lindzey 1957; Sherman 1971).

Briefly put, Freud held that normal female development and the emergence of a healthy, mature, female personality is contingent on a successful passage through the so-called Oedipal crisis and subsequent penis envy. Here, the small girl's wish for a penis has to be and normally is transferred to a wish for a child. Desire for motherhood, therefore, in this view, represents a successful resolution of the Oedipus complex and normal compensation for the lack of a penis. This desire is considered indicative of normal female personality development. Conversely, any rejection of the wish for motherhood signifies abnormal psychological adjustment.

Within such a framework, abortion seeking indicates that a woman is maladjusted. Moreover, actually having the abortion is considered to lead her to even further disorder. According to a well-known psychiatrist, for example, abortion "reactivates castration fears causing guilt and depression" (Lidz 1954, p. 279). Another psychiatrist elaborates:

> Despite protests to the contrary, we know that woman's main role here on earth is to conceive, deliver, and raise children. Despite all other sublimated types of activities, this is still their primary role. When this function is interfered with, we see all sorts of emotional disorders. . . . This is not just textbook theory as all who practice psychiatry very well know. (Bolter 1962, pp. 314-15)

Yet another approaches the topic in a much less complicated way:

A woman is a uterus surrounded by a supporting organism and a directing personality. In advancing this proposition I am neither facetious nor deprecatory of womankind. I am biologically objective. In elaboration of this position, I would add that from the psychiatrist's viewpoint the strivings that animate the female can best be understood in terms of the functioning of the uterus. . . . In the light of all this, I think it is fair to argue that abortion must be looked upon as an eventuation that runs counter to the biological stream of life . . . we are confronted both with a sick person and a sick situation. (Galdston 1958, pp. 118-19)

Prior to 1966, reflecting this view, the conclusion was reached almost without exception that abortion inevitably causes trauma, posing a severe mental health threat to the woman involved (Taussig 1942; Deutsch 1945; Dunbar 1954; Wilson 1954; Galdston 1958; Bolter 1962). Research findings were presented along with the observation that completing an unwanted pregnancy was psychiatrically preferable to abortion in virtually every case. This view among medical and family-planning professionals was clearly evident at a Planned Parenthood conference on abortion held in 1955. The subsequently published conference proceedings concluded that "abortion, whether legal or illegal, is a traumatic experience and in many instances its commission does not solve the basic problem" (Calderone 1958, p. 182).

Such conclusions were reached in studies typically consisting of impressionistic reports on a few cases rather than data acquired through systematic research on larger groups. Recently, many reviewers of the literature have given testimony to the overly strong opposition to abortion and the weak research data used to support it in these studies (Simon and Senturia 1966; Fleck 1970; Walter 1970; Beck 1971; Pohlman 1971; David 1972; Osofsky and Osofsky 1972 and 1973; Sarvis and Rodman 1973; Friedman, Greenspan, and Mittleman 1974; Blumberg and Golbus 1975). In the words of one of these reviewers:

It is, however, sad to have to report that psychiatrists oblivious to their contamination by irrational traditions, albeit deeply ingrained social attitudes . . . justify blanket refusal of abortions because of alleged subtle, buried psychological aftermaths based often on a single case report—aftermaths rarely of a clinical magnitude. (Fleck 1970, p. 45)

To some extent this trend has been curbed in very recent years, but its influence has been and still is pervasive. As another reviewer, George Walter, has said, "A whole generation of professional health workers refuses to let the myth die out that abortion will irreparably harm a woman. . . . (1970, p. 482).

Current Orientation

In the late 1960s and early 1970s, more systematic research was reported. These studies attempted to clarify two important psychiatric questions which were often confused in earlier research: (1) Are women who seek abortion psychologically different—more emotionally disturbed—from other women? and (2) Does induced abortion result in psychological harm to the patient?

This latter question, as we have discussed, was initially answered in the affirmative. Abortion was considered likely to produce severely harmful after-effects. With more precise research, however, it was concluded that these after-effects, if they existed at all, were almost always mild and short-term (Peck and Marcus 1966; Niswander and Patterson 1967; Simon et al. 1967; Patt, Rappaport, and Barglow 1969; Margolis 1971; Ford, Castelnuovo-Tedesco, and Long 1972; Athanasiou et al. 1973)—even positively therapeutic (Notman 1973; Payne et al. 1973). Using comparison groups of women continuing their pregnancies to term, it was concluded that abortion is no more psychologically damaging, perhaps less so, than giving birth (Athanasiou et al. 1973).

While scientific opinion on the harmful aftereffects of abortion has shifted dramatically, opinion on another previously unquestioned finding, that women who seek abortion are a psychologically abnormal group, has not significantly changed. Two frequently cited abortion studies from the post-1966 period reached the following conclusions about the women in their study populations:

> Women who come to therapeutic abortion are highly selected in terms of their psychopathology. The high incidence of sadomasochism, depression and rejection of the feminine biological role supports this. . . . Pregnancy in many cases fulfills the role of gratifying the woman's unconscious masochistic wish, while abortion gratifies the sadistic impulse (directed against the fetus) as well as the masochistic wish (assault on the self). (Simon, et al. 1967, pp. 64-65)

and:

> Contrary to the popular belief that shame over pregnancy out of wedlock is the major motivation for abortion, we observed that . . . much more important was the woman's rejecting of motherhood with all of its attendant demands. Our impression is that these women tend to be narcissistic and regard the fetus as a competitor for the succorance and dependent care they themselves obviously require. (Ford, Castelnuovo-Tedesco, and Long 1972, p. 551)

Such assessments of women seeking abortion appear to be elaborations of the Freudian theme stated by Lidz in the 1950s: "The need to undergo an abortion is proof of inability and failure to live through the destiny of being a woman" (Lidz 1954, p. 279). In their critical review of this literature, Rosen and Martindale (1975) refer to this view as an attitude of "blaming the victim."

The conclusions of most of these studies once again were based on clinical judgments. These judgments seem to have been influenced by a particular view of women and abortion. For example, it was concluded that women who sought abortion were women who had unconsciously desired to become pregnant (Aarons 1967; Sandberg and Jacobs 1971; Ford, Castelnuovo-Tedesco, and Long 1972). This conclusion was determined by the fact that they did not use contraceptives,* the underlying explanation for which was "psychic conflict" over pregnancy. Luker (1975) has called this interpretation of unplanned pregnancy the "intra-psychic conflict theory." She points out the tautological reasoning used in such a view: "There is no such thing as an unwanted pregnancy because if a woman gets pregnant she must have wanted to" (p. 27).

One of the few studies which did not use clinical judgments found contradictory results. This study set out to examine whether abortion-seeking women were significantly different from nonpregnant women through using a Neuroticism Scale (Kane et al. 1973). No differences between the two groups were found.

In summary, the clinical judgments reported in many psychiatric studies of abortion patients appear to have been biased by the researcher's ideological positions. In addition, the women about whom these judgments were made represented only a tiny segment of all women having abortions—a segment already self-selected for indications of mental illness. Thus, even within the already narrowly defined scope of patient pathology, the medical-psychiatric literature is impossible to assess accurately.

Restricting ourselves to the most recent and most systematic of these studies, we are left with the suggestion that abortion experience is not psychologically catastrophic in the long term, but that it cannot be considered completely benign either. This research suggests that women who seek abortion are not characteristically different in personality disturbance from other women.

SOCIOLOGICAL AND SOCIAL-PSYCHOLOGICAL LITERATURE

Within the broad scope of sociological research, studies of abortion have tended to be limited to investigations of large-scale social trends, particularly demographic, epidemiologic, and public opinion surveys. Studies reflecting a

---

*An alternative explanation for women not using contraceptives is discussed in Chapter 5.

sociological perspective on the level of abortion experience or the abortion patient are almost nonexistent. In this review, we consider the large-scale studies first. Then we discuss the few studies which take a more social-psychological orientation.

Surveys and Organizational Studies

Large-scale sociological research on abortion can be subsumed under three types: (1) surveys of attitudes toward abortion (Rossi, 1966 and 1967; Peyton et al. 1969; Westoff et al. 1969; Blake 1971 and 1973; Maxwell 1970; Moore 1973; Jones and Westoff 1973; Pomeroy and Landman 1973; Zelnik and Kantner 1975; McCormick 1975; Arney and Trescher 1976); (2) demographic-epidemiological studies on the incidence of abortion and characteristics of abortion populations (Gebhard et al. 1958; Tietze and Lewit 1969 and 1973; Aitken-Swan 1971; Steinhoff 1973; Smith et al. 1974; Weinstock et al. 1975); and (3) studies of the social organization of abortion (Bates 1954; Bates and Zawadski 1964; Ball 1967; Lee 1969; Manning 1971; Davis 1973). Since legalization, the thrust of this latter research has shifted from the structure of the illegal system to the organization of delivery of abortion services (The Alan Guttmacher Institute, 1975; Shelton, Brann, and Schultz 1976). All these studies focus on the society or the organization of abortion services within society as the unit of analysis. Many are oriented toward social policy concerns. Findings from these studies have already been discussed, having provided the picture of the current abortion scene presented in Chapter 1—that is, the frequency of abortion in the United States among specific sociodemographic categories, the current structure of abortion attitudes, and the changing shape of abortion services from illegitimate to legitimate. Some of these findings are also reported in subsequent chapters.

While the emphasis in sociological research has been on institutional structures and large-scale societal trends, some attention also has been placed on the patient and the social situation of abortion.

Studies of Abortion Experience

As we mentioned previously, sociological research at the level of the person experiencing abortion is very scarce. What few studies do exist have tended to lack a clearly stated theoretical or conceptual focus. Hence, they are either purely descriptive and, therefore, analytically weak or else they lack analytical direction and are therefore often unclear in their central findings.

At least part of the problems with most of these studies appear to arise from the absence of a definite sociological perspective. This is of fundamental importance since, without such a perspective, many of these researchers rely on the "psychological" notions of guilt, anxiety, depression, and stress. The power of sociological analysis—in the sense of examining people's daily lives and experiences from the standpoint of the person's participation in ongoing social groups and social relationships—is lost. The abortion patient tends to be viewed as acting alone in a vacuum or else is studied in terms of broad sociodemographic categories, without regard for the impact of her immediate social world.

Another characteristic of these studies is that they have tended to focus on a single phase or aspect of abortion experience. Thus, there are studies of the abortion decision phase (Pearson 1973; Diamond et al. 1973; Dobrofsky 1974) and, in the context of the illegal period, studies of trying to secure an abortion (Lee 1969; Manning 1971; Davis 1973). Still others have emphasized the emotional or "psychological" response to abortion (Henslin 1971; Rosen and Martindale 1975; Adler 1975). Only Lee's study, and Davis's to a lesser degree, have given attention to the processual nature of abortion passage.

Despite the weaknesses of this literature, we will review briefly each of the studies since these studies constitute the only source of sociologically oriented findings that touch on the concerns of the present research, as discussed in Chapter 1.

Abortion Decision Making

Pearson (1973) in research conducted in England studied single pregnant women, half of whom continued pregnancy and half of whom terminated it. His purpose was to compare the two groups on a number of preconception and postconception factors. He found no differences between the two groups in terms of preconception contraceptive behavior except that the abortion group was more likely to have accepted the idea of using contraception. The only other preconception difference was that the women later choosing abortion were more likely to have been involved with the potential father in a relationship that was "uncertain, less meaningful than previous ones, or a social rather than a romantic one" (p. 454). Subsequent to conception, the two groups were more differentiated. The abortion group was found to be comparatively more sensitive to stigma and the fear of being discredited, more accepting of abortion, and less accepting of unmarried motherhood. Women having abortions were more likely also to find themselves in a relationship that had ended or was likely to end once the prospective father learned of the pregnancy.

Diamond et al. (1973) studied a group of women in Hawaii who all conceived during the same two-month period. This group, referred to as a "conception cohort," was matched according to whether they decided to complete the pregnancy or seek an abortion. A model was constructed with the following variables as predictors of the decision: whether or not coitus had been expected, whether pregnancy had been planned, and whether birth control methods had been used. They found, as expected, that almost all women planning pregnancies had not used contraception and chose to continue their pregnancies. Unexpectedly, they found no relationship between type of contraceptive used and abortion decision. Both marital status and religion were related to the decision: single women were more likely to choose abortion than married women and Protestant and "no religion" subjects were more likely to choose abortion than Catholics.

Dobrofsky (1974) studied a group of pregnant women with the hypothesis that their role and status orientations would predict their decision to continue or terminate the pregnancy. She distinguished between orientation of primary socialization group and adult reference group. She found that the adult reference group had more influence in the decision-making process than the primary socialization group.

These findings as a whole suggest that women may enter into abortion because of the social characteristics of their immediate situations as much as because of attitudes or beliefs learned earlier.

Reactions to Abortion

The remaining social-psychological studies deal with various aspects of abortion after the decision has been made. In discussing women's passage through the abortion and the meaning of the experience in their lives, these studies all place central emphasis on emotional states.

Henslin (1971) made the assumption that women having abortions feel guilt because they have committed a deviant act. With that assumption as a base, he interviewed women seeking abortion and presented the various ways by which these women "neutralize" their guilt. He observed that these neutralization techniques shielded the self-concept from blame among women who had internalized cultural norms. Thus, he concluded that the abortion had few negative consequences for identity. Henslin did not independently determine the existence of guilt nor did he distinguish those who internalized norms from those who did not.

Rosen and Martindale (1975) also considered the emotional response to abortion. They suggested that, since abortion indicates independence and a nontraditional view of family life, women seeking abortion should be feminist in orientation. Their findings supported this suggestion. They hypothesized that, reflecting this feminist orientation, women should exhibit a mild emotional response (low levels of guilt and internal conflict). Their findings also supported this hypothesis.

Alder (1975) asked women having abortions to select appropriate responses from a whole range of emotional reactions to abortion. She then factor analyzed these responses and came up with three types of emotional responses.

She speculated from the clustering that the circumstances surrounding the creation of pregnancy and its termination were central in affecting emotional intensity.

These studies provide evidence for several points made previously. The Henslin research seems to suggest that women having abortions recognize the fact that abortion is not morally legitimate in American society. The Rosen and Martindale study further confirms recent psychiatric studies concluding that abortion aftereffects are not severe. And, thirdly, Adler draws attention to the importance of situational factors in the experiencing of abortion.

Securing an Abortion

None of the research reviewed thus far described the actual situation of abortion along the lines of the questions posed in Chapter 1. Three studies exist, however, which point in that direction. All these are studies which emphasized the abortionist search during the illegal period.

Lee (1969) was primarily interested in establishing the nature of the communication networks used to locate an abortionist. She also, however, described the stages in the abortion process from the decision-making period into the post-abortion period. She was unable to follow a systematic method of obtaining subjects, and consequently her study group was found to be atypical of American women in terms of most standard sociodemographic indicators.

In her book, Lee dealt first with the discovery of pregnancy and the decision to seek abortion. She concluded that many of the women she studied had difficulty accepting the pregnancy and attempted to deny it. Most were involved in a stable, loving relationship with the prospective father and informed him of the pregnancy. Most of the couples agreed upon abortion. In cases where they did not agree, most frequently the man tried to persuade the woman to have the child rather than the woman trying to convince the man that she should continue the pregnancy. Most of the women rejected the pregnancy without ambivalence and without rejecting childbearing or children in general. Most of the women consulted only a few persons besides the man involved; parents were generally avoided. Those persons consulted were generally favorable to the abortion decision. Lee observed that most of the women seemed to select the persons they consulted on the basis of whether that person was likely to agree with their own tentative decision for abortion.

Next, Lee considered the search for the abortionist. She discussed the length of the communication chain, the number of "fresh starts," and the type of persons contacted.

The abortion procedure itself was considered as the third phase. Here, Lee's discussion was technical for the most part—the kind of medical procedure performed, the cost, satisfaction with the abortionist, and so on.

The fourth phase considered was the aftereffect and the return to normality. Lee found that few of her subjects reported any physical symptoms. Somewhat fewer than half reported "mild depression." Lee noted that the incidence of depression seemed associated with the woman's impression of the abortionist. Abortion, she concluded, was a time of crisis for most couples. More than half of her subjects reported that their relationship with the man involved got worse or deteriorated completely. Relationships with other persons were generally unchanged.

Lee concluded that, in coming to terms with their abortion, most of the women did not consider abortion experience as being like any other experience. Most had to take some kind of attitude toward it. Two modes of reaction to abortion characterized Lee's study group. One group of women "encapsulated" the experience, isolating it from the rest of their lives by breaking off relationships with others involved in the abortion and keeping the event secret. The rest of the women "politicized" the abortion, making it the basis of political conviction and action. These women focused on abortion as a time of revelation and change. Lee did not attempt to find consistent patterns of variation throughout the process, nor did she attempt to explain differences among the women studied.

Manning (1971) also focused on the abortion search, but his study was much more limited in scope than Lee's. He presented findings similar to Lee's concerning the initial anxiety and denial which characterize the discovery of pregnancy. Manning, however, did not discuss emotional states. He found that his subjects (unmarried college women) tended to avoid contacts with others. Manning suggested that this avoidance was done in order for the women to protect their identities.* This need for protection was due in part, he hypothesized, to the fact that society holds women responsible for their pregnancies.†

Both Lee and Manning addressed the question of what happens in abortion situations. Their research was conducted in the illegal system and suffered from the difficulty of contacting representative groups of women. Lee gave a great amount of description, but she did not attempt to link the various stages in the abortion process nor did she discuss patterns of passage through these stages. In addition, little attention was paid to the dynamics of interaction and how this might affect the woman's passage through abortion.

Davis (1973) in her study of the abortion market included a section presenting data from interviews with abortion clients. Some of her respondents had

---

*Henslin also focused on the protection of identities, but through cognitive rather than behavioral mechanisms.

†Sorensen (1973) supports this observation. In a study of adolescent attitudes, he found that adolescents held the female accountable for pregnancy when peers became pregnant.

secured legal abortions; others had had illegal ones. There was great variation in the length of time since the abortion among her subjects. As she acknowledged, her unsystematic sampling procedure produced a study group "biased in an unknown direction."

Like Lee, Davis organized her discussion of these women according to their chronological movement through the process.

The first stage was "defining the problem," which involved the women determining what was happening to them physically, how it had happened, and what the consequences would be. As in previous research, Davis concluded that fear, anxiety, and confusion characterized this stage. The second stage involved the construction of alternatives. Davis pointed out the importance of others during this process, observing that the rejection of solutions by friends, lover, or parents might prove "shocking." After the construction of alternatives, the woman contacted help. At this stage, the decision may have been redefined by others. Davis suggested that shifting solutions increased the level of guilt.

At this stage of the abortion procedure, Davis pointed to the significance of the professional persons associated with it—especially counselors. Davis noted that the existence of this professional structure was the element of change which separated her study from previous ones.

The final stage Davis discussed was the postabortion period. In support of Lee, Davis found that relief was the most immediate reaction. Turning to the question of how women evaluated the experience, Davis found no single set of perceptions which characterized the women in her study group. In approaching the "expressed psychological experience" of the women, Davis focused on her own estimates of the amount and patterns of stress which the women experienced. She found variation in terms of stress patterns, with the modal one being moderate stress before and normal one month after. The variation was not explained.

IMPLICATIONS OF THE LITERATURE

The theoretical points of departure for this study have been established in terms of an interactionist approach. Of primary importance is the view that situations are defined, are acted upon, and derive their meaning through social interaction. Social-psychological research on abortion has not typically been interactionist in approach. It has, however, generally supported an interactionist view of social life in that characteristics of the immediate situation, particularly relationships with others, have been suggested as important. These have not been adequately explored as yet. Most research, instead of focusing on the dynamics of the woman's interaction with others and the quality of emergent meanings, has concentrated on the isolated women, particularly their emotional states. As a consequence, abortion has not been studied as a real social process but rather as a static series of events. While variation at each stage has been established by previous research, no attempt has been made to link each stage and to establish the patterns by which women pass through abortion. This is the task of the present study.

3

ABORTION IN MIDVILLE: THE SETTING AND RESEARCH STRATEGY

INTRODUCTION

The women upon whom this study is based all resided in one particular midwestern community and its immediate surrounding area. This community will be referred to as Midville.*

Midville has a metropolitan area population of approximately 165,000. It is a relatively prosperous community. Midville is a solid, pleasant place to live. Moreover, in the words of one of the women interviewed for this study, it is "kind of conservative." This characterization probably is due in part to the fact that Midville is the political center of a politically conservative state, oriented to the traditional values of the rural Midwest. While there are many people in Midville who can be accurately characterized as conservative and traditional, there are others holding considerably more liberal views.

The existence of vocal, opposing groups and the political atmosphere typical of a governmental center mean that Midville residents are likely to be particularly cognizant of current political and social controversies such as abortion. The city has a visible antiabortion contingent which has actively held rallies and distributed leaflets door-to-door within the past few years. A primary target has been one group of local physicians who reportedly are the only physicians in town willing to perform abortions. It is safe to say that probably few Midville residents remain unaware of the intense opposition to abortion.

---

*All names of persons and places reported here are fictitious.

With some idea of Midville and its abortion climate, let us turn to the structure of abortion services in the city.

OBTAINING AN ABORTION IN MIDVILLE

Abortions are readily available in Midville. They typically are obtained by passage through one of two channels within Midville's network of abortion services (see Figure 3.1). The first of these is best termed the "traditional medicine route": A woman suspects that she is pregnant and contacts her physician; the physician confirms the pregnancy and either arranges to perform an abortion in

FIGURE 3.1

Channels to Abortion for Midville Residents

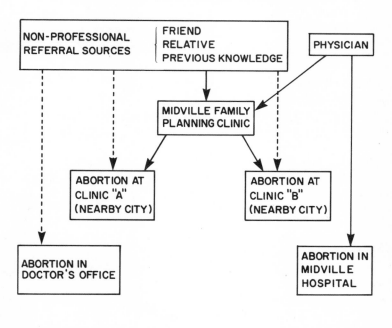

SELDOM USED - - - - - - - - - - -

FREQUENTLY USED ————

Source: Compiled by the author.

a local hospital or refers the woman to another physician who will. The other network can be described as the "specialized clinic alternative": Here, the woman contacts the public health department's family-planning clinic to have her pregnancy confirmed. Upon confirmation and after appropriate counseling, a staff member makes an appointment for her at one of the two freestanding clinics in a large nearby city which are devoted primarily to performing abortions. She travels there for her abortion.

The possibility of a third channel exists in that there is a physician in a neighboring town who performs abortions in his office. Very few persons in Midville, however, are aware of this option, for neither the family-planning clinic nor Midville physicians refer patients there. Most staff members at the family-planning clinic do not approve of office abortions.

The two major channels do not necessarily function independently of each other. Local physicians in Midville are aware of the specialized clinic alternative and frequently refer their patients to it either because abortion at one of the clinics is generally cheaper (Table 3.1) or because the family-planning clinic offers professional counseling as part of its abortion services. These professional abortion counseling services are the only ones available in Midville. Switching from one network to the other may also occur when a clinic patient decides to have her abortion done in a local hospital and is referred to a private physician.

TABLE 3.1

Cost of Abortion for Midville Women by Type of Abortion Facility and Length of Pregnancy, 1975

Type of Abortion Facility	Length of Pregnancy (in weeks)	Total Cost of Abortion (in dollars)
Hospital	–	550.00
Specialized clinic A	through 12	150.00
	13–14	250.00
	14–15	375.00
	15–17	575.00
Specialized clinic B	through 12 only	155.00
Physician's office	–	50.00

Note: Abortion here refers to the dilatation, suction, and curettage (vacuum aspiration) method.
Source: Compiled by the author.

Regardless of the channel they use, most women having abortions in Midville have at least some contact with the family-planning clinic. (This clinic will be referred to hereafter as Midville Clinic.) The clinic is centrally located in Midville in a relatively new, modern building near several other medical care facilities. Midville Clinic is just one of several types of clinic run by the public health department. The clinic's professional staff consists of both nurses and social workers. One physician is available on a part-time basis.

Most of the activity at Midville Clinic is centered around birth control services, pregnancy testing, abortion referral, and related counseling. The clinic is used by a diversity of local residents; however, clients from middle- and lower-middle-income/occupation levels are most common.

Hospital abortions in Midville generally must be scheduled at least a week in advance. The women taking this route are told very little about the procedure beforehand. They arrive at the hospital and are admitted in routine fashion. They are taken to a hospital room which they frequently share with another patient (not necessarily another abortion patient). Here they are put in bed, prepared for the abortion procedure, and given a general anesthetic. The procedure is performed using the dilatation, suction, and curettage technique (also known as vacuum aspiration). When the woman has recovered sufficiently from the anesthetic, she is allowed to go home. The entire procedure takes about eight hours. No overnight stay is involved. A woman having a hospital abortion in Midville has only minimal contact with health care professionals—typically with the nursing staff. She sees her physician only briefly. Rarely, if ever, would she be given a detailed technical explanation of her abortion procedure. The cost of a hospital abortion in Midville (including physician's fee) is roughly $550 and is paid for in the same manner as any other hospital medical procedure.

Abortions performed in the specialized, freestanding clinics can be scheduled much more quickly—within one or two days of the procedure. Both clinics use the same medical technique as the hospital: dilatation, suction, and curettage. Before going to the abortion clinic, each woman is given an instruction sheet at Midville Clinic and is told in detail what the facility and the actual abortion procedure will be like. In both abortion facilities, the entire procedure takes usually five to six hours. In contrast to the hospital setting, a woman having a specialized clinic abortion has contact with a variety of health care professionals. In addition to the physician and nurses, she sees a number of clerical and medical assistants as well as an abortion counselor.

The major difference in medical procedure between the two facilities is that Clinic A performs abortion through the seventeenth week of gestation while Clinic B does not perform abortion for anyone who is more than 12 weeks pregnant (first trimester). Because of this difference, Clinic A has a slightly larger medical staff—the additions being two anethesiologists and two operating room attendants. Also related to this difference is the fact that Clinic A has a sliding fee scale whereas Clinic B has only one standard fee. Clinic A's fee is nearly the same as Clinic B's up through week 12, but increases incrementally thereafter as the number of weeks of pregnancy increase (see Table 3.1).

Both clinics follow similar routines in the delivery of their services. Clinic A's client routine will be described to exemplify both clinics' operating procedures.

The client arrives at Clinic A and enters on the main floor. The receptionist refers her to an admissions office where she pays a portion of her fee. A medical chart is made up for her and she is asked to sign a general consent form. The woman is then sent to the second floor. Here she pays the remainder of her fee, based upon the number of weeks she was found to be pregnant in her initial pregnancy test at Midville Clinic. She signs another consent form specifically covering her abortion procedure. At this point the person or persons accompanying her (each woman is asked to bring at least one person with her so that she does not have to drive after the abortion) are taken into the visitor's waiting room. No one is allowed to accompany the client past this point. Next, the woman is given blood and urine tests. Then she goes to a patient's waiting room, where she is asked to complete a third consent form. The next step is a pelvic examination. When she returns after the examination, she must pay an additional amount if the results reveal that her pregnancy is more advanced than was previously indicated. At this point she goes into a counseling session.

The counselors at Clinic A are trained by other clinic personnel at the clinic. They are all women hired on the basis of what the clinic considers an "appropriate educational background" and/or "relevant experience." While not an explicit qualification, many clinic counselors have themselves had an abortion. The primary employment criterion, taking precedence over background qualifications, is that the counselor be able to establish rapport easily with the clientele.

Counseling takes place in separate counseling rooms. The women are seen either individually or in groups of two to four. Group sessions are the rule. When feasible, women are put into groups on the basis of similarities; age, marital status, student status, and religion are among possible criteria. Frequently, patients who happen to get to know each other in the waiting room will be counseled together.

The counselor begins the session by asking the women if they have any problems concerning their abortion decision. If so, these problems are discussed. Most often, the women say very little and the counselor turns to giving a detailed description of the abortion procedure. The counselor also goes over a list of the risks involved in an abortion. She then discusses the proper after-care procedures and talks to the women about their future use of contraceptives. After the session the clients return to the waiting room.

Next, the woman is called to prepare for the abortion. She undresses and puts on a gown and slippers. She then goes into a specially designated room to await the abortion. The procedure itself lasts only a few minutes. The woman's counselor goes into the procedure room with her. The counselor offers to hold her hand and talks to her while the doctor performs the abortion. Afterward she is taken to a recovery room shared with one or more than one woman. Here she is given crackers and a soft drink and a heating pad if she wants one (to relieve pain from cramping). She stays in the recovery room for about an hour, dresses, and goes home.

In contrast to hospital abortion, the freestanding clinics seldom use general anesthetic. Clinic B never gives it. Clinic A is equipped to administer it but does not typically do so. Both clinics use a local anesthetic, a paracervical block (zylocaine). Both clinics also offer the woman a mild pain reliever if she so desires.

While their procedural routines are nearly identical, there are some basic differences between the two clinics.

Clinic A was begun in 1971 and claims to be one of the first freestanding abortion facilities in the central United States. It is housed in a 50-year-old, plain, square brick building, located in a lower-income, predominantly black area on the northernmost edge of a large city, about an hour-and-a-half drive from Midville. The structure resembles an old schoolhouse rather than a hospital or medical facility. It presents a somewhat bleak image in the rather desolate area which surrounds it. There is little landscaping, and patients must park in an unfinished mud and gravel parking area on the side of the building. At the time of this study, the main floor of the building was vacant except for the admissions office. The basement was occupied by a nursing home for area residents. The clinic itself was housed on the second and third floors.

Clinic B was begun in 1974. It occupies two office suites in a new, professional office building located along a major highway in the midst of a busy shopping area in a suburban part of the same large city some distance from Midville. Like Clinic A, Clinic B is not housed in a structure which resembles a hospital or medical facility. Clinic B's building, with its wrought-iron trim and balconies, looks more like an apartment building or a hotel than a clinic. It is well maintained and landscaped, with a large concrete parking area in front.

Neither clinic has any sort of sign or marker to indicate its identity. Even if there were signs, each clinic has a name so euphemistic that no indication of the purpose of the clinic is revealed. Both clinics are owned by separate private corporations. Although the two clinics are only 20 minutes apart, little contact occurs between them. It is interesting to note that just about the time Clinic B opened, Clinic A initiated an incentive plan to increase its referrals. With this plan, each referral source (Midville Clinic is one such source) can send one nonpaying client for every 15 paying ones. No relationship between the initiation of this program and the opening of Clinic B was mentioned to the investigator by the staff of Clinic A.

At the time of this study Clinic A was performing abortions on three days of every week, with a total of approximately 80 to 90 a week. Clinic B was performing abortions two days a week with approximately 50 to 60 a week.

The clientele of Clinic A differs somewhat from that of Clinic B. Clinic A's patients are predominantly from blue-collar families: 40 percent are Catholic; the rest, Protestant. Twenty percent are black; the rest are white. Clinic B, on the other hand, reports that its clientele tends to be from white-collar families and has a relatively high level of education. Fifteen percent are Catholic and only a very small proportion are black. Both clinics perform slightly more than half their abortions on single women between the ages of 18 and 22.

The differences between clinic clientele are paralleled by another difference, one in the interior decor and atmosphere of each clinic. The emphasis in both clinics is on avoiding the "hospital look." A hospitallike atmosphere is thought to produce patient anxiety and therefore make the experience more disruptive. According to one staff member, "We don't want to make them [the clients] feel like we are sterile robots." The accepted view of the staff is that "nothing is as depressing to patients as white walls." A nonhospitallike decor is thought to be relaxing, less traumatic, and related to greater patient confidence. (The degree to which the desired image is achieved in the perceptions of the clientele will be discussed in a later chapter.) While both clinics agree on the general image they want to promote, differences occur in the way each clinic has attempted to achieve this sought-after, nonhospital look.

As previously described Clinic A is located in an older building. During the time of this research, the clinic was just finishing a do-it-yourself redecorating project. All the rooms had been newly painted in pastel shades: lavender, turquoise, yellow, and so on. Some walls and ceilings had a sparkling substance added to the paint to produce a glittering effect. Another feature was the use of posters, paste-on flowers, and brightly colored contact paper on doors and walls. Rock music played over the speaker system.

Clinic B's building, on the other hand, is new. The building interior is thickly carpeted and there is a feeling of elegance. The interior of the clinic suites is less ostentatious with the emphasis on bright colors. The decor approximates a Scandinavian Modern style, relaxed rather than severe. Clinic B's interior appears to have been done professionally in contrast to the do-it-yourself appearance of Clinic A.

Both clinics are self-conscious about their appearance. This feeling is not limited to the interior decoration. It also includes the demeanor of the staff. Both clinics are working to "individualize" their staffs; this means that they are seeking a personal, informal style in patient–staff interaction rather than an impersonal, "professional" style which they associate with traditional medicine. This is in keeping with the "nonhospital" philosophy described above. It is evidenced, for example, in the fact that counselors and other staff members tend to wear casual street clothes rather than uniforms. The medical staff in Clinic A may be uniformed, but even here the emphasis is on subtlety, on not appearing "too formal." Thus, for example, pastels are preferred over white uniforms. The push toward an "individualized" staff is also evidenced by the fact that counselors are hired less for their professional–educational qualifications than for their personality, interaction style, and personal experience with abortion.

With some idea of the abortion services network of Midville, we can now discuss the specific research procedures employed in the study.

THE NATURE OF THE DATA

We have taken the view that persons facing problematic situations construct their actions and the meaning of those actions jointly, through interaction with those around them. To conduct research using such a view requires information both about *sequences of action*—specifically, what do women do in their passage through an abortion situation and how are their actions responded to by others—as well as information revealing *the actor's interpretation* or perspective on these events.

Perhaps the best way to fully comprehend the interrelated aspects of an event, situation, or social world is to observe it directly. Numerous sociological studies have employed direct observation to uncover interaction patterns and actors' perspectives. Some good examples are the study of medical school life by Becker et al. (1961), Julius Roth's (1963 and 1972) work in hospitals, Lofland's (1966) study of a religious cult, and Wiseman's (1970) research on skid row. These studies all were conducted in public or at least in settings which were accessible to the researchers.

There are, however, some events or experiences to which access is restricted. Abortion is one such experience. The interaction sequences which form a woman's passage through abortion are largely of an intimate nature and are conducted in virtually nonobservable settings. In order to observe adequately the dynamics of an abortion situation, the observer would have to follow a woman through the course of her everyday life over a period of several months. Only a very tiny portion of this interaction would occur in a location accessible to the researcher, making the task of adequate observation impossible.

It is precisely because of this difficulty in observing some kinds of social situations that most observational research is conducted with persons who play out most of their daily life in institutions—hence, the quantities of research on hospitals, prisons, skid row, and similar places. In contrast, there are comparatively few studies using direct observation of family or home life.

The problems with observing abortion situations are compounded by the complexity and emotionality of the attitudes which surround abortion. It is a particularly sensitive topic, an event seldom discussed and rarely revealed to others by those who have experienced it. Frequently, deliberate measures are taken to avoid the subject altogether. Thus, in the discourse of everyday life, abortion as a personal experience is an action that the average person cannot be openly curious about.

An alternative method to firsthand observation is to secure descriptions from persons who have themselves participated in the experience being studied. In the case of abortion, the only consistent source for this type of information is the woman who has undergone abortion. This is the source which was used to provide the data for the present study.

Descriptions of abortion experience were obtained using the intensive interview method. This method was carried out following the approach of Lofland (1971). He describes the intensive interview in this way:

> Its object is not to elicit choices between alternative answers to pre-formed questions but, rather, to elicit from the interviewee what [s]he considers to be important questions relative to a given topic, his [her] descriptions of some situation being explored. Its object is to carry on a guided conversation and to elicit rich, detailed materials that can be used in qualitative analysis. Its object is to find out what kinds of things are happening, rather than to determine the frequency of predetermined kinds of things that the researcher already believes can happen. (Lofland 1971, p. 76)

Following Lofland's strategy interviews were "guided" by a flexible yet coherently organized interview guide. Each woman was encouraged to describe in her own words what happened over the course of her abortion experience. She was guided through her account by the interviewer. The entire range of subtopics outlined on the guide was consistently covered in each interview, although not always in the same order. Hence, there was comparability from interview to interview.

SECURING THE INTERVIEWS

All the women who were interviewed for the present study were clients of Midville Clinic. Most followed the abortion services route previously referred to as the "specialized clinic alternative." A few of the women had their abortions performed in the local hospital. One woman, acting on her own, located a doctor in a neighboring town who performed the abortion in his office.

The investigator arranged to contact the women at Midville Clinic. Beginning in February of 1975, each clinic staff member (either a nurse or a social worker) whose responsibilities included talking with abortion-seeking patients was given copies of a letter describing the present study, signed by the investigator (Figure 3.2). Attached to the letter was a second sheet, a form containing a statement of consent and a brief questionnaire asking age, marital status, occupation, education, and place of residence.

All of the staff members had been explained the nature of the research project. They were instructed to give a copy of the letter and the form to each

FIGURE 3.2

Introductory Letter to Prospective Interviewees

January 6, 1975

Dear Friend,

    I am a social scientist from the University of Minnesota. I am working here in _____ with the cooperation of the _____ Health Clinic.

    I realize that the present time may not be an easy time for you, but because of your experiences you can be of help to a study of women which I am conducting. This study is designed to provide knowledge of women's life experiences in an area where very little is now known. It is my hope that this study will be of help to many women as well as to the clinics which serve them.

    You can help if you would be willing to talk privately with me about your experience with abortion. What I will do, if you agree to participate, is to telephone you in about 6 weeks and arrange a time convenient for you when we can talk together. I want to emphasize that this conversation will be *completely confidential*. No record will be kept of your name or address or anything else which would identify you. All that is important for the research is your own first-hand experience which, of course, only you can give.

    If you are willing to participate, please write your name on the following page along with a telephone number where you can be reached in about 6 weeks. If your first name is all that is necessary for me to reach you at this number, then you needn't write your last name. If, on the other hand, your last name is necessary, let me assure you again that I will keep it in the strictest confidence.

    If you have any questions, you may reach me at the following number: _____

Sincerely,

Mary K. Zimmerman

Source: Compiled by the author.

of their abortion clients at the time each woman was scheduling her abortion. They were asked to disregard any woman who had previously had an abortion and/or any woman who was too advanced in her pregnancy for the vacuum aspiration method to be used (more than 17 weeks pregnant).

The decision to limit this study to women having their first abortion was made in order to standardize the women's own prior experience with abortion. Excluding those with a prior abortion put all the women on a common baseline in this respect as they entered their abortion passage. It was felt that having had a previous abortion might well influence the woman's perceptions and interpretations and actions as well as those of others directed toward her. This feeling is based on the supposition that people are likely to react less favorably to a second abortion than to a first.* The experience of an abortion repeater might, therefore, be characteristically different from a woman "naive" about abortion. Within the confines of the size desired for the study group, this source of possible variation could not be adequately handled and so it was eliminated.

The decision to limit the study to only those women undergoing the dilatation, suction, and curettage method (vacuum aspiration) was made for similar reasons. In this network of abortion services women whose pregnancies are within the first 17 weeks are aborted by this method. Women whose pregnancies are more advanced must undergo a more complicated procedure, involving more medical risk and a greater degree of medical attention, including hospitalization overnight. These differences significantly alter the nature of the abortion experience and might be expected to affect the perceptions of the woman as well as the nature of her interactions with others. For these reasons, this source of possible variation was also eliminated.

Each of the staff members at Midville Clinic was asked to have her client read the letter immediately and was instructed to answer any questions about the study the client might have. If the woman were willing to participate, then she was asked to sign her name—she was told that, if she preferred, only her first name was necessary. Participating women were also asked to give a phone number or some other means by which they could be contacted approximately six weeks after their abortion was performed. This name and phone number, given by the woman herself, was the only record of personal identity made in the course of this research.

Regardless of whather the client chose to participate or not, she was asked to complete the short questionnaire, which asked for basic sociodemographic information. These were collected for all the women contacted and given to the investigator by the staff members. If, for some reason, the client left an incom-

---

*There appear to be no survey data available to support this contention. Quotations from the women in this study, presented in Chapter 7, do provide support. In addition, Luker (1975) suggests the same phenomenon in her book.

plete questionnaire, the staff member was instructed to supply the missing information from clinic files.

At the request of the clinic director, staff members were asked not to give the client the letter, consent form, and questionnaire if, in their judgment, it would be inadvisable clinically. In such cases, where clients were not told of the research, questionnaires were completed from clinic files. These questionnaires were specially marked so that the investigator would know that the woman had not been asked to participate.

Thirteen percent of all the women seeking abortion within the given time frame were not informed of the research (see Figure 3.3). Not all of these women were passed over for clinical reasons, however. Several were included in the "not told" category because the nurse or social worker inadvertently forgot to hand out the material. The women who were excluded for clinical reasons tended to be under 22 and not married. Staff comments on the questionnaires of these women indicated that the typical case where the research was not mentioned consisted of a client, young and single, accompanied to the clinic by her mother, and involved in conflict and hostility with her mother throughout the period of contact with the staff member.

The number of interviews desired was set at 40. This size was chosen because it provides an optimum balance between the scope which a large number of cases allows and the manageability for analysis possible only with a smaller number.

The women were interviewed in sequence. Approximately six weeks after each woman had her abortion procedure, the investigator contacted her in the manner previously indicated and arranged for an interview. Most interviews were conducted between six and ten weeks after the abortion. Each interview lasted between one and two hours.

The interval of at least six weeks was chosen because of previous research findings (Davis 1973), corroborated in consultations with the social work staff at Midville Clinic. Six weeks has been found to be a long enough period of time for women to "recover" from the abortion and to reestablish an everyday routine. It was reasoned that any alterations in life style or social world which are more than short-term aftereffects should be observable at that time. In addition, the women would have ample time to establish a definition and perspective on the entire abortion experience—a meaning for the act. Since both interruptions or alterations in social worlds and the meanings attached to abortion experience are of central importance in this research, six weeks appeared to be an appropriate interval. Certainly, longer-term effects and definitions are also of considerable interest; however, time constraints precluded longer intervals from being included in the present study.

Interviews were conducted until 40 women had been interviewed.

As indicated in Figure 3.3, eight women who had originally agreed to participate were not contacted because the desired number of interviews had

FIGURE 3.3

Interviewee Selection Procedure

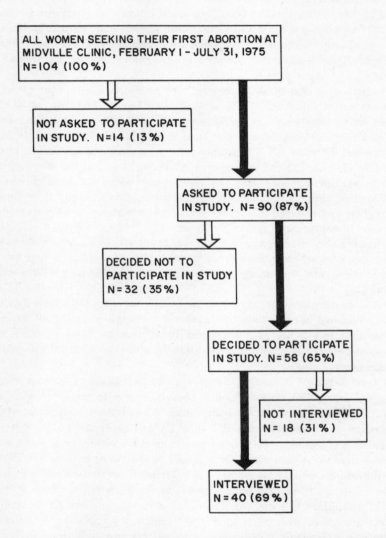

Note: Of those "not interviewed," two were contacted at the appropriate time but refused the interview, four were contacted at the appropriate time but were found not to qualify, four could not be located, and eight were not contacted because the desired number of interviews already had been achieved.

Source: Compiled by the author.

already been obtained. Only two of the women who had earlier consented to be interviewed decided not to be interviewed at the time they were contacted. Four could not be located at all. Another four women, when contacted, were discovered not to qualify for the research—two had had previous abortions, another had cancelled her initial abortion appointment and eventually had to have another type of abortion procedure done, and the fourth changed her mind at the last minute and decided to continue her pregnancy to term.

REPRESENTATIVENESS OF THE INTERVIEW GROUP

Of those informed of the research, 65 percent agreed to participate (Figure 3.3). In order to know whether any particular characteristic differentiated those refusing to participate from those who agreed, the two groups were compared in terms of age, marital status, religious affiliation, occupation, and amount of education completed. The differences between the two groups are small (see Table 3.2). Compared to the participant group, the refusal group was slightly less well-educated, was slightly older, had a slightly higher proportion of never-married women, and had a slightly higher proportion of Protestants and a correspondingly lower proportion of Catholics.

This comparison gives credibility to the contention that, at least socio-demographically, the women refusing to participate were not substantially different from those agreeing.

Another important question concerns how well the interview group represented all the women seeking abortion at Midville Clinic. The interview group, when compared to the entire clinic population of abortion-seeking women during the given time frame, appears to be quite similar in composition (see Table 3.2). The notable differences, small in magnitude, showed that a slightly greater proportion of divorced, separated, and widowed women were selected to be interviewed and a slightly lower proportion of never-married women. Also, a higher proportion of Catholics was included in the interview group as well as a relatively low proportion of those claiming no established religion.

In all of the other categories of age, marital status, religion, occupation, and amount of education completed, there were no notable differences. Thus, we are able to suggest that the group selected for this study is reasonably representative of the entire clinic population.

Another important question concerns how representative Midville Clinic women are of all Midville women who seek abortion—in other words, how accurately does the study group represent all these women?

The group of women interviewed would appear to accurately represent all Midville women with the possible exception of slightly underrepresenting those in the upper socioeconomic levels. For example, very few women who are themselves professionals or are married to professionals are clinic clients. The extent to which these women experience unwanted pregnancy and abortion is

TABLE 3.2

Comparison of Frequencies of Clients by Selected Sociodemographic Characteristics among (1) Those Not Asked to Participate in the Study, (2) Those Asked Who Declined, (3) Those Asked Who Accepted but Were Not Interviewed, and (4) Those Interviewed

All Midville Clinic Abortion Clients, February–July 1975

Characteristic	Not Asked to Participate N = 14[a] N	Percent	Asked, Declined to Participate N = 32 N	Percent	Asked, Agreed to Participate, Not Interviewed[b] N = 18 N	Percent	Interviewed N = 40 N	Percent	Total[b] N = 104 N	Percent
Age										
14-17	5	(36)	9	(28)	7	(41)	11	(28)	32	(30)
18-22	6	(43)	13	(40)	8	(47)	19	(46)	46	(44)
23-29	3	(21)	7	(22)	2	(12)	9	(23)	21	(20)
30-39	0	(0)	3	(10)	0	(0)	1	(2)	4	(6)
Marital status										
Never married	11	(79)	21	(65)	14	(82)	24	(60)	70	(68)
Married	3	(21)	4	(13)	1	(6)	6	(15)	14	(14)
Divorced/separated/widowed	0	(0)	7	(22)	2	(12)	10	(25)	19	(18)
Religion										
Catholic	—		5	(15)	0	(10)	11	(28)	16	(18)
Protestant	—		23	(72)	13	(76)	27	(68)	63	(70)
Jewish	—		0	(0)	1	(6)	1	(2)	2	(2)
None	—		4	(13)	3	(18)	1	(2)	8	(10)
Occupational status										
Student	—		9	(28)	5	(30)	15	(37)	29	(33)
Employed outside home	—		15	(47)	7	(41)	16	(40)	38	(42)
Not employed outside home	—		8	(25)	5	(29)	9	(23)	22	(25)
Education completed										
Some high school	—		12	(37)	6	(35)	13	(33)	31	(35)
High school graduate	—		16	(50)	4	(24)	17	(42)	37	(42)
Some college	—		4	(13)	7	(41)	9	(23)	20	(22)
College graduate	—		0	(0)	0	(0)	1	(2)	1	(1)

[a] Data limited to age and marital status.
[b] One questionnaire with incomplete data.
Source: Compiled by the author.

46

not known; but if and when they do, they are likely to take the "traditional medicine route," bypassing the clinic. We should note on the other hand that it is also possible that some women who ordinarily would take the traditional medicine route might come to the clinic in order to obtain secrecy.

CHARACTERISTICS OF THE INTERVIEW GROUP

The typical woman interviewed for this study was single with no children, was between the ages of 18 and 22, and was either a student or had a full-time job (see Table 3.3).

Most of the women were white. The proportional representation of black and Spanish-surnamed women within the interview group, while small, nevertheless generally corresponded to the proportional representation of these groups within Midville as a whole (Johnson 1974). Similarly, the proportion of Catholic women interviewed also corresponds to the proportional representation of Catholics in Midville (Bureau of the Census 1973).

The distribution of women older than 22 and younger than 18 was roughly the same, with a few more in the younger group.

Women were categorized as either blue collar or white collar on the basis of their own occupation if they were regularly employed. For those who were not regularly employed, category assignment was made on the basis of the occupation(s) of their parent(s) or husband, whichever was appropriate in the case at hand. The problems encountered in measuring women's social class standing in research on abortion has been documented previously (Steinhoff 1973). In the present study, the blue collar/white collar distinction was used because it was considered the most accurate way to measure social class in a group of women who had diverse occupational and familial patterns and who represented various stages of the life cycle.

As indicated earlier in this chapter, the women in the study group, while all received the counseling services of Midville Clinic, took diverse routes through the abortion services network. Specifically, one woman had her abortion in a doctor's office, four women (10 percent) had their abortions in a local hospital, and the rest (35) went to one of the two specialized, freestanding clinics in the nearby city: 24 women (60 percent) went to Clinic A and 11 women (27.5 percent) went to Clinic B.

The criteria by which some women were referred to Clinic A and others to Clinic B were largely the discretionary ones of Midville Clinic staff members. The only structural factor affecting referral practices was the fact that only Clinic A could take women over 12 weeks pregnant. Another factor which may have encouraged more referrals to Clinic A was the fact that Midville Clinic staff members frequently expressed more confidence in Clinic A since they had been working with it for a much longer period of time than they had with

TABLE 3.3

Frequency of the Women Interviewed by Selected Sociodemographic Characteristics

Characteristic	N	Percent
Age		
14 and younger	1	(2)
15-17	10	(25)
18-22	19	(48)
23-25	5	(13)
26-29	4	(10)
30-34	—	—
35-39	1	(2)
Marital status		
Never married	24	(60)
Married	6	(15)
Divorced/Separated/Widowed	10	(25)
Number of living children		
0	26	(65)
1	4	(10)
2	5	(13)
3-4	4	(10)
5+	1	(2)
Religion		
Catholic	11	(28)
Protestant	27	(68)
Jewish	1	(2)
None	1	(2)
Occupational status		
High school student	11	(28)
College student	4	(10)
Employed full-time outside home	12	(30)
Employed part-time outside home	4	(10)
Not employed outside home	9	(22)
Education completed		
Some high school	13	(33)
High school graduate	17	(43)
Some college	9	(22)
College graduate	1	(2)
Racial/cultural group		
White	35	(88)
Black	4	(10)
Spanish surname	1	(2)
Family's social class		
Blue collar	22	(55)
White collar	18	(45)

Note: Age, marital status, occupational status, religion, and education completed were all recorded at the time the abortion procedure was scheduled. Other characteristics were recorded at the interview.

Source: Compiled by the author.

Clinic B. Clinic B's relative newness appeared to be a source of doubt for some Midville Clinic staff members, possibly affecting the rate of referrals.

Despite no specific criteria for referral to one clinic rather than the other (other than length of pregnancy restrictions), and notwithstanding most staff members' claims that there were no particular reasons for sending some women to Clinic A rather than Clinic B, a definite pattern was found. Of the 24 women referred to Clinic A, 18 (75 percent) were from blue collar families. Of the 11 referred to Clinic B, only three (27 percent) were from blue collar families. It is possible that this inequity is simply a reflection of the fact that blue collar women had disproportionately more pregnancies terminated beyond the twelfth week of gestation.

As Table 3.4 indicates, it is indeed the case that the women whose pregnancies were more advanced were blue collar women. Nevertheless, looking

TABLE 3.4

Frequency of Referral to Abortion Clinics A and B by Social Class, Controlling for Length of Pregnancy

| | Clinic to Which Referral Was Made | | |
	Clinic A	Clinic B	Total
12 weeks pregnant or less			
Blue Collar			
N	9	3	12
Percent	(60)	(27)	(96)
White collar			
N	6	8	14
Percent	(40)	(73)	(54)
Total			
N	15	11	26
Percent	(58)	(42)	(100)
More than 12 weeks pregnant			
Blue collar			
N	9	—	9
Percent	(100)	—	(100)
White collar			
N	0	—	0
Percent	(0)	—	(0)
Total			
N	9	—	9
Percent	(100)	—	(100)

Source: Compiled by the author.

only at those pregnancies reported to have been terminated by the twelfth week, we see that the tendency was *still* to send blue collar women to Clinic A and white collar women to Clinic B. This analysis does not suggest that such a pattern was intentional. It would appear that it was unrecognized by the staff of Midville Clinic.

The question of the representativeness of the study group has already been discussed vis-a-vis Midville Clinic and also vis-a-vis Midville's general population. The sociodemographic data also enable us to pose the question of how similar the women interviewed are as compared to all abortion-seeking women in the United States. Comparisons can be made on the basis of age, marital status, race, and number of living children (there are no national totals reported to compare to the remaining variables covered in Table 3.3). As indicated in Table 3.5, national data for 1975 shows proportionally more women 20 years old and older having abortions than does the Midville Clinic interview group. Of the three age groupings, national abortion data show the 25 and over group to be the most frequent abortion clients. This group is the least represented in the present study group. The interview group also has proportionally more women 19 and younger than does the national population. According to the Center for Disease Control, however, the state in which Midville is located (designated "Midwestern State") reported age data more in line with the Midville group (Table 3.5). Even so, the Midville women are proportionally younger.

The Midville group is also different from the national population in that it has a higher percentage of unmarried women, and lower percentages of non-white women and women with one or more living children. The lower proportion of married women and women with children is most likely related to the fact that our study group was somewhat younger. Again, data from Midville's state are less divergent than national data.

The differences, in excess of the previously noted statewide differences, exist for at least two reasons. First, as we have already pointed out, Midville Clinic does not attract women from upper socioeconomic levels. When it does, these are usually teenagers. The older women from these levels, if they desire an abortion, are much more likely to go the traditional medicine route. This pattern would systematically exclude a number of older married women with some living children from a specialized clinic group but would not exclude such women from the Abortion Surveillance Report, which includes hospitals as well as clinics.

Another reason for the Midville Clinic group being younger, less frequently married, and with fewer living children than the national population is that our study group includes only women who have never had an abortion before. The national and state data are not limited by number of previous abortions. Of all United States women having abortions in 1975, 15.8 percent had already had at least one previously (Center for Disease Control 1977). It might be suggested that women with previous abortions, excluded from the present study, might

TABLE 3.5

Percentage Distribution by Selected Characteristics of U.S. Abortion Clients, 1975, Midwestern State Abortion Clients, 1975, and Midville Clinic Interviewees, 1975

Characteristic	U.S. Abortion Clients, 1975*	Midwestern State Abortion Clients, 1975*	Midville Clinic Interviewees, 1975
Age			
19 and younger	33	44	52
20-24	32	28	28
25 and older	35	28	20
Race			
White	68	79	87
Nonwhite	32	19	13
Unknown	—	2	0
Marital status			
Married	26	22	15
Unmarried	74	78	85
Unknown	—	0	0
Number of living children			
0	47	59	65
1	20	16	10
2	16	13	13
3-4	13	9	10
5 and above	4	2	2
Unknown	—	1	0

*Source: Center for Disease Control: Abortion Surveillance, 1975.

tend to be older and hence might also be married and/or have children. If the present study group had included women with previous abortions, then the differences between it and the state and national populations would most likely be reduced.

GATHERING THE DATA: VALIDITY AND RELIABILITY

At the time the interviews were scheduled, the women were told that they could choose to be interviewed either in their own homes or at Midville Clinic,

whichever was most convenient. The majority (32 out of 40) chose to be interviewed in the clinic setting. The women were also asked to choose the day and
time for the interview. Most interviews were conducted within one or two days
of the postabortion telephone call. Occasionally there was some delay so that
the length of time between the abortion procedure and the interview varied from
six to ten weeks. Each women was asked to set aside at least two hours for the
interview and was requested to come alone since it would be a rather long wait
for anyone accompanying her. Several hours preceding the scheduled time, when
possible, a reminder telephone call to the woman was made. Most appointments
were kept. Occasionally, a woman forgot and the interview was rescheduled.

The interviewee was instructed to present herself to the receptionist, when
she arrived at the clinic, in the same manner as all other incoming patients. She
then indicated to the receptionist that she had come to see the investigator,
whereupon the receptionist rang the investigator's office. The investigator then
came out to the main desk, introduced herself, and escorted the woman back to
the office. This procedure followed normal clinic routine as closely as possible
but avoided the possibly disturbing effect of the interviewee's having to fill out
the standard patient form (asking the nature of the visit) and having to sit in the
noisy, crowded waiting room. The aim was to make the investigator's role as well
as the interviewee's role as "normal" and unproblematic as possible.

In carrying out the interview, the investigator was aware of the issues of
validity and reliability as they relate to this particular type of research.

Reliability refers to the consistency of the data (Selltiz et al. 1959). Thus,
data can be said to be reliable if an independent but identical investigation
would obtain the same findings.

Concern with reliability requires that the researcher take precautions beforehand to eliminate as many sources of distortion or error in the data as
possible. In this study a number of extraneous factors which might have served
to influence the interviewee's remarks were considered. Such factors could have
arisen from the preinterview mood or temperament of the interviewee. They
also could have come from some ulterior motive on the part of the interviewee—
for example, seeking advice or hoping to get a refund from the clinic. Another
source of bias might have been an attempt on the part of the interviewee to
choose answers which she thought would please the interviewer. Other factors
biasing the content of the interviews might have been some disruptive element
in the way the interviews were arranged and carried out, or some element
emerging in the interview situations themselves.

Recognizing the possibility for the intrusion of any or all of these factors,
the researcher took the following steps in carrying out the interviews.

First, each woman to be interviewed was selected in as unbiased a manner
as possible (a description of this procedure has already been given).

Secondly, each interview was carefully structured so that no disruptive
event would occur and so that each interviewee would be interviewed in ap-

proximately the same setting and atmosphere. As pointed out above, the majority of interviews (80 percent) took place in the same setting, a family-planning clinic private office. The remainder took place in the women's own homes. In the latter cases, care was taken that no other persons were present at the time of the interview. For the office interviews, additional measures, such as those governing the woman's arrival at the clinic and the preparation of the office, were taken to eliminate disruptive factors. These measures were discussed above.

It was anticipated that the most difficult and touchy part of the investigator's preinterview comments would be getting permission to use the tape recorder. Each woman was told that it was very important for the investigator to keep a complete record of everything said so as not to misunderstand or leave out anything. The women were told that, for this reason, the tape recorder had been found to be the best way of recording the interview. They were then asked if they would have any objections to its use. Only one woman objected. That interview was conducted with the investigator taking notes as she went along. All the other interviews were tape-recorded.

Thirdly, the investigator tried to establish good rapport with each woman. An important part of this process was to develop confidence in the investigator. To help achieve this, the investigator tried to clarify her own identity and professional credibility, to eliminate any possible barriers to frank discussion.

To begin with, all interviewees were informed that the investigator was a sociologist conducting research independently. It was pointed out that, although she had received help from the clinic, she was not working for the clinic. This fact was established so that the women would not identify the investigator as a staff member, thereby possibly choosing their comments accordingly.

Next, the interviewee's possible fears were allayed concerning the confidentiality of her remarks and the purposes for which their content would be used. Each woman was assured that no mention of her identity or the identity of any person she might talk about in the course of the interview would be recorded. This explanation appeared to be readily accepted. The women were also assured that the interview tapes would be heard only by the investigator in the course of data analysis. Furthermore, each interviewee was told that the purpose of the study was to discover general trends and patterns and that her own personal case would not be presented in detail in any report of the study's findings. She was told that the research was being conducted to provide an understanding of what abortion is really like and that it was important for each woman to give as clear a picture of her own situation as possible.

In addition to having confidence, an interviewee must be relaxed in order to give a good interview. To help achieve a more relaxed atmosphere, the investigator explained ahead of time the nature and organization of the interview. The interviews began with questions concerning the woman's daily life prior to the discovery of pregnancy. In this way most interviews began on a relaxed level with nonsensitive, nonthreatening subject matter and worked gradually toward the more intimate areas of pregnancy and abortion.

The issue of validity is closely related to reliability. Wiseman (1970) has posed the problem of validity for the depth-oriented, qualitative researcher:

> . . . the validity problem is not whether the empirical indicators used to operationalize concepts are indeed valid representations of this phenomenon from an objective or scientific point of view (or even the so-called rational or reasonable man's point of view), but whether or not the investigator has represented the social world of the actor as the actor himself sees it. (Wiseman 1970, p. 280)

The problem of correctly representing the actor's perspective and actions has been dealt with in this research at two points. First, as just described, strategies were employed at the time the data was collected. Here, the aim for valid data impinges on the issue of reliability; that is, to the extent that data are unreliable, they lack validity (Selltiz et al. 1959, p. 178). Thus, enhancing reliability also means enhancing validity. The second point at which validity must be considered is in the data analysis. Throughout the interviews several techniques designed to increase validity later in the analytic phase were used. First, to help eliminate any idiosyncratic misunderstandings of questions and to be sure to get the woman's complete meaning, the investigator asked the major questions in several different ways. When puzzled by a particular response, the investigator reintroduced the question, perhaps rephrased, later in the interview. Finally, note was made of obvious facial expressions and gestures, such as smiles, tears, or frowns, which might not be evident on the tape.

The interview tapes were transcribed verbatim into typewritten form and the contents analyzed. The results of these analyses are presented in the chapters that follow.

4

APPROACHING PREGNANCY:
THE WOMEN AND THEIR LIVES

INTRODUCTION

The purpose of this chapter is to introduce in more detail the women whose abortions are the subject of this study. During the interviews the women all described themselves as they recalled their lives two or three months before they became pregnant. In this chapter we analyze these descriptions, delineating specific qualities and patterns. Starting with this point in the women's lives enables us to establish the kind of immediate social environment with which they entered into their abortion experience.

As mentioned in Chapter 1, the interview excerpts in this book frequently include in parentheses the interviewer's questions. Following each excerpt, also in parentheses, is the interviewee's identification number.

AFFILIATED AND DISAFFILIATED LIVES

At first glance, what is most notable about the women is their diversity. This diversity is quite evident in the range of their sociodemographic characteristics (see Chapter 3). It is also evident on a deeper level when we consider the complex reality of their everyday lives—their roles, their relationships, their life styles, and the various stages in the life cycle which they represent. While these concrete, substantive differences (differences in content) are numerous and intricate, when they are viewed analytically they take a much clearer shape (differences in form). Qualitative analysis reveals that the differences among the women revolve around the nature of their integration into society. When this issue was examined, the women fell into two groups. Underlying this division are notions of certainty and involvement—the idea of being "imbedded" or "well-rooted" in social groups. Let us examine this dichotomy more carefully.

In one group, the women were well-integrated or "tied in" to their social worlds. These women were clear about their obligations, expectations, and futures. They knew who they were and where they were going. This pattern is designated as *affiliation*, a pattern characterized by persons who are securely rooted or enmeshed in social life. The women in the second group were less firmly attached to their social worlds. These women could be described as being in flux. They had fewer and weaker social ties, role relationships, and other forms of systematic social participation. They also appeared to have less of a sense of purpose than the former group. This pattern is designated as one of *disaffiliation*, of being detached or loosely tied in to social life.

The two patterns can be seen more clearly when we consider the women's lives in terms of four components:

1. leisure or "volunteer" activities such as sports, clubs, hobbies, crafts, and so on
2. the nature of relationships with other people—family members, male partners, other friends
3. continuities and discontinuities in the central activities of their lives—primary group roles, employment, residence, and so on
4. orientation toward the future

Leisure Activities

The women could be dichotomized easily on the basis of leisure activities: roughly 55 percent were unable to identify any activity other than their usual occupational work and watching TV; the remaining 45 percent were involved in at least one additional activity, usually more than one. Many of the women who were not involved reported that their lives were centered around their male partners. This occurred among married as well as unmarried women. As one woman put it, "The only interest I have is him." The daily life of one of these women was explained in this way:

(Going back to last fall, I'd like to know something about your activities.) Mostly work and taking care of the kids. That's about it. No outside activities. (In a normal day, what would you do?) Go to work and come home and cook and clean house and watch TV and take care of the kids. . . . I really got kind of tired of doing that all the time . . . (What were you interested in?) I didn't do hardly anything at all. I'm not involved in anything. I don't have any hobbies. . . . I lead a very dull life. (1)

The other group of women, in direct contrast, reported many activities. Some were involved in sports such as motorcycling, bowling, or softball. Others participated in social and service organizations. Still others pursued various hobbies and crafts.

Relationships with Others

All the women had casual or "acquaintance" relationships with others. What we are concerned with here, however, are primary relationships—those with friends, with male partners, and with parents and/or siblings. Each woman was asked to comment about the nature of her relationships with these three categories of persons.

On the basis of the number, variety, and intensity of each woman's relationships in these categories, a basic distinction among the women appeared. In one group, comprising nearly two-thirds of the women studied, the women reported close relationships with at least two out of the three categories of persons. Twenty-five percent of this first group cited close relationships with all three types of persons. On the other hand, a second group—the remaining third of the women studied—could be characterized as more detached. Most of those in this latter group said they were close to only one of the three categories of persons. A few claimed not to be close to anyone.

In addition to this dichotomy, another interesting feature of the reported closeness to others was that no one type of relationship was cited as being close any more frequently than the others. Thus, closeness to parents was reported just as often as was closeness to friends and male partners.

Continuity in Central Activities

Here again, the women fell into two distinct patterns. Slightly over half the women (52 percent) had experienced a relatively constant and stable period during the six months prior to pregnancy—for example, living with the same persons in approximately the same type of living environment, having the same set of occupational obligations and expectations, etc. The other 48 percent, however, had had much more disruptive, discontinuous biographies. Some had dropped out of school recently; others had erratic attendance patterns. Others had moved in and out of the labor force. Several had made major changes in their life styles and living arrangements. One woman, for example, six months before she became pregnant had been living with a female friend and attending the local university. Then she quit attending classes, dropped out of school, and moved in with her boyfriend. After living with him for a couple of months and being employed and at home all the time, she moved back with her parents and got a job as a waitress. Then, after a month or so and shortly before she became pregnant, she joined the military and left for basic training.

Orientation toward the Future

Half of the women could be characterized as being uncertain or indefinite about their futures. These women varied in the degree to which they expressed concern for the future. Some were seemingly unworried and appeared to be living just for the moment. Others, however, while hesitant, were very concerned and could be described as searching:

> (What were your plans?) I'm thinking about trying to go to school and be a dietitian if I'm financially able to do it. . . . I'm trying to save money for it, but I can't really say it's definite because I don't know whether I'll be able to, but I'd like to. (If you went ahead with this, what would your expectations be for the future?) I don't really know . . . I'm just trying to get that far before I plan anything else because, like I said, I can't even plan too heavily on that at the time. (OK, let's go back to last fall. Did you have any particular interests?) Well, mainly . . . I was trying to use that time so that I could get myself to kind of clean up the path or whatever. So, mainly I spent the time just trying to figure out what I was going to do in the future. . . . (11)

In contrast to the disregard or ambivalence toward the future of the above group, the remaining women (50 percent) were definite. Some anticipated their present way of life continuing and, thus, saw the future as already laid out. Others had a definite set of steps outlined and, unlike the previous group, had no reservations about pursuing this path:

> (Do you have any particular plans?) Oh, yes. As soon as I graduate from college—five more semesters—I'm going to a technical institute in Europe for a five-year program in engineering. . . . (36)

The Two Patterns

Looking at the study group in terms of each of the four components, two patterns, affiliation and disaffiliation, are indeed clear. Each component has been viewed as a dichotomy, and these dichotomies, in turn, have been found to be interrelated. While there is a small degree of overlap, on the whole the women who appear in one category for one component follow the same pattern in categories for the other three components (see Figure 4.1). In terms of the

FIGURE 4.1

Presence or Absence of Selected Components of the Women's Lives During the Six Months Prior to Pregnancy

Components	Yes	No
Participation in Leisure Activities	12, 22, 31, 14, 34, 35, 26, 36, 17, 37, 28, 19, 29, 39, 10	11, 21, 1, 2, 3, 13, 23, 33, 24, 15, 25, 16, 27, 32, 18, 38, 8, 9, 20, 30, 40
Close and Varied Social Relationships	21, 22, 31, 6, 8, 34, 35, 26, 36, 17, 37, 28, 19, 29, 39, 10	11, 12, 5, 13, 23, 33, 24, 14, 15, 25, 16, 27, 32, 18, 38, 9, 20, 30, 40
Continuity in Central Activities	3, 4, 12, 22, 14, 34, 35, 16, 26, 36, 6, 17, 37, 28, 19, 29, 39, 10	2, 11, 21, 13, 23, 33, 24, 15, 25, 27, 32, 18, 38, 8, 9, 20, 30, 40, 31, 1
Certainty Toward the Future	3, 4, 5, 12, 22, 14, 34, 35, 26, 36, 17, 37, 28, 19, 29, 39	1, 2, 11, 21, 13, 23, 33, 24, 15, 25, 6, 16, 27, 8, 32, 18, 38, 9, 20, 30, 40, 10, 31

Note: Each of the interviewees in this study was assigned a number. Those numbers underlined indicate the women who exhibited pattern one, "disaffiliation." The numbers that are not underlined indicate the women exhibiting pattern two, "affiliation." Designation by one pattern or the other was made according to whichever pattern was indicated by at least *three* of the four components. Three women, numbers 6, 8, and 31, were split between the two patterns. All were of college age. One was attending college and also had strong social ties. She was categorized as "affiliated." Another had dropped out sometime before, but had decided to return. She also had strong social ties and was categorized as "affiliated." The third woman had dropped out recently and was extremely uncertain of her future. She was categorized as "disaffiliated."

Source: Compiled by the author.

specific categories, women who were involved in some sort of leisure activity tended to be those who also had close relationships with a variety of other people, who had experienced continuity in the central activities of their lives, and who had a fairly well-defined view of the future. On the other hand, the women who were not involved in any activities other than work and television also tended to have very limited close relationships with others, lacked continuity in past central activities, and lacked a definite picture of the future.

Regarding frequency distribution, Figure 4.1 shows that just over half the study group (21 women) fell into the affiliated pattern and slightly less than half (19) fell into the disaffiliated pattern.

Two questions remain concerning the affiliation-disaffiliation dichotomy: Do particular types of women tend to be disaffiliated (or affiliated)? Is the affiliation-disaffiliation dichotomy related to any other patterned differences within the interview group?

FACTORS RELATED TO AFFILIATION-DISAFFILIATION

Two possibilities for variables associated with affiliation-disaffiliation seem most likely for sociological reasons: *social class membership* (lower-class persons are frequently considered to be more alienated than other socioeconomic groups) and *stage of life* (young, single persons are frequently considered to be more alienated than somewhat older and/or married persons).

Social class and the configuration of the women's lives appear to be somewhat related (see Table 4.1). Among affiliated women, there is a slightly higher proportion of white collar women. In the same way, among disaffiliated women, there is a higher proportion of blue collar women.

TABLE 4.1

Configuration of the Women's Lives by Social Class

| Configuration | Social Class | | | | | |
| | White Collar | | Blue Collar | | Total | |
	N	Percent	N	Percent	N	Percent
Affiliated	11	(52)	10	(48)	21	(52)
Disaffiliated	7	(37)	12	(63)	19	(48)
Total	18	(45)	22	(55)	40	(100)

Source: Compiled by the author.

The stage of life the woman was currently in also appears to be related to the configuration of her life. Four stages of life can be distinguished: "late childhood," "first independence," "entering adult vocation," and "established in adult vocation."

The first stage has been termed late childhood because, while these women were able to conceive and bear children, they were in many respects still themselves children; that is, they lived with their parents and typically were dependent upon their parents both emotionally and financially. These women were still in high school, had never been married, and had never before been pregnant. Some were anticipating becoming independent and were actively challenging their parents' authority. Many of these women were sexually inexperienced.

The second stage refers to that period of time when the soman has left her parents' home and is out on her own, independent and searching for a vocation. These women were somewhat older, 18 to 22. They were generally either working or in college and were uncertain of their futures. They were unmarried and without children. Some had had previous sexual experience; others had not.

The third stage refers to the beginning of adult life. Women at this stage had a definite future in mind and were actively preparing for it. They, too, were in the 18 to 22 age range and were either planning to be married soon or, in the case of one woman, planning postgraduate training to prepare for a career. What differentiated them from women in the second stage is that these women were not searching. They had made a choice about their adult life. These women were often living with their parent(s), an arrangement which they considered practical (to save money) and temporary. They had been sexually active for some time.

The fourth category of women included both presently married and previously married women, most of whom had children. These women were older than the others (23 to 39). They were either living with their husbands or, in the case of those who were separated or divorced, living alone. One divorced woman had moved in with her parents after first living on her own for a year. These women had established life styles which were relatively permanent. They had a routine. There was continuity to their lives in terms of role involvement. These women were well established in their adult vocations—for most, this involved an occupation outside as well as one within the home.

As indicated in Table 4.2, the women in this study were distributed fairly evenly over these four stages. Furthermore, stage of life and the configuration of the women's lives were shown to be related. It appears that, at least among the women in this study, those who were about to leave childhood and those who were newly independent after leaving home were the ones who tended to be disaffiliated. Such a relationship is consistent with the idea that periods of transition involve a certain amount of change and adjustment—for some women this apparently meant detachment. Conversely, the women who had chosen and were embarking on a particular adult vocation (career and/or marriage) as well as those who had previously done so and were now established were the women

TABLE 4.2

Configuration of the Women's Lives by Stage of Life

	Configuration		
	Affiliated	Disaffiliated	Total
Late childhood			
N	4	8	12
Percent	(19)	(42)	(30)
First independence			
N	2	7	9
Percent	(9)	(37)	(22.5)
Entering adult vocation			
N	5	1	6
Percent	(24)	(5)	(15)
Established in adult vocation			
N	10	3	13
Percent	(48)	(16)	(32.5)
Total			
N	21	19	40
Percent	(52)	(48)	(100)

Source: Compiled by the author.

who tended to be imbedded in their social worlds (affiliated). Their lives were organized. They had achieved a definiteness and permanence which the former group lacked.

Another important aspect of the women's social worlds prior to the discovery of pregnancy was the nature of their attitudes toward abortion. How much did they know about abortion? Did they approve of it? Under what circumstances? How did they think others in their community felt about abortion? In the next two sections, these attitudes, as reported by the women themselves, will be considered—first, personal views, and then, perceptions of general community attitudes.

PRIOR ATTITUDES TOWARD ABORTION

Prior to becoming pregnant themselves, the women had definite moral opinions but very little factual knowledge about abortion. All of them knew it was legal but many knew virtually nothing beyond that. A third of the women said they knew absolutely nothing about what was involved in an abortion. Another smaller group had read about abortion and had heard indirectly about persons who had gone through an abortion. These women, however, had no personal acquaintance with anyone who had an abortion. In effect, they knew little more than the former group. The remaining half of the women had either a friend or relative who had experienced abortion. Few of these friends or relatives, however, had discussed their abortions. Thus, even these women had a very limited knowledge of what is actually involved either technically in an abortion procedure or social-psychologically in the woman's passage through an abortion. Such lack of knowledge is consistent with the cloak of secrecy typically cast around abortion but nonetheless surprising given the current frequency and controversial status of abortion.

The cloak of secrecy which has obscured abortion over recent decades is well illustrated in the images which abortion reportedly evoked for the women in this study. These images suggest an occurrence very far away from normal, everyday lives—something belonging to an underground, deviant side of society:

> It was dirty, you know, and a thing that you didn't tell anybody about. Something that you sneak off and do in quiet and keep it a secret for the rest of your life. (15)

Abortion was envisioned as something unsafe, unclean—even sinister:

> In our life we were raised up with this thing of abortion being a butcher with a big knife, you know. And you'r going to come out and bleed to death. Abortion became a dirty word. It really did. You know, people, when you say "abortion," they just kind of shudder. (31)

> Well, I thought of it more as a back-alley thing—hush-hush type of thing, you know. (17)

This sterotypic view of abortion was a subtle yet powerful lens through which most of the women had formed their prior abortion attitudes as well as one through which they were to perceive the events of their own abortion passage. For one woman, this imagery appeared to provide such ambivalence that she was unable to reach any opinion about abortion:

> I really didn't know anything about abortion. I knew that it was something that a lot of people really disagreed on and they were—I don't know. It was really kind of a dark thing. I really didn't know. It wasn't close enough to me that I would stop and think about it. I—for some reason, I always blocked abortion out of my mind because I didn't know how I felt. I was very confused about it. (6)

While this woman and one other—the youngest of the interviewees—were the only ones unable to articulate their prior abortion views, there is little doubt that this imagery served to encourage ambivalence and disruptive feelings for nearly all the women studied. This will become clearer in subsequent chapters.

One might think that women who have abortions are largely those who have previously approved of abortion. This follows the widely held principle that previously held attitudes correlate with subsequent behavior. It is striking, therefore, that only 30 percent of the women in this study characterized themselves as having been completely favorable to abortion prior to their own experience. It is also noteworthy that some of the women reported very intense opposition, inasmuch as they themselves were later to choose that very path:

> . . . I decided I would never have an abortion. I was entirely against it. I felt that it was murder, first degree, and that I would never have one. I felt like that up until I got pregnant. (Were you opposed to abortion just for yourself or in general?) I was opposed to it in general. I felt like a mother is a protector, a vessel . . . she is responsible for that child's birth, for maintaining and not doing anything to harm it in any way, and to insure that she does her part to get it safely here. My feelings on abortion were so intense that I always felt that even if I did get pregnant, I would go ahead and have the baby. (21)

The most common response, made by approximately two-thirds of those interviewed, was that their previously held opinion about abortion was a qualified one—not as permissive as complete approval but not as restrictive as unconditional disapproval. Hence, most of the women disapproved of abortion under certain circumstances and approved of it under others.

The qualifications or conditions for approval of abortion varied. The most restrictive women gave their approval only in cases of rape:

> Before, I thought it was horrid for a woman to get an abortion. I always thought there could be some way they could work things out. Other than rape or something like that. I've always kind of felt if she was older, then she knew what she was getting into. (24)

As suggested by this woman and by the next, age was also a factor in abortion attitudes. Very young women who get pregnant and then have an abortion presented an acceptable set of circumstances for abortion, even among the most restrictive.

Those with slightly less restrictive approval also included danger to the prospective mother's life as an acceptable condition for abortion:

> I'd have said I believe in abortion in the case of rape for girls that were young—a white girl raped by a black man, something like this—

somebody that was too young to know what was going on, or in
the case of where it would save the mother's life, things like this. I
don't believe in going out and getting an abortion just for the hell of
it . . . I don't see this. I can't see this. I still don't. I didn't before and
I don't now. But, like in cases of rape or where it would save the
mother's life, I'm all for it. (29)

Women who were yet a little more accepting of abortion added financial
inability as an acceptable reason for having the procedure done:

> . . . my girlfriend had an abortion last year and I did everything but
> beg her not to have an abortion . . . I was against it. I was against
> abortion. No, I was against it in her respect. I've never been against
> abortion down pat because I feel there's a lot of people who need it.
> But, I mean, she was married, she only had one child. Her husband
> and herself draw plenty of money. I mean, you know, they can af-
> ford another child and I felt it was wrong for the reasons she wanted
> to have the abortion. . . . I thought that was thoroughly wrong. (5)

Not only was this woman suggesting that those who can afford a child should go
ahead and continue the pregnancy, but she also seemed to suggest that married
women, particularly those with just one child, are also women for whom abortion is not appropriate.

Health, financial ability, and rape are all addressed in the following comment by another woman, along with an additional theme—the idea that women
should have to "suffer the consequences" of getting pregnant:

> The way I saw it, I couldn't see just letting a woman have an abor-
> tion just to have it, just because she wanted it. I couldn't see that be-
> cause—well, it was her fault she got pregnant. With the pill and
> everything else nowadays I couldn't see that. When it comes to her
> health or that there could be something genetically wrong with her
> or her husband, and the baby could be like a Mongolian, you know
> . . . or that that she couldn't afford it—that the baby might have to
> be put in a home . . . things like that I can see. When I was studying
> abortion in school, I took the same attitude about it because I
> couldn't see a woman who could afford having a baby—single having
> a baby—like these women that are single and can have children and
> then go and get an abortion, but yet the only reason they get the
> abortion is because they don't want a baby. With contraceptives,
> why should they get pregnant in the first place? Like, I'm always
> reading about cases of rape—that's one reason, if they get raped and
> get pregnant, I think they should have an abortion right off. (21)

This "crime and punishment" theme for pregnancy and abortion was addressed particularly to unmarried women. It reflects the traditional view that the

woman is to blame for pregnancy—that she is the one who must control sexual activity outside of marriage. When such women get pregnant, therefore, they should "pay" for their mistake. They shouldn't be able to "get off the hook" too easily. Thus:

> I kind of thought, if they can be dumb enough to get into that position, then they should go ahead and have it [the baby]. (39)

Or:

> I don't think she should get an abortion just because she doesn't want it [baby]. . . . I think that women should suffer the consequences and go ahead and have the baby. And, if she doesn't want that baby, she should just put it up for adoption. But I don't feel she should have an abortion if she really doesn't have a good reason for doing it. (Who do you think is responsible if a woman gets pregnant?) I think it's really her responsibility. I think it's her fault because she could be on the pill or IUD or whatever. She doesn't have to get pregnant anymore. That's her fault and I think she should go ahead and suffer the consequences. Stand up and be a woman and accept it. That's what she should do . . . I guess it depends on how old she is, too. But, like I'm talking about a person in her late teens or early twenties. There's no reason why she shouldn't know about birth control. (1)

For many of those who placed some restrictions on their approval of abortion, what was primarily important was that the woman seeking abortion have some reason *other than* not wanting a child. Said the other way around, a woman had to have a reason for an abortion other than just wanting one. Thus, "abortion on demand" was a concept approved by very few of the women in this study. Even the women who were most favorable toward abortion hesitated at the idea of abortion for no other reason than not wanting a child:

> (Did you have a generally favorable or unfavorable view of abortion before you got pregnant?) It was generally favorable, really. I never was against it . . . like I had no doubt about something like that— like, I mean, if the mother is going to die, or like if the baby was going to be terribly deformed or something like that and if the mother and the doctor and the woman's husband decided that they wanted an abortion, I don't think that a court or legislation has anything to do with it. I didn't really ever think about that—like, just if somebody got pregnant and they didn't want the baby. I never—I don't really think I ever thought about the area too much. (8)

We have examined the reasons for abortion which the women considered to be acceptable prior to their own abortion experience. The conditions varied from the most restrictive (abortion was acceptable only if the woman's life is endangered) to the least (abortion was acceptable for most reasons as long as it is not just a matter of not wanting a child). The order of conditions for acceptance among the women in the study group parallels the order consistently found in the attitudes of the general public (see Table 4.3).

TABLE 4.3

Abortion Attitudes of the General Population of the United States under Specified Conditions, 1965, 1972, and 1975

Condition of Abortion	Percentage Approving		
	1965*	1972†	1975†
Pregnancy is dangerous to the woman's health	71	83	88
Pregnancy is a result of rape	56	74	80
Strong chance of serious defect in the baby	55	74	80
Family has a very low income and cannot afford any more children	21	46	50
The woman is not married and does not want to marry the man	18	40	46
The woman is married and does not want any more children	15	38	44

*Source: Rossi, A. 1966. "Abortion Laws and their Victims." Trans-Action (September): 9. (National Opinion Research Center data).

†Source: Arney, W. R. and W. H. Trescher. 1976. "Trends in Attitudes Toward Abortion, 1972-1975." Family Planning Perspectives 8 (May/June): 117-24. (National Opinion Research Center data).

Another finding of previous research on abortion attitudes is the fact that a person who morally disapproves of abortion may also at the same time believe that it should be legal. As one researcher put it, "sin is not necessarily equivalent to crime" (Moore 1973, p. 5). Such a view was also found among the women in the present study:

> We both realize that we've done something wrong, something immoral. It goes against our beliefs—taking a life is wrong. . . . I've always been pretty much in favor of abortion being a legal opportunity. (19)

The legal right to have an abortion was viewed as a way to ensure the "lesser of evils" in resolving unwanted pregnancies. Thus, while abortion might not be viewed as a desirable thing to have done, it was seen as the best alternative under some circumstances:

> I always thought they should have the right to do it because it would be better to have that than for somebody to have a child that they didn't want and then not to take care of it or something. That's the way I always felt about it. (40)

It should be noted here that the concern for the potential child expressed in this last comment was atypical. Most women emphasized the potential mother and not the future of the potential child.

A more subtle variation on the abortion-should-be-legal-but-it-may-not-be-moral theme consisted of the view, "It's OK for other women, but not for me." For example:

> I didn't have any bad feelings against the idea. I wouldn't be prejudiced against a person—you know, even years ago—just because they had an abortion. I feel like that's their decision and they know what's right for them . . . and yet, I didn't think I could ever do it . . . I always did think of it as something I wouldn't want to be involved in, you know. But it was all right for other people. (17)

Their willingness to accept abortion in other women but not in themselves implies that, perhaps, these women viewed themselves as being "different" from other women. When questioned in detail about this, some women acknowledged that they had tended to stigmatize women who had abortions:

> I was kind of surprised at some of the people that I found out had an abortion. You know, it really surprised me because I didn't think of people that were going to school with me as having abortions. I thought of it as something beyond me, beyond my age. The getting pregnant time was way off, as far as I was concerned. (Where did you think pregnancies and abortions were located? Whose world did you identify them with?) People with problems . . . the normal, good student, those kind of people just—either they are smarter or in their growth and development they are not ready for that. (20)

> Well, before I got pregnant I figured that there wasn't that much need for them . . . (Would you say that you tended to be against abortion?) Pretty much. Well, I figured, it's their own fault. If somebody did it, it didn't bother me, but me myself, it was no. Other people, if that's what they wanted to do, fine, but I didn't think there was that much need for it. Like, they got themselves in that

situation, you know, and they're just going to have to figure out what to do about it. (Would you have tended to look down on that?) I probably would have in a small way. I would have tried to catch myself and keep myself from doing it, but I'm sure way back in the back of my mind I was still probably thinking it. (22)

Not only did this last woman tend to stigmatize women having abortions, but she tied this negative view to the notion, discussed earlier, that such women should pay for their mistakes. While these two ideas did not appear together explicitly in the comments of many of the women, they very likely go together in underpinning many people's thoughts about women who have abortions.

Returning to our central dichotomy, affiliation-disaffiliation, let us briefly consider whether or not it can be related to the women's reported prior abortion attitudes. We find that it can. As Table 4.4 shows, complete approval of abortion

TABLE 4.4

Abortion Attitudes by the Configuration of the Women's Lives

Abortion Attitude	Configuration of the Women's Lives					
	Affiliated		Disaffiliated		Total	
	N	Percent	N	Percent	N	Percent
Complete approval	9	(75)	3	(25)	12	(30)
Disapproval with exceptions	12	(43)	16	(57)	28	(70)
Total	21	(52)	19	(48)	40	(100)

Source: Compiled by the author.

occurred disproportionately more often among affiliated women. Similarly, disapproval occurred more frequently among those who were disaffiliated.

Two explanations for this relationship are possible. First, disaffiliation may mean that these women are indecisive and hesitant, unable to completely approve of a controversial action—and/or it may be that because of their own insecurity they are particularly prone to criticize others, adopting rather negative views of controversial actions. A second possibility is that both affiliated and disaffiliated women may have selectively recalled their prior abortion attitudes differently, reflecting their current situations. Either way, the most dramatic trend remains that by far the majority of the women studied (70 percent) reported that they had disapproved abortion to some degree prior to their own experience with it.

In summary, the prior abortion attitudes of the women studied here indicate that abortion is considered acceptable only under specific circumstances. The majority of the women would be likely to disapprove an abortion unless the woman had been raped, unless she had health problems relating to her pregnancy, or unless she were financially unable to take care of a baby. Interestingly, their own abortions did not always fall within these circumstances.

Such an apparent contradiction is not unusual; abortion attitudes have been found to contain many seeming contradictions. Perhaps most important among these is the fact that approval of the *legality* of abortion does not imply that one approves the *morality* of abortion. A similar point was made previously (Chapter 1) in our discussion of the current abortion scene in the United States. The statement was made that abortion is legal but not moral. The views of the study group confirm this. Many of the women claimed that they had approved of abortion but then later qualified that statement by saying, "But I never thought I would have one myself" or "It's the lesser of two evils." None of the women stated their approval without some qualifying remark. The fact that most of these women did not appear to enter into their abortion experience with complete and unqualified approval of abortion is certainly noteworthy. We shall see later, in Chapter 9, whether or not these attitudes changed.

To complete our consideration of the women's prior views on abortion, we now turn to their perceptions of community attitudes.

PERCEIVED ABORTION ATTITUDES IN MIDVILLE

Disapproval also characterized what the woman perceived as the typical attitudes of fellow Midville residents. Of the 40 women 32 (80 percent) believed that the majority of their fellow citizens disapproved of abortion. This was described by one woman as follows:

It's very closed. It's obvious because—well, when we went through this thing with the hospitals, they make it very expensive because they don't want to do it. They don't want it done in town. A lot of parents protest that they even offer the services that this clinic does as far as birth control is concerned. And abortion is even worse than that. So the people in this town have really—"We don't want that here,"—I think that's the general opinion . . . abortion, that's really—that's like mortal sin. This is a pretty conservative town. I would say most people morally are against abortion. (20)

Several women spoke in terms of the intensity of feeling against abortion which they perceived—the view of abortion as a crime or sin:

> Well, the people that I know, most of them feel like it's something that shouldn't be done. They feel like if you get pregnant you should just stick in there and handle it, go ahead with it, and not get rid of it. I think they believe that's the worst thing to do. (1)

> They look at it as being murder or something bad. (10)

> They think that it's killing a child—a life or something like that. (32)

To account for such strong opposition in their community, some women cited the particular residents' background or experience. One such explanation was that people who are against abortion are generally those who have never experienced it themselves:

> I think the better percentage would say that it's murder. They think it's bad and that it should be illegalized just because they haven't gone through it. (15)

> I just wonder, you know, if the situation ever came up how they would handle it—if the shoe was on the other foot and they couldn't feed their family or something like that and came up with another kid. How would they feel then? (17)

> Well, I feel sorry for the people who are so much against it. What about all these congressmen, you know? They don't know what a female goes through. They can never have children. (23)

Another frequently stated theory, refuted by recent research (Zelnik and Kantner 1975), was that community opinion is divided by generation—the older ones against and the younger ones in favor. One woman mentioned the impact of religion as well as age:

> It would depend on what age they were. It seems like the younger generation would be more for it. I think that they'd probably be for it. Of course, like if it was a Catholic person, then they're going to be against it. (16)

It has been pointed out that most Americans, according to public opinion research, do not approve of abortion as a freely available option. Instead, they approve of abortion only under certain restrictive conditions. These findings have been supported by the women themselves in their own attitudes. In perceiving the attitudes of their own community, however, even more restrictiveness is suggested. Some women expressed doubt about the degree to which these "acceptable" conditions are *really* acceptable:

> They are against it. Some of them are for it in cases where it's needed for health reasons or something wrong with the baby or something like that. But I think they're pretty much against it. (23)

> I would say probably that most people would not be for abortion in just any case. I think most people—in fact, I think a lot of people don't even believe in abortion when there might be a medical problem or something. . . . I think they are pretty much antiabortion. (8)

While the vast majority perceived local residents to be strongly opposed to abortion under almost any circumstances, three women saw a somewhat different climate. Their perceptions were that most members of the community were neutral, taking an "it's not part of my life" attitude. These women also suggested the existence of a familial theme—the idea that "abortion is OK for someone else, but not for me." They implied that surface approval is a mask for ambivalence and possibly for disapproval. As one woman put it:

> I think the general attitude in [Midville] is for abortion for another person. They never face up to it themselves. It's fine for the unwed mother or someone like that. . . . Underneath it all they say, "fine for Amy Lou, but I could never do that." (17)

None of these women perceived their community in terms of an overall and genuine approval of abortion. From this fact and from the fact that the women's own personal views prior to abortion were reported to have been generally negative, we can conclude that for most of this group, abortion was entered into with the view that it represented a form of deviance. For the women involved in abortion to perceive that others in their community disapproved of abortion and for them to have frequently disapproved of abortion themselves implies that their own pregnancy must have constituted, for them, a highly problematic situation.

AFFILIATION-DISAFFILIATION AS AN ANALYTIC TOOL

The study group has shown consensus to a large degree in their own abortion attitudes and in their perceptions of their community's attitudes. Thus far, the central factor on which there was not uniformity at the point of entry into pregnancy is the configuration of their social worlds—whether the women were affiliated or disaffiliated with respect to ongoing social life. Having isolated this conceptual distinction, we must now be prepared to use it as a tool to observe whether it discriminates the way the women experience the various stages of their abortion passages.

In subsequent chapters, therefore, we will be examining whether affiliation-disaffiliation is related to the way in which pregnancy is initially reacted to, the nature of the decision-making process, the actual experiencing of the abortion procedure, the nature of the postabortion "recovery" period, and/or any subsequent changes in the women's lives.

5

INTRODUCTION

The preceding chapters have revealed who the subjects of this study were and what their lives were like before they became pregnant. In this chapter we move to the period when pregnancy was discovered.

Becoming pregnant is a sequence of activity initiated by the biological event of conception. This sequence is a product of subsequent physiological changes in the woman's body and a related process of recognition, culminating in the woman defining that these changes indicate pregnancy. From conception to recognition to medical confirmation of pregnancy, the woman is interacting with others and applying socially constructed meaning to her condition. Therefore, in analyzing this experience, it is important to consider her social world, particularly those persons she is closest to.

Thus far in our analysis, we have identified a general pattern in the women's social worlds. This pattern has divided the study group on the basis of each woman's attachment or integration within the society around her. With our social process view of becoming pregnant, we need to know some additional things about these social worlds at the time of conception. Who were the intimate other persons in each woman's life? What person(s) was she closest to? Was she using any form of birth control? What was her view of birth control? How did she first recognize she was pregnant? What was her first reaction to pregnancy? Did she consider herself responsible?

INTERPERSONAL RELATIONSHIPS AT PREGNANCY

So far the women's relationships with others have been touched upon only briefly. Their general scope and intensity provided one of the four components

74

upon which the women were categorized as either affiliated or disaffiliated in the last chapter. One important aspect of relationships with others has not been discussed—which other person each woman felt closest to. Such a person can be described as the one who most clearly served as her significant other.

Significant others are central participants in the establishment of meaning and in the organization of action. They are persons whose interpretations of an actor's behavior are incorporated by the actor herself (Mead 1934). Such persons, therefore, serve to validate or invalidate claims of appropriate conduct (Goffman 1959). They provide a point of reference (Merton 1957) or social comparison (Festinger 1954) for an actor. In studying an act with the potential to be highly problematic, such as abortion, it is particularly important to delineate significant others and their roles during the course of experience.

In Table 5.1 the study group is categorized according to the type of "other" indicated by each woman as the closest to her at the point she became

TABLE 5.1

Frequency of Types of Significant Others as Perceived by the Women Studied

Type of Significant Other	N	Percent
Husband (permanent male partner)	10	(25)
Boyfriend (nonpermanent male partner)	13	(33)
Friend	8	(20)
Parent(s)	9	(22)

Source: Compiled by the author.

pregnant. For more than half the women the male partner was the central other person. For another 22 percent parents (along with, in some cases, siblings) were central. The remaining 20 percent were friend-centered, their peers serving as significant others.

Because of his biological and social involvement with the woman's pregnancy and abortion experience, and also in light of the fact that he was most frequently the woman's central reference point at pregnancy, we now turn to a more in-depth discussion of the woman's relationship with her male partner.

The women in this study typically became pregnant within fairly stable and exclusive relationships. These tended to be serious relationships with at least some degree of mutual commitment. The majority of the women had been involved sexually before. For 28 percent, however, this was the first time they had

had a sexual relationship. Lee (1969) found the same percentage of first sexual relationships among the women she studied. Lee also reported that a few women in her group had doubts about the identity of the potential father. In this study none of the women reported any such doubts.

Of the relationships with the male partner, 38 percent were characterized either by marriage or formal engagement or by the partners cohabiting for at least one year. Thus, more than a third of the women became pregnant in the context of an enduring relationship, generally with substantial commitment for the future.

The largest portion of the relationships, 45 percent, could be termed serious but with limited commitment in terms of the future. Most of these relationships (11 of 18) had been going on for at least six months; some had existed as long as two or three years. These couples saw each other frequently, and exclusively, and most of the women felt quite close to the men involved.

The remaining 17 percent of the women became pregnant in relationships of a more casual nature. A few of these relationships had lasted for several months; however, they were characterized by friendship rather than by the intense involvement of the relationships discussed above. Four of the seven casual relationships were extremely casual: the woman had seen the man only a few times. In two of these cases, the sexual encounter occurred while the woman and a more serious partner had temporarily broken up.

Previous research on similar groups of women has shown patterns in women's relationships with their male partners like the ones found in the present study (Lee 1969; Pearson 1973). Specifically, these studies, as well as the research reported here, all suggest that most women who become pregnant and have an abortion do so in the framework of a steady and meaningful relationship. The promiscuity which is sometimes stereotypically associated with unwanted pregnancy and abortion is not validated here.

In addition to the nature of her relationship with the male partner, another important aspect of the woman's situation at the time she became pregnant is her pattern of birth control use.

BIRTH CONTROL PRACTICES PRIOR TO PREGNANCY

Why does a woman who ends up having an abortion become pregnant in the first place? Does she want to have a baby and then change her mind? Did the birth control method she was using fail? Was she herself careless? Or was she uneducated about the functioning of her body and the ways to control conception?

Questions such as these are common reactions to cases of pregnancy termination. Professional answers vary widely. Those within a social work or family-planning framework tend to emphasize problems in birth control availability (Shah, Zelnik, and Kantner 1975) and the lack of knowledge about birth control (Reichelt and Werley 1975; Presser 1974) which lead to unwanted pregnancy, particularly among younger women. Psychiatric investigators have argued that women *do* understand the "facts of life" but that underneath they actually want to become pregnant (Aarons 1967; Sandberg and Jacobs 1971; Ford, Castelnuovo-Tedesco, and Long 1972). Feminist writers point to the inadequacies of existing birth control methods and to the large number of women who become pregnant simply from the "normal" failure rate of these techniques (Rossi 1966 and 1967). While each of these explanations may fit one or two women interviewed for this study, none is adequate to explain the majority of the pregnancies. A more careful examination is required.

The Nature of Contraceptive Use

To begin with, respondents in the present study can be described in terms of their contraceptive use during the six-month period prior to pregnancy by one of three general qualities—conscientiousness, carelessness, or complete indifference. As indicated in Table 5.2, most of the women studied can best be characterized as careless. Few were completely indifferent. Even fewer were conscientious users whose method failed.

A *conscientious user* is one who uses a reliable method of birth control and who, when questioned, reports consistent use of that method. "Reliable" methods are so defined on the basis of the relatively low percentage of women who get pregnant while using them. Such methods include oral contraceptives (the pill), the intrauterine device (IUD), and the diaphragm used with spermicidal jelly. These methods have been demonstrated to result in far fewer pregnancies than the other available methods, which we have termed "unreliable." The latter include contraceptive foam, douching, condoms (prophylactics), "withdrawal" (coitus interruptus), and the so-called "rhythm" method (abstaining from sexual intercourse during ovulation, estimated to occur around the fourteenth day of a normal menstrual cycle).

Just three women (7 percent) of the entire study group could be characterized as being conscientious users (Table 5.2). Two had an IUD in place at the time they became pregnant and a third reported that she had used a diaphragm in the correct manner (with spermicidal jelly) during all her sexual activity. This proportion is substantially smaller than the 30 percent reported as contraceptive failures in Lee's (1969) study of women who had abortions. Most of Lee's contraceptive failures were diaphragm failures. Her study was conducted nearly a decade ago when the pill was just beginning to have widespread use. The larger number of failures reported in her study probably reflects the greater dependence on the diaphragm during those years.

TABLE 5.2

Frequency of Type, Usage Pattern, and Method of Birth Control Use as Reported by the Women

Type and Usage Pattern	Method	N	Percent	Total N	Total Percent
Conscientious					
Consistent use of a "reliable"	IUD	2	(5)		
method	Diaphragm	1	(2)	3	(7)
Careless					
Sudden discontinuation of a	Pill	15	(38)		
"reliable" method	IUD	2	(5)		
Sporadic use of a "reliable"	Pill	3	(8)		
method	Diaphragm	1	(2)	32	(80)
Sporadic use of an "unreliable" method*	Foam, condom, "rhythm," douche, withdrawal	11	(27)		
Indifferent					
Not using any method	—	5	(13)	5	(13)

*Two of these women using an "unreliable" method reported consistent use.
Source: Compiled by the author.

A *careless user* is one who is unsystematic, using contraceptives during sex at some times but not at other times. Careless users in the present study followed one of three patterns: (1) consistently using a reliable method and then suddenly deciding to quit, failing to adopt another reliable method; (2) using a reliable method but using it inconsistently—for example, leaving the diaphragm in the drawer during intercourse or not taking the pill for a day or two or more; and (3) using not only an unreliable method, but using it inconsistently. With respect to this last pattern of carelessness, it is noteworthy that almost all the women who used unreliable methods also tended to be inconsistent users. Only two women reported that they had used an unreliable method consistently—in both cases, the method used was contraceptive foam.

Carelessness characterized a large portion of the women studied (Table 5.2). Eighty percent followed one of the above three patterns. Earlier studies indicated that well over half the aborted women studied had tended to be careless users (Lee 1969; Pearson 1973). A more recent study (Luker 1975) supports the somewhat higher proportion found in this study. In all of these studies, including the current one, the women generally have been found to be familiar with, rather than ignorant of, birth control practices.

A final group are those women who ignored birth control altogether. They have been termed *indifferent users*. Thirteen percent of the women studied reported that they had used no method of birth control during the six months prior to and including the approximate time of conception (Table 5.2). Four of these five women reported that they had *never* used any method of birth control. While Lee in her research did not report those who had never used birth control, she did report that 20 percent of her study group had failed to use any contraception in the month in which conception occurred. It would appear, therefore, that the current study group was characterized by fewer nonusers than Lee's group.

It also appears that lack of contraceptive education is *not* a key factor in explaining indifference. When the women in this study were questioned, they reported that they *did* understand bodily function and that they were aware of various methods of birth control. Previous research (Pearson 1973; Luker 1975) corroborates this point. As will be discussed later, for the women in this study, ignoring birth control is better related to lack of stability or to uncertainty in their lives than to lack of contraceptive education. For a few, ignoring birth control might even be considered a form of rebellion.

The questions asked at the beginning of this section can be easily answered for those who were conscientious users. They became pregnant because of the failure of the birth control device they were using. The cases of women who were careless or who did not use any form of contraception are less easily understood. We now consider them.

Abandoning the Pill

As shown in Table 5.2, 32 of the 40 women exhibited some form of careless birth control use. Of these careless women, over half had been consistent users of a reliable method and then suddenly quit. The others were nearly all sporadic users of either reliable or unreliable methods, mostly unreliable ones. In this section, the first group to be considered is composed of those who discontinued a reliable method. This group included women on both the IUD and the pill; the vast majority were on the pill, and two women had IUDs. These two had health-related problems with the IUD and each had to have it removed following the recommendation of her physician. Neither woman, however, adopted another method of birth control and both soon became pregnant. As we have said, the rest of the women were using the pill. In the remainder of this section, their sudden abandonment of the pill will be examined.

Abandoning the pill was the most frequently occurring pattern leading to pregnancy (see Table 5.2). Some of these women used an alternate method, albeit an unreliable one. The vast majority, however, used no replacement method. Most of the women reported that they became pregnant just a few months after discontinuing the pill.

For the observer, such behavior raises several questions. Why did the women stop taking the pill? And, once they did, why did they not adopt another relatively effective method of contraception? How did these women feel about the risk they were taking? Were they aware of it? Did they worry about becoming pregnant?

Why Did They Stop?

Three conditions appeared to precipitate discontinued use of the pill.* The women were distributed fairly evenly among these three. Some stopped after a change in their relationship with a male partner. Another group quit when their prescription ran out and they had to return to the doctor or clinic for another. A third group stopped for medical reasons—either the fear of or the actual experiencing of side effects. The only exception was one woman who stopped the pill because she and her boyfriend had decided to have a baby. After she discovered she was pregnant, their relationship disintegrated and she decided to have an abortion. Her pregnancy reportedly was intentional. (The subject of intentional pregnancy will be considered in a later section.)

The most common condition precipitating discontinuation of the pill was a change in the woman's relationship with her male partner—specifically, a break in the relationship:

> (Were you using birth control then?) Yes. (What were you using?)
> Pills. (Then, did you go off the pills?) Yes. When we were separated,
> I quit taking them. (11)

In the case of this woman, the "break" was a legal separation. For others, it was the termination of a dating relationship, or, in some cases, simply a severe argument:

> (Were you using any method of birth control?) I *was* and then we
> broke up for a month. (What were you using?) Pills. And I just—well,
> my big mistake was I quit taking them. (When you started seeing

---

*Recently, Luker (1975) has reported similar findings. The data reported here were gathered and analyzed without the investigator having knowledge of Luker's research, adding to the validity of the findings.

him again, were you doing anything to . . .) No. That's what I did wrong. (25)

Unlike this last woman, most did not return to the previous partner. They became pregnant by another man. This new partner, however, was often a man with whom the woman had established a fairly stable relationship by the time pregnancy was discovered.

Why did the termination of a relationship signal cessation of the pill? The women's comments indicate that for them the termination of a relationship also meant the termination of their sexual activity. They did not appear to envision themselves engaging in sexual intercourse with other men.

> (Were you using anything for birth control at the time you got pregnant?) No. (Had you been using anything?) When I was married I did and then, after that for a long time . . . for a long time I just didn't take the pill anymore because I figured, "What the heck," you know, "I don't need it". . . . (35)

Sooner or later, however, these women did "need" the pill. They resumed sexual activity—frequently after a very short time. When they did, they were unprotected. In some cases, the women were sexually active for several months without protection. Others lacked protection only during a brief encounter. One woman, for example, had a series of arguments with her boyfriend during which time she saw another man:

> When I started seeing this guy, I had gone off the pill because he wasn't able to father any kids. (He had had a vasectomy?) Right. And so, with that, I couldn't see any reason to continue taking the pill because I wasn't planning on messing around or anything. And then, I kind of let myself get talked into something one night and that's when it happened. (With another guy?) Yes. (39)

Her comment that she "wasn't planning on messing around" further illuminates why the women thought they wouldn't "need" the pill. *The pill is a symbol of planned sex.* It symbolizes the intention to engage in sexual activity. According to the viewpoint of these women, sexual activity should occur in the confines of a permanent or potentially permanent relationship. Because they did not see themselves as sexually active persons except in the context of such a relationship, they did not see the "need" to prepare for "outside" sexual activity. When the relationship was severed, they continued to define themselves as not sexually active outside ot it. They *did* have other sexual activity, but they were unprepared:

> Well, when me and [my former boyfriend] broke up, I went off the pill because I had promised myself that I wouldn't do it with another

guy again. (Did you feel uncomfortable about having sex with him?) No, because I loved him . . . and then when [my new boyfriend] and I started having it, I said, "Well, shall I go back on the pill?" and he said, "Well, let's think about it." And then, I got pregnant. . . . (3)

Although by the time of pregnancy these "new" relationships were fairly stable, the women were still hesitating to admit their sexual activity by starting an effective method of birth control.

Clearly, the values which have traditionally regulated the sexual lives of women did not prevent the women in this study from engaging in nonmarital sexual activity. They did, however, influence the women's definitions of the situation. This has been illustrated above and will be shown again later when we discuss the sporadic users and those indifferent to birth control.

Not all of the women who quit taking the pill when their relationships with their male partners terminated were certain why they stopped:

(Do you remember why you went off?) I don't know . . . I don't really remember why I quit taking them. I guess I just didn't feel like messing with them. I don't really remember why I quit taking them. (11)

The notion of sexual activity being tied to a "permanent" relationship may be subtly carried out. The pill may be stopped without the woman always being completely aware of the power of these societal constraints in shaping her action.

This last woman's remark that she "didn't feel like messing with them" suggests the second set of conditions under which women reported that they stopped. A woman's supply of pills would run out and she would "not get around" to contacting a doctor in order to get another prescription:

I was on the pill up until about six months before I got pregnant. I don't know what made me quit taking it. I just thought, "Oh yuk, I'm tired of taking these pills." I think one reason was that I didn't want to go back to the doctor for a physical. That was a stupid reason, but I just didn't want to go. I thought, "I've had enough of them anyway. I'll just stop taking them for awhile." (12)

I wasn't on the pill at the time. I got pregnant because I couldn't come up—see, I needed more and I had nobody to take me and get some. So, I got in trouble. (13)

Moving to a new city appeared to compound these circumstances in an explanation offered by another woman:

What happened is I came to town with a prescription of birth control pills, just two months of birth control pills that my doctor had left me. I didn't get to a doctor in time to get a new prescription before my old prescription went out and I was off my pills for a month. It only takes one month. And, I got pregnant. (5)

A third group of women reported that they quit taking the pill for medical reasons. They were concerned with the pills's side effects. For one woman, the fear of side effects and the idea of discontinuing the pill were generated by her doctor:

I went and got a regular gynecologist—you know, here in town—and he told me that you are supposed to go off your pills every two years and some doctors say every four years because, I guess, you become sterile. That's what he made it sound like—you would become sterile if you didn't go off of them. So, I went off of them for three months and that's when I got pregnant. (15)

Others actually experienced side effects which precipitated their quitting:

I started taking the pill and I took about ten different kinds and I just couldn't take them. I was sick all the time. I wasn't gaining weight. And then, I stopped taking them and then about a month after that I got pregnant. (9)

When I was taking them, it would just come back up. (Do you mean you'd get sick to your stomach?) Yeah. (After you'd take the pills?) Yeah. (Then what did you do?) I quit taking them because I couldn't hack it anymore. (2)

I used the pill for a long time, probably about three years. Then, I had an ovary taken out and I quit taking it, and then I started taking it again two months later. . . . My doctor told me to stay off of it for awhile and then he told me it was OK to go ahead and start them again. So I did. And then, from being off them, I could really tell what a difference it made when I went back on them. They make me nervous, they make me depressed, and they make me feel really icky. They really do. And they made me retain my fluid. . . . And so, I quit taking it because I thought it made me feel bad. (31)

Why Not Another Method?

In addition to the question of why these women went off the pill in the first place, another question was posed: Why didn't the women who had quit taking the pill choose one of the other relatively effective methods of birth control (IUD or diaphragm) as a replacement?

Their comments reveal that they were quite hesitant and indecisive:

I went off thinking I would get an IUD and I never did . . . I was kind of waiting on my period and my period never did come. . . . I was using that foam stuff, but I knew it wasn't really safe . . . I thought, "I'll just go ahead and use the foam until I have my period." (31)

(Did you use anything?) No, nothing. We just tried to—I just tried rhythm for awhile and that's basically what I was doing when I did get pregnant. (12)

The same reluctance was shown in considering a return to the pill:

(Did you talk about birth control?) Yeah. We had decided that—I had decided that I was going to see the doctor and get the pill, and I had never gotten around to it. (Were you using anything?) Nothing. (35)

Other comments emphasized the "difficulty" in using the less effective methods that many women seemed to prefer:

(Were you using any other kind of protection?) At that time, no, I wasn't. . . . My husband and I had a hassle about that because I told him to go and get something and he said he wasn't going. He didn't want to go and buy something. He's embarrassed. . . . I told my husband, "Leave me alone," but he won. (5)

We had been planning it out—when to do it and when not to do it. And, that was the weekend we planned not to do it, but it didn't work out that way. . . . We went to a party that night and we got kind of drunk. I knew it and he knew it, but we completely forgot. . . . (3)

For another woman, such methods were not necessarily difficult but they were certainly undesirable. In her view, they ruined the spontaneity of sex:

(Did the doctor give you another method?) Well, yes, but I never used it. We just didn't do anything—well, we did, but not very often, like once a month and then just the rhythm method. . . . (What did the doctor suggest that you use?) Rubbers, things like that, but we didn't use them. It's hard to say, "Wait a minute, stop right here." It kind of takes everything out of it. (15)

While disruption of spontaneity is sometimes suggested as a major reason why couples do not use birth control devices, this was the only woman in the study group who indicated as much.

This same woman was also the only one to indicate another frequently suggested reason for ignoring birth control—the notion that abortion is viewed by women as an *alternative* to contraception. She appeared to be substituting abortion for contraception in that she reported using no birth control but, at the same time, reported coming to Midville Clinic every month for a pregnancy test:

> I was coming up here. I came up here three times—well, once a month—and took pregnancy tests because I wanted to know as early as I could if I did get pregnant. I wanted to know real early. (15)

It can be suggested that she wanted to know early so as to be sure of being able to secure an abortion. Again, it must be emphasized that this woman was the only one who seemed to be substituting abortion for contraception.

What is striking in most of the women's comments is the indication that most were consciously oriented toward using birth control. They did not lack knowledge; nor did they want to get pregnant. Why, then, were they so lax? Since most of the women studied were not married (87 percent of those who abandoned the pill), it seems plausible to return once again to the norms governing the sexual activity of unmarried women. Because it is not proper to do so, unmarried women do not generally think of themselves as sexually active persons. They may engage in sexual activity, but that is viewed differently from being a sexually active person. As we have said, reliable methods of birth control suggest a *commitment* to sex. To obtain them, a woman must visit a physician. This constitutes an overt admission of the intention to have sex, validating for her that she is sexually active. Thus, it can be suggested that many women shy away from such a situation. Moreover, reliable methods are such that they must be obtained well in advance, adding to the notion of "planned sex."

For the woman, an alternative to the identity threat posed by the reliable methods is to use an unreliable one. These can be obtained more discreetly or, in the case of "withdrawal" and "rhythm," involve no device at all. These latter two involve no tangible evidence of sexual activity, no evidence of having "planned" sexual activity and, thus, may be considered the least implicating to the self. Unfortunately, they also are among those providing the least protection.

Risk Taking

The final question concerning abandoning the pill has to do with whether or not the women were aware of the risk they were taking. Did the women worry about becoming pregnant?

In general, most women seemed to be relatively unconcerned. Their comments indicate that they realized they "should" be protected; and, in that sense, they perceived the risk of becoming pregnant. Nevertheless, most women took the view that they were invulnerable—in their words, "It couldn't happen to me":

> I said, "No, I couldn't get pregnant. It's just not possible." (Did you worry about getting pregnant then?) Not really. I just thought, "It's not going to happen to *me*," you know. But it did. (35)

Rather than worry, they appeared to place confidence in their unreliable methods—or in the element of chance:

> I didn't think anything about it. I don't know. I just must not have thought it was that time of the month when I could have gotten pregnant. I must have miscalculated it or something. (12)

> (Did you worry about it at that time?) Well, I figured I was close enough to my period that I was beyond getting pregnant. I *thought*, but I wasn't. (39)

Myths or rumors also helped the woman not to worry:

> (When you stopped taking them [pills], were you using any kind of protection then?) No. (Had you thought about the possibility of getting pregnant?) Oh, I really didn't think too much about it. I don't know. I knew there was a chance I would, but I had always heard—this probably isn't true—but I had always heard that women that have taken the pill and then stop, it's real hard for them to get pregnant. And, I guess that's why I didn't use anything. (9)

In summation, the women who abandoned the pill did so with very little provocation. They frequently appeared to have acted on impulse. They frequently appeared to have acted on impulse. They reported nothing about having thought carefully about a replacement method. It could be inferred that few of these women had considered the implications of their actions. In the words of one woman:

> I don't know. I don't know why I did it. That's the thing I can't understand. (Why you. . .?) Took the chance. I mean, everyone knows it only takes one time for this to happen. That's the thing that bothers me the most, I think, about the whole thing is that I took the chance. (31)

While they spoke in terms of having very little hesitation in deciding to go off the pill, there was a great deal of hesitation in returning to it or to another similarly effective method. We have suggested that this indecision reflects the force of cultural constraints placed on the nonmarital sexual behavior of women. This helps explain why carelessness occurred even in the context of relatively stable relationships. Although relationships with new partners became stable and exclusive, the women continued to hesitate; or, even when a stable relationship was only briefly disrupted, the women discontinued effective birth control immediately. The women were aware, at the time, that they had taken a risk— that they could become pregnant—but the majority were relatively unconcerned that pregnancy might actually occur.

Off and On Contraceptive Use

The other pattern of carelessness found among the women studied is one of inconsistent, erratic use of birth control. Not only were these women inconsistent users, but the methods they used were generally the unreliable ones. As indicated in Table 5.2, less than a third of the inconsistent users employed an effective method such as the pill or diaphragm. While most of these women were not using the pill, many of them said that they had been considering it. Like the women discussed in the last section, however, they hesitated in getting started. Also like the previous group, myths or rumors and the notion that "this couldn't happen to me" characterized their hesitation:

(Were you using any kind of birth control when you got pregnant?) He was using condoms, but he just didn't a couple of times, I guess. . . . Before, we decided that he or I ought to do something and he decided he would do that . . . I think I thought about birth control pills, but somebody told me—I'm too gullible, I guess, and I'm still not sure about this—but when I was a freshman my roommate got birth control pills and she said you had to be 18 or something to get them . . . and I said that. He was kind of hoping I wouldn't have to do anything, so he asked me if it was all right and I said, "Sure." (When he didn't use one, did you think about it?) I don't think I even thought about it. (8)

I didn't think it would affect me. I thought, "Well, I'll go on and this will never happen to me"—that kind of naive attitude. (Were you using something?) Withdrawal. According to everybody, it shouldn't even be classified as a method for birth control. (20)

Both these women were aware of the need to protect themselves against pregnancy, but, like the careless women discussed above, they remained relatively unconcerned and tended not to worry.

Two women provided significant exceptions to this trend. They worried about getting pregnant. What is interesting is that despite their worry they still did not use a consistent and reliable birth control method. Their comments illustrate the dilemma introduced earlier—the dilemma an unmarried woman faces between protecting her personal identity as a nonpromiscuous woman and at the same time protecting herself against an unplanned, unwanted pregnancy:

(Before you found out that you were pregnant, had you ever suspected that you might be pregnant?) Yeah. I'd say, "What if I
get . . . " because he wasn't using anything and I wasn't and, before,
he'd just stop. (You mean, withdrawal?) Yeah. Ugh. But then,
after awhile, he just couldn't and I . . . I would get so nervous that
I'd break out in hives. I'd start itching all over every time he would
come in my room, you know, because I knew that—and I'd think,
"Oh, God, what if I get pregnant?" (Did you ever discuss birth
control?) Yeah—well, I had a problem with my periods. I had one
that lasted a couple of months and I went to the doctor and he gave
me birth control pills. I don't know, I just felt like I was—I always
get that dirty feeling if I was taking the pill. . . . I just felt like if I
took it he'd know, "Well, she's taking the pill. I can do it all the
time." I didn't want that. I wanted him to be with me because he
wanted to be with me, not to fool around. (Did you ever discuss
condoms?) Yeah. He went and bought some one time, but he just—
he didn't like it. He'd just take it right off. (30)

I would always tell him, "No, I don't think we ought to do this,"
because I was kind of afraid of it. And he'd say, "Oh, don't worry."
(Had you talked about using birth control?) Yeah, but he didn't . . .
I couldn't get pills or anything like that because I was afraid Mom
would find them lying around the house or something . . . I wouldn't
know what to do if she found them . . . I really would have been at a
loss about what to tell her. (How do you think she would have reacted?) I don't know. It would have been more embarrassing for me.
I don't know how she would have reacted, but I just know I would
have been really embarrassed. (How about any other things?) Well,
he didn't want to use anything else. (Do you mean a condom?)
Yeah. I asked him to and he said, "No," he didn't want to . . . he
doesn't like them. (How about an IUD?) I had thought about that,
but I didn't know how to go about getting one and I had heard they
weren't too dependable, so . . . I would say something and he'd
say, "What time of the month is it?" And then he'd say, "Well, it's
OK." But the way I was so *irregular*—he didn't really grasp the idea
that I was trying to tell him it wouldn't make any difference. (40)

Preparing for sexual activity ahead of time with a reliable method such as the pill or an IUD may stigmatize a woman as being promiscuous or immoral.

Fearing this stigma from others and in order to protect her own concept of self, a woman may choose to leave herself vulnerable to pregnancy. Less effective methods are less stigmatizing and less threatening to the woman's identity. They do not imply a permanence to sexual activity. A condom, foam, withdrawing, or "watching the time of the month" all allow her to demonstrate some concern for avoiding pregnancy and, at the same time, imply nothing more planned than a one-time encounter. With one of these methods, a woman need not feel that she is or will be considered "always ready." Also, in order to use a reliable method, the woman must visit a doctor, openly acknowledging that she is sexually active. Many single women find this too threatening an admission to make—or, at least they are prone to postpone such a visit. Instead, they continue to think of their sexual activity as limited to only one man—or to a very special relationship; and they either suffer the continual fear of pregnancy or, as was more frequent in this research, they convince themselves that *they* could never become pregnant.

The idea that an unplanned pregnancy may result when a woman cannot accept herself as a sexually active person is not new (Pohlman 1969; Cutright 1971; Lessard 1973). It has typically been offered, however, as an explanation for pregnancies among women who are becoming sexually active for the first time—particularly teenagers (Miller 1973; Cobliner 1974). The findings of the present study suggest a slightly different interpretation. They suggest that an unwillingness to accept oneself as sexually active may be tied to societal norms which restrict nonmarital sexual activity for *all* women. Thus, such norms can be expected to affect women with sexual experience as well as those with none.

In comments concerning their use of birth control, their recognition of the risk, and their definition of that risk, sporadic users are similar to those women who abandoned the pill. They are hesitant to use a reliable method, yet they know there is a possibility of getting pregnant. This inconsistency is overcome by their not thinking about it or by their adopting the notion that pregnancy could never happen.

Nonusers

At the beginning of this chapter, it was pointed out that only three of the 40 women studied could be classified as conscientious birth control users. A similarly minimal number (five women) reported that they had used *no* birth control method at all during their sexual activity in the six months prior to becoming pregnant. In fact, among these nonusers, only one woman reported that she had *ever* used any method of birth control.

The practice of not using birth control and then voluntarily terminating the resultant pregnancy draws attention to several questions raised previously. Were these women unaware of birth control? Had they considered using birth control even though they hadn't used it yet? Or did they want to become pregnant?

With respect to the first question, like all the other women interviewed, these nonusers had discussed taking the pill. Several themes familiar from the other groups discussed appeared in their comments—for example, the association of the pill with promiscuity (immorality) and the fear of stigma:

> Everything that I've been hearing about the pill . . . I thought it was really bad. Well, since I've been taking it, I don't think it's all that bad. I have aunts and cousins that are taking it. They're taking it to regulate their periods. I mean they're—like they don't drink, they don't smoke, and they're a really close family, and if they don't see anything wrong with it, then I don't see why everyone is talking about it. (But, before, you thought there might be something wrong with it?) Right—that like people who took them always wanted to go to bed or something like this. This is what I got the impression of. (32)

Another theme found previously was the susceptibility to myth or rumor:

> (When you started having sex, was there any discussion about using birth control?) Yes, there was. I told him that I wanted to get on the pill before anything started, you know, and he said, "Well, the pill doesn't help you all that much," and like a dummy . . . I listened to him and then I got pregnant. (How about other alternatives?) He didn't think they were worth the time. (Even a condom?) No. He just said they were a waste—I mean, he didn't get any pleasure out of it or something like that. . . . (32)

It should be noted that such an attitude toward the use of the condom has appeared in several of the comments presented here. Thus far, it has generally been the male who was reported to be the one to reject the condom; however, women, too, discouraged its use. This attitude, along with the susceptibility to rumor, is illustrated in the following:

> (Did you talk about whether you were going to use birth control?) Well, we started talking about it before, but I was afraid the pill would mess me up or something and that was the only thing I thought about. I couldn't imagine using something else—the pill at that time seemed a neat thing. I mean, I couldn't see using anything I had to insert or anything like that. (Did you talk about a condom?) Not really, because I wouldn't think—to me, that didn't seem fair to him. We just always talked about the pill for some reason. . . . We talked to this one lady and she told us that if I ever got on it, I'd have to be on it all my life; and if I ever quit taking it, I'd have a

baby automatically. She was this friend who worked in a tavern. It kind of scared us, you know, so we decided "No, uh-uh." (Were you using any kind of protection?) No, I wasn't. (14)

From these comments, it is evident that nonusers were not only knowledgeable about birth control methods, but they had actually discussed using an effective method.

Turning to the last of the three questions, we considered whether or not the nonusers failed to use birth control because they, in fact, wanted to get pregnant. Here, there is a notable difference between these women's comments and the comments of the women discussed previously. The nonusers' remarks indicated more ambivalence toward pregnancy—less commitment to not getting pregnant—than did the remarks of the other women:

> (Had you talked about the possibility of your getting pregnant?) Yeah. We had talked about it, you know, and he said he really didn't care if I got pregnant because that would be one way I could marry him faster. (Were you trying to get pregnant?) Not exactly. We weren't: "Hey, let's get pregnant tonight." It wasn't that type of deal, but it was just—it was out of love more than anything. It wasn't that I was trying to marry him that quick because—I don't know. (If you had really *not* wanted to get pregnant, do you think you would have tried harder to take birth control?) Yeah. If I had been worried about it and if I wasn't engaged—you know, if I had not been wanting to be married—then I would have worried about it a lot more. (14)

One woman had even reportedly considered becoming pregnant a desirable condition:

> (How about your own feelings about getting pregnant?) Well, it was kind of like—I was rebelling against my parents and I thought if I got pregnant maybe that would stop them for awhile; because, after my girlfriend had got pregnant and had her abortion, she got really close with her parents . . . I was trying anything to get close to my parents, you know. I ran away. I was doing everything I could possibly think of and I thought if I would have got pregnant or if I told them that I was pregnant or something like that, then maybe they would sit down and finally just listen to me for awhile. . . . (Did you think about what you would do with that pregnancy?) Umm, not really. I didn't really know anything after that. (32)

In this case, however, the desirability of pregnancy was related to what impact it might have on others rather than to actually wanting a baby.

FACTORS RELATED TO BIRTH CONTROL USE

Do certain categories of women tend to follow one birth control pattern more frequently than another? This is an important question in the area of fertility and fertility control. To answer it, we will examine each of the four major patterns found among the women under study: conscientious use, abandoning a reliable method, sporadic use, and no use at all.

Two of the patterns must receive qualified attention because of the small number of women to whom they apply. As previously noted, conscientious use was found among only three women; five women used no method at all. Despite the small numbers of women characterized by these two patterns, age was related so consistently that it should be pointed out. All the conscientious users were in the over 21 age category (see Table A.1, Appendix A). In contrast, all the nonusers were in the 21 and under category; all but one were under 18.

These younger women were also all high school students living at home with their parents. They were distinguished, however, from similar high school students in the study in that they were all, to some degree, actively rebelling against their parents (see, for example, the previous comments of interviewee 32). All five nonusers could be characterized as rebellious. In addition, all but one of these students reported they were doing poorly in school. Looking at their affiliation or disaffiliation from social life, four of the five nonusers were categorized as disaffiliated (see Table A.6, Appendix A).

The other two patterns can be viewed with somewhat greater confidence since larger numbers of women were involved. In analyzing these two patterns, of major concern will be the question: What type of woman might follow one pattern of carelessness rather than the other?

The group who abandoned a reliable method of birth control tended to be slightly older (over 21) than the group of sporadic users (see Table A.1, Appendix A). More important than age for the abandoning group, however, was marital experience (see Table A.2, Appendix A). Proportionally, those who quit a reliable method included more women either currently married or who had previously been married than did the sporadic group.

Differences based on religion were relatively small. Catholic women were proportionally overrepresented among the abandoning group and underrepresented among sporadic users. The reverse was true for Protestants (see Table A.5, Appendix A). Perhaps related to the earlier observation that abandoning the pill frequently occurred after a change in the relationship with a male partner, those who abandoned the pill tended to be disaffiliated in comparison to sporadic users. Thus, sporadic users included proportionally more women categorized as affiliated (see Table A.6, Appendix A).

Another feature of the abandoning group was that they included a proportionally higher number of blue collar women (see Table A.4, Appendix A). This was particularly the case among the women 29 and younger (see Table A.7,

Appendix A). Young, white collar women tended to be sporadic users of unreliable methods whereas young, blue collar women tended to go on the pill and
then quit. One of the high school students interviewed made reference to this
latter pattern among her peers.

> . . . the way that everybody had been talking about it, they had
> taken the pill for three or four months—I knew three girls who had
> done this—and then they got off it. They said it didn't help—well, it
> helped and everything, but they thought they could use something
> else. (32)

Those who used birth control sporadically were almost all in the younger
age category. Only two of the 15 sporadic users were over 21. Despite their
youth, sporadic users were slightly better educated (Table A.3, Appendix A)
and, as mentioned above, included proportionally more white collar women
(Table A.4, Appendix A). Again, it is suggested that the advantages of using unreliable birth control (for example, avoiding the implication of promiscuity)
rather than ignorance of birth control was the key influencing factor among
these women.

In summary, conscientious use as well as complete indifference toward
birth control seemed to be related primarily to the age of the woman. The two
patterns of carelessness—abandoning a reliable method and using a typically unreliable method sporadically—reflected not only age differences, but marital
experience, social class, and educational differences as well.

We now move from the issue of conception to the process of becoming
aware of pregnancy.

SUSPECTING THE PREGNANCY

The women in this study—with two, possibly three, exceptions—did not
plan to become pregnant. They were careless in using birth control. Being careless, however, does not mean that they were planning to become pregnant.

Not having planned pregnancy, as one might expect, the women also
tended not to have anticipated becoming pregnant. As one woman put it, "I
thought I'd be lucky." Eventually, of course, all began to suspect. Most often, it
was the inevitable physiological changes associated with pregnancy which generated the suspicion.

For some of the women studied (15 percent), however, pregnancy was
anticipated even before symptoms began to be experienced. These women reported that they had feared becoming pregnant from the time they had unprotected intercourse. These women were not obsessed with fear of becoming pregnant, but neither were they as casual and unconcerned as the others.

Most of the women, while neither planning nor anticipating pregnancy, did, nevertheless, recognize and correctly interpret pregnancy symptoms within a relatively short time. More than 75 percent of the women identified the signs and, within a week or so of first experiencing them, were definitely suspecting pregnancy. This finding contradicts that of a recent study in which the author concluded that "women who were truly surprised by pregnancy (nonplanners)" not only failed to anticipate the cues of pregnancy, but they also "did not recognize their meaning when they occurred, and went initially to a (nonobstetric) physician for diagnosis of 'illness' rather than confirmation of pregnancy" (Miller 1975, pp. 18-19). The majority of women in the present study *did* accurately and rather quickly perceive pregnancy. In addition, only two of the 40 women studied went to a physician seeking treatment for something other than pregnancy. Other studies also have reported how quickly pregnancy was recognized among "nonplanners" (Lee 1969; Pearson 1973), supporting the findings of the present study.

Let us turn to considering how the women came to an awareness of the fact that they were pregnant. What made them first start suspecting?

For a majority of the women (68 percent), missing a menstrual period was the central factor in their recognition of pregnancy:

> (Let's go back to the first time you can remember thinking you were pregnant . . .) I guess it was when I was about three days late . . . I was three days late and I knew, I just knew I was. I didn't have any signs. Nothing. But I just knew I was. (12)

> (What was it that made you start suspecting?) Well, when I missed my period a week I thought, "Oh, no." I said, "I'll wait another week because they said here that you have to wait two weeks before you can come in. . . . I didn't have any symptoms. I wasn't sick or anything . . . I had no doubt in my mind. I knew when I came down here that they were going to tell me it was positive. (30)

Some of these women had experienced other symptoms of pregnancy before missing a period—symptoms such as feeling tired or sick or noticing enlargement of the breasts. Usually, they only momentarily connected such symptoms with pregnancy, if at all. Until the period was missed, prior symptoms tended to be normalized:

> (You didn't worry until you missed your period?) Right. Well, I was getting kind of—starting to get dizzy, and when I would stand up real fast or something like that—I wasn't having any morning sickness or anything. (Did you think about that in terms of pregnancy before you missed your period?) No. I just kind of thought it was something else because . . . I had been working so much and so I just

really didn't think a whole lot about it until I missed my period. (How many days was it before you started worrying?) About three days. (39)

At first I thought it might be something else. Then, when I didn't have a period—that's when I really started worrying. . . . (29)

(How did you start suspecting that you might be pregnant?) I just felt tired all the time. I didn't have the energy to want to do anything else. And . . . I was getting sick in the morning—not really, really sick, but I just felt so nauseated and . . . I missed one and then I thought, "I *know* this is it." Before then I thought, "Well, maybe not," but when I missed it, I thought, "This is it. . . . " There was just no doubt in my mind that I was. . . . (35)

For other women, these symptoms came at about the same time as the missed period, adding to its significance.

Most of the women with a history of regular menstrual cycles frequently dismissed their earliest symptoms, but they seemed unable to disregard or normalize a late or missed period. While several indicated that they thought there might be a reason other than pregnancy for the missed period, they went ahead and made an appointment for a pregnancy test. Only one woman denied the implications of her missed period in any notable way. She was able to accept the possibility of pregnancy only after a friend questioned her:

(When you missed that first period, what went through your mind?) Oh, I just thought that . . . I was kind of nervous about a few things. I was just moving into the new apartment and moving in with a new girl and everything. And I was kind of nervous and I just thought that that was probably it. . . . And then, well, my roommate knew I had been acting really funny and she—you know, you live with somebody and they can tell when you are not having your period, I guess. So she asked me. She said, "Have you been missing your periods or what?" And I go, "Yeah." And she sat me down and she said, "What are you going to do?" (31)

For the remaining third of the women in the study group, missing a period was a less important factor in the events which led them to awareness of pregnancy.

Ten percent of the women were certain that they were pregnant before a period was ever missed (in a couple of cases the period was *not* missed even though the woman was, in fact, pregnant):

Well, the earliest I started thinking about it was when I started getting sick. . . . I missed a bunch of days at work because I was so sick. I didn't have this morning sickness; I had afternoon sickness. That was when it first dawned on me that I was pregnant—because it was so obvious. I mostly kept trying to talk myself out of the fact that I was pregnant because I hadn't missed a period. Then I decided I was definitely and so I was trying to decide what I should do about it. (11)

As mentioned previously, another two women did not identify any cues of pregnancy. Instead, they consulted a physician (in both cases, gynecologists) in order to get their periods regulated. For both of these women, pregnancy came as a complete surprise:

(Why don't we move to the point when you actually started suspecting that you were pregnant?) I never suspected, that's the thing. . . . I wasn't that regular . . . and then I had cramps for two weeks straight, so I had made an appointment to go see a gynecologist for the reason of getting something that would straighten me out . . . and I had to cancel it because I was spotting at the time . . . and I made another one and I went to that. That's when he told me I was about two months pregnant. I go, "Oh, really?" (You had no idea?) No. I didn't know. . . . I wasn't suspecting it. (28)

The remaining women (17 percent) were those who said that they were not regular with their periods. For this reason they could not easily distinguish a missed period from a late one. In the cases of these women, a combination of the "late" period and the increasingly obvious symptoms resulted in eventual recognition. As with many of the other women, the early and less severe symptoms were normalized. As the days passed and the signs became more and more revealing, it became exceedingly difficult to continue the denial:

(How did you first start suspecting it?) Well, I didn't—I should have, but I didn't really recognize it. I did have just a tiny bit of morning sickness and I just thought that I hadn't been eating the right kind of foods or something. But it never really hit me . . . that I was pregnant . . . physically, my stomach got bigger and I noticed my breasts were a lot tenderer . . . and mentally I thought I was a lot more sensitive to situations than I would have normally been. (How did you react to those things?) I was beginning to get concerned and I kind of just pushed it off to the side—"No, that's not—" . . . because I considered it at different times before when I was late starting my period and that wasn't really the case. I was just late again. Like, sometimes it happens, and so I wasn't really that concerned until all of it started coming together. (When did it finally come together?) Well, my husband had bought me a new pantsuit for Christmas and we were going out in the evening and I had put it on and I couldn't get it buttoned and I kind of decided that I hadn't been eating more than I normally eat. As a matter of fact, I had been eating less . . . so that was kind of when I decided I was. (7)

Three of these "irregular" women continued normalizing symptoms until the approximate time for a second period had passed:

> (When did you first start suspecting?) Well, my period—I missed one and a half, and when that second one didn't come rolling around like it was supposed to, I kind of got worried. Just about that time, I started getting sick all the time. I have stomach trouble anyway and I kind of just thought, "No, I've got an ulcer or something." (40)

In the case of this particular woman, the normalization of symptoms escalated into a full-scale process of denial, which meant a delay in the woman seeking medical confirmation. The signs of pregnancy became so obvious that her mother finally noticed them and forced her into coming to terms with them:

> . . . I just kept putting it off, saying to myself, "No, it couldn't be. I couldn't. There's no possible way." (Were you trying to convince yourself that you weren't?) Yeah. Well, I *had* convinced myself that I wasn't. It was my mother that finally said, "Hey, you know these symptoms look kind of familiar for something." And, I said, "No, Mom, you don't think I'd be doing anything like that, do you?" She's the one that finally convinced me that I had to do something and find out. . . . (40)

To summarize the recognition process, the majority of the women in this study suspected pregnancy when they missed a menstrual period. Their suspicion began within just a few days of this happening. For women who did not have regular periods, recognition took a little longer and was frequently based on other symptoms. While it was common for the women to normalize their earliest symptoms, they did not tend to normalize the more obvious signs. Thus, when a woman who was generally regular with her periods missed one, or when a woman became continuously ill for several days, the conclusion was quickly reached that these signs indicated pregnancy. Although these women were not looking for pregnancy in the sense of planning or anticipating, they responded to the appropriate symptoms.

CONFIRMING THE PREGNANCY

Once suspicion was firmly aroused, most women sought medical confirmation right away. Thirty of the women arranged for a pregnancy test as soon as possible after they became aware that they might be pregnant. Some may have, as one woman put it, "kind of held out a little hope," but generally the pregnancy test simply added scientific validity to something they had already established for themselves as fact.

It was the symptoms which they could not successfully normalize that brought them to an awareness of pregnancy. This point is particularly well-illustrated by the few women whose first pregnancy test was negative. Even though these women did not want to be pregnant, and even though medical expertise indicated that they were *not* pregnant, they persisted in defining themselves as pregnant because of symptoms they could not normalize:

> Well, things started going kind of funny. My periods were getting . . . closer together and then my stomach started bloating up down here and I thought, "Gee, that's odd," you know, because I generally have a pretty flat stomach. . . . Then I started not feeling too good. I've never had morning sickness or anything like that, but I was just tired, run-down. . . . Well, finally it [IUD] came out. . . . And I was just absolutely panic-stricken—I mean, hysteria hit. . . . And, of course, there is nothing you can do, but immediately you want to know if you are pregnant. So I had to wait maybe two weeks to take a pregnancy test . . . and all during this time I knew that I was pregnant. . . . I kind of held out a little bit of hope, you know, but then I went down to get that pregnancy test and the signs became more obvious . . . and then not to have it confirmed the first time was completely crushing. (What did you do when they told you it was negative?) I said, "Oh, my God." Well, I told them, I said, "I know I am." Then I came back, I think ten days later, and gave them another specimen and then, of course, the results were positive, which I already knew. (17)

Another woman in a similar situation at first believed the negative test results, but she, too, was faced with symptoms she could not normalize:

> The first time the test was negative and I was really happy about that. And then I came back down because everything started getting worse. I started gaining weight, you know, and that's unusual because I usually don't gain weight during school when I'm playing tennis and volleyball and things like that. So I came back down here and the second test was positive. (32)

Becoming aware of pregnancy and seeking medical confirmation were the products of a struggle which for some women was short-lived but for others went on for several weeks. The object of the struggle was for the woman to hold on as long as possible to the idea that she was not pregnant. For those who typically had irregular periods and who now experienced little physical discomfort or change, normalization was easier and continued longer than for those whose periods had been regular and who now were experiencing striking physical changes and discomfort.

For the pregnancy test which all eventually had, the women either went to Midville Clinic (72 percent), to a private physician (20 percent), or to a local laboratory service (8 percent). Two-thirds of the women went alone for their pregnancy test. One-third were accompanied, most of them by friends. Thirteen percent, however, were accompanied by the involved male. Only one woman was accompanied by a parent.

While most women were very prompt to make arrangements for a pregnancy test after recognizing that they might be pregnant, this was not typically their first action. Initially upon suspecting pregnancy, most women first confided in another person. In fact, all but three of the women studied had told at least one other person before calling for a pregnancy test. For nine of the women (23 percent) this other person actually took the initiative in making the pregnancy test appointment. In two of these cases, the person encouraged the woman to make the appointment; in the remaining seven cases, the other person actually called and made the appointment.

Who were the confidants? The male partner involved in the pregnancy was told *before* the pregnancy test by 65 percent of the women. The man also was the most frequent "other person" told of the suspected pregnancy. This is not surprising since he was considered as "significant other" by a large number of the women. Fifty-three percent of the women told a friend. Parents and siblings or other family members were least likely to be confided in. Thirteen percent of the women told a parent and 10 percent told a sister. An additional three women told the mother of a friend; two were their boyfriend's mothers.

In previous research it was found that another common action for women to take early in an unwanted pregnancy was to try to "bring on the period" with various home remedies. Lee (1969) reported that over half the women she studied used at least one of these "methods." In contrast, only one woman in the present study spoke of pursuing this type of activity:

> Do you really want to know what I did? I did exercises. I ran up and down my trailer. I took douches that were real strong, thinking, "Oh, God, I just can't be." (12)

Whether such activities represented attempts at creating spontaneous abortion is unclear. Other women interviewed, however, mentioned that friends or acquaintances had claimed to have produced spontaneous abortion through more dangerous practices—for example, by having someone jump on the abdomen or by using a vibrator belt.

Thus far, we have followed the women from their earliest suspicion through medical confirmation of their pregnancy. The next section will complete our discussion of the process of becoming pregnant. It deals with what the women recalled as their first reaction to being told they were indeed pregnant.

INITIAL REACTIONS TO PREGNANCY

The women's first reactions to medical confirmation of pregnancy varied in degree of intensity as well as in direction of sentiment. The majority of the women took a negative view of their pregnancy. Sixty-eight percent reported that they initially reacted in terms of not wanting to continue it. Fifteen percent said that they were uncertain about what they wanted to do. Seventeen percent said that their first reaction was to want to continue the pregnancy and have the baby. The women's reactions can be separated analytically into two dominant patterns, discussed in the section that follows.

Rationality-Emotionality

A little over half of the women reacted to their pregnancy in a relatively calm, matter-of-fact way. For the most part they had what we will call a *rational* response. Certainly, there was emotion involved, but it was pragmatism that was preeminent. Now that they knew what their condition was, these women were immediately thinking ahead to their decision. Relatively certain that they were pregnant, they came for the pregnancy tests prepared for positive results. Once they were told, they tended to respond by organizing a plan of action rather than by expressing emotion. Their attention was focused on problem solving, on how they could arrange to terminate the pregnancy:

> I already knew that I was and I was thinking to myself, I said, "Why waste the seven dollars? I already know I am." (It wasn't a shock then?) No, because I already knew I was and I knew I had to do something about it. . . . (39)

> (How did you feel when they told you?) I knew it. When she [the social worker] said, "How do you feel since I have confirmed it?" I really didn't feel any different because I already knew. I mean there was just no doubt in my mind that I was and I was prepared for it. (35)

Some women who generally took a matter-of-fact view of medical confirmation also spoke of experiencing other feelings as well:

> I pretty much knew before I came down here, you know, what it was going to be. . . . It was no big surprise. . . . (Do you remember how you felt when they actually told you?) I was prepared for it, but still, it kind of shook me a little bit. I still had that little bit of hope in me—you know, maybe it's not. (How did you feel?) I just kind of let things come as they come. Everything usually moves its

way. . . . I guess the first thing was making sure I kept it from Mother. I don't know what else. . . . Not really fear, just—I was kind of worried about what other people would think of me because I knew what I thought of other people before and I guess I was mostly worried about that, and making sure not very many people knew about it. . . . I'll say I was—the thought of it, you know, was kind of a dark thing in my mind. I didn't know what was going to happen and what all the procedures were. Ignorance is probably what, if anything, made me scared—but I wasn't that scared. (22)

These themes—feeling upset, being afraid of the reactions of other people, particularly the reactions of parents, and being anxious about what was involved in the abortion procedure itself—were common among all the women in this study. For the rational women, illustrated above, these were secondary concerns. For others, however, *emotional* reactions took precedence. Forty-five percent of the women could be categorized as reacting emotionally to medical confirmation of pregnancy. Shock, fear, confusion, depression, and happiness were the words they used to describe their feelings. Fear and shock were the two reactions most commonly reported:

It just kind of hit me . . . I said, "How am I going to tell my mother?" That's about what I thought. How do you tell your parents that you're pregnant? But I was. I was just kind of—I don't know . . . I was stunned. (28)

(What was your first reaction?) I went and got hysterical. I just— deep down I knew that I was, but I didn't want to believe it. I didn't want to accept it. And I just went crazy. I didn't even know what to do and I started crying and I just felt like everything had fallen out from under me. (Were you scared?) Yes. Very. Because I knew I couldn't tell my parents, just by the way they had raised me and the way I knew [they] felt about it. There was no way I could tell them. (6)

(How did you feel when they told you it was positive?) I kind of—I just sank. It just—it hit me like an atom bomb. I almost vomited. I was just sitting there and I was going, "Oh, you've got to be kidding." It was really ridiculous. Somehow, it just came as a shock—I mean all this time I knew, but it just came as a shock to me for some reason. I don't know why. (14)

As these statements indicate, the women were shocked upon actually hearing what they had expected to hear. That they still registered shock reflects the stigma they attached to pregnancy. It is difficult to accept deviance in oneself. The same kind of denial that had led them to ignore the possibility of pregnancy while they were engaging in unprotected intercourse affected their recognition of pregnancy once it occurred. As one woman said in describing her response to being told she was pregnant, "I just couldn't believe it—me!"

Because they defined their behavior as deviant, most women feared what others would think or how others would react to them in light of their pregnancy. The fear of being stigmatized by others, as well as the shock of confronting one's own stigmatizable actions, appear in the following comment:

> I had it in my mind that I was—I mean, I was just sure that I was, but I was kind of shocked when she said it. I was so sure on the outside but there was this little thing in the back of my mind—it just seemed like, you know, it can't happen to me. Of course, you say that about everything. (What do you remember feeling when she told you you were pregnant?) I was nervous. I thought, "Oh, no." . . . I was happy but I was scared about what Mom and Dad was going to say and how I was going to tell them. . . . I was afraid my dad was going to beat me and I was afraid I was slowly going to be tearing up my mom. . . . I was just wondering what [my boyfriend] was going to say—whether he was going to drop me or. . . . (16)

Fear of a possible negative reaction from the man was also the concern underlying another woman's emotional reaction:

> (When they told you that you were pregnant, how did you feel?) I started crying. It was because I knew what he was going to say. . . . I wanted to have it because it was his, and he just didn't understand. (25)

Shock and fear tended to appear among the unmarried women. Two women, both of whom were married, characterized themselves as depressed upon finding out they were pregnant. One of these women expressed her reaction in this way:

> When I really knew that I was pregnant, you can't imagine the depression I went into. I was just completely a different person. As a matter of fact, my daughter came up finally one day and she said, "Mommy, why isn't anything funny anymore?" You know, I was that bad. I didn't laugh at anything. Life was just—the prospect of another child to me was just something that I couldn't bear. (17)

While these married women reacted emotionally to their pregnancy, in an overall sense they were more oriented toward the practical matter of terminating the pregnancy than were the unmarried women who had strong emotional reactions.

The women's modes of initial response to pregnancy constitute a second major dichotomy in this study. In order to determine whether there is any relationship, we will compare it to the first.

Initial Reaction and the Women's Lives

Returning to our first major pattern of affiliation-disaffiliation, which distinguished the women before they became pregnant, and comparing these findings to the contrast found in the mode of initial response to pregnancy, we do indeed find a relationship. As Table 5.3 shows, 15 (79 percent) of the women classified as disaffiliated also claimed to have had an emotional reaction to official confirmation of their pregnancy. A similarly large number of those classified as affiliated, 17 (81 percent), exhibited the opposite reaction, one of rationality or pragmatism. The pattern is clear: the nature of the woman's life as she entered into her abortion passage divides the women into almost the same two groups as does the mode of her initial reaction to pregnancy.

TABLE 5.3

Mode of the Women's Initial Reaction to Pregnancy Confirmation by the Configuration of Their Lives

| Mode of Initial Reactions | Configuration of the Women's Lives | | | | | |
| | Affiliated | | Disaffiliated | | Total | |
	N	Percent	N	Percent	N	Percent
Emotional	4	(21)	15	(79)	19	(48)
Rational	17	(81)	4	(19)	21	(52)
Total	21	(52)	19	(48)	40	(100)

Source: Compiled by the author.

The differences in reaction take on further meaning when they are examined in terms of the role played by the women's significant others (see Figure 5.1). Rational reactions (even among those who were disaffiliated) were almost uniformly given among women who were friend-centered. Rational reactions also tended to be exhibited among women whose significant other was a permanent male partner (husband). While the women oriented toward friends and permanent male partners tended to have a rational mode of response to preg-

FIGURE 5.1

Frequency of Affiliation-Disaffiliation in Terms of the Relationship between Mode of Initial Reaction to Pregnancy Confirmation and Type of Significant Other

Mode of Initial Reaction	Type of Significant Other			
	Husband	Boyfriend	Friend	Parent
Emotional	15 21 $\underline{37}$	2 13 16 18 24 25 30 32 38	$\underline{14}$	1 6 27 $\underline{28}$ 33 $\underline{40}$
Rational	$\underline{4}$ $\underline{5}$ $\underline{7}$ $\underline{10}$ $\underline{17}$ 23 $\underline{35}$	$\underline{3}$ $\underline{8}$ $\underline{19}$ $\underline{29}$	9 11 $\underline{12}$ 20 $\underline{22}$ $\underline{31}$ $\underline{36}$	$\underline{26}$ $\underline{34}$ $\underline{39}$

Note: Underlined numbers indicate affiliated women; numbers not underlined indicate disaffiliated women.

Source: Compiled by the author.

nancy, those oriented toward boyfriends (nonpermanent) and parents generally had an emotional response.

To be sure, larger numbers of women and statistical analyses are required to substantiate these trends. Even so, we can suggest some theoretical explanations.

The women who were affiliated had, accordingly, an established sense of identity to the extent that it made the meaning of their pregnancy clear. That is, the significance of pregnancy for them was clear. Hence, their initial mode of reaction was rational. The basis for this interpretation is that the integration of persons in social groups provides them with a sense of identity. Persons know who they are by virtue of their ordered relationships with others. As Foote (1951) has pointed out so well, having ends in view and knowing what path is necessary to meet those ends (for Foote, "motivation") is integrally related to participation in ongoing social groups. Having a sense of identity, rooted in one's interactive roles with others, gives one a path to follow. On the other hand, being detached or disaffiliated from social life leaves identity unfirm. Establishing meaning for an event or situation is difficult. If a woman is unsure of who she is, then how is she to know what to do? Thus, the reaction to a problematic situation is emotional, not rational.

Reaction to pregnancy is also affected by the other people in one's life, particularly those one is closest to. For an unmarried woman who learns she is pregnant, social support is important in order to provide validation for her threatened identity. Women closest to parents and nonpermanent males can be expected to consider themselves a high risk in terms of getting validation. Support for this point is evident in the comment, for example, "How am I going to tell my mother?" Those closest to friends and husbands can be expected to be more confident of getting support. It can be suggested that the former group is more vulnerable and, hence, initially has a more emotional response to pregnancy; the latter is more secure and has a more rational response.

One additional emotional response to becoming pregnant must be mentioned—anger. The response of anger was reported by women who otherwise reacted calmly, as well as by those who did not. Anger, directed toward the self, was the most commonly expressed emotional reaction to pregnancy:

> I was mad because in my case there wasn't any sense in me getting pregnant. . . . (37)

> I wasn't satisfied with—well, I could have been more careful. I thought, "You stupid little nut," because I had—because it led to an abortion. (36)

> I was mad at myself because I was stupid and I knew right away that I had messed up. But, you know, aggravation was the only thing that I can remember. . . . I wasn't really scared . . . but I was just kind of frustrated because I had allowed it to happen. . . . I felt like I should have known enough to take precautions so that it wouldn't happen. . . . I was just pretty irritated with myself. (11)

> I was mad at myself. I just thought, "Oh, brother! I've really pulled a goody now." (39)

In making statements of anger toward themselves, these women were, in effect, blaming themselves for their pregnancy. Blame and the issue of personal responsibility are the subject of the next section.

TAKING RESPONSIBILITY FOR PREGNANCY

In American society, women have the role of governor or regulator of sexual interaction. This is particularly true for unmarried women. They are the ones who are expected to act as the controlling agent—they are the ones who are expected to indicate when things have gone far enough, to "blow the whistle." Societal standards portray the male as the aggressor and the female as the checkrein. While it is true that out-of-wedlock pregnancies are often expressed

in terms of "he got her pregnant," in a much more fundamental sense the
woman is held responsible. For centuries it has been the woman who has been
punished for nonmarital sexual activity, not the male. By definition of her role
in sexual activity, American culture prescribes that the woman be the party
responsible for controlling conception. She should have been the one to say
"No."

This interpretation was supported by the women interviewed. When asked
whom they felt most people held responsible for an unwanted pregnancy, almost all responded that it was the woman. While they, themselves, tended to
think that both parties should take responsibility, they recognized that was not
generally the way things worked in practice:

> I just think that I should be the one in our marriage—not all the time
> that the lady should, but I think in most cases that men don't, they
> don't think about that. They might think about that, running
> through the back of their mind, but they won't do anything. And I
> think I should. . . .

This woman continued, directly addressing her own responsibility for her pregnancy:

> That was kind of dumb on my part—I'll say on both our parts, but
> more so on my part. (37)

Similarly, over half the women in this study acknowledged that they were
responsible for their pregnancy. They blamed themselves for becoming pregnant.
Statements of anger directed toward the self, as presented earlier, and more
direct statements, such as the following, were common:

> When she first told me, my whole face just turned red. I don't know
> why. I just felt real stupid. . . . I kind of felt like it was all my fault;
> and that was a big burden. (7)

> I had worried about it, but, you know, I guess when you shouldn't
> be doing things that you do, you always worry about it. . . . It was
> making me kind of feel like some kind of dummy. I had gotten my-
> self into a situation that I don't think I was really—I don't think I
> should have been in. (28)

The somewhat less than half who did not take responsibility tended to
avoid the issue of blame altogether. Very few attempted to assign blame else-
where, although, as discussed in a previous section, several women offered
various excuses for not having used proper birth control. Those who did not
directly take responsibility themselves or make a self-derogating statement

typically said nothing at all, leaving feelings of remorse or lack of them undiscussed.

Who were the women who did make statements about their own responsibility? Were there particular factors distinguishing them from the others?

Taking responsibility for pregnancy did not relate to the emotionality of the woman's response to pregnancy. Those who responded in an emotional way tended to be just as likely to take responsibility as did those who reacted calmly. Neither did taking responsibility relate to the configuration of the woman's life prior to pregnancy, that is, affiliation-disaffiliation was not a factor.

Looking more closely, what did make a difference was the type of relationship the woman had with the male involved. Of those women with marriage, engagement, or cohabiting relationships, only 20 percent took responsibility for pregnancy. On the other hand, of those who had particularly casual relationships, 75 percent took responsibility. Thus, women with fairly permanent relationships did not appear to assume responsibility, while those with more casual relationships—those least resembling marriage relationships—seemed likely to do so.

This pattern reflects the normative conditions in American society under which it is most and least acceptable to become pregnant. It would appear that the more "deviant" pregnancies (as defined by the acceptability of the conditions under which pregnancy occurred) were associated with the tendency for the woman to explicitly accept responsibility herself for becoming pregnant.

THE PROCESS OF BECOMING PREGNANT

Thus far, the passage into pregnancy and through abortion has been characterized by commonality among the 40 women studied as well as by variability. Almost uniformly, the study group tended to use birth control carelessly during the time they became pregnant. The women's relationships with the male involved tended to be stable and exclusive. The women tended to be unworried about becoming pregnant; and when the signs of pregnancy began to appear, they initially tried to normalize them. Then, when the symptoms became so obvious that they could not be reasonably attributed to "normal" events, most women readily recognized pregnancy and quickly made an appointment for a pregnancy test. Again, almost uniformly, the *first* thing they did after recognizing that possibly they were pregnant was to confide in either a friend or in their male partner or, sometimes, in both. Finally, at the time of receiving a positive pregnancy test result, most of the women were negative about the pregnancy: they didn't want to continue it. The fact that these trends were found to hold for such a large portion of the women is particularly interesting since, as we indicated in the last chapter, the women were quite diverse in many social and demographic characteristics.

Becoming pregnant was not a completely uniform process. It involved a major point of difference among the women in affective modes of reaction. This difference has been described in terms of a rational-emotional dichotomy. Specifically, slightly over half of the women reported they took a matter-of-fact attitude and the remainder reportedly reacted more emotionally. It is significant that this difference was associated with the other major difference found among the women, a difference in their affiliation with the society around them. If the general configuration of the women's lives helped to shape their initial reaction to becoming pregnant, then it may also be similarly related to patterns in subsequent stages of the experience.

6

CHOOSING ABORTION: "THERE WAS NO OTHER WAY"

INTRODUCTION

This chapter concerns the decision phase in abortion passage. Again, we find the women characterized by a dichotomous pattern. For some women, what to do about pregnancy began to be considered right along with the gradual recognition of pregnancy. For others, the question of continuing or terminating became a serious problem only once the pregnancy was certain. For some women, the decision to have an abortion was clear, established from the first awareness of pregnancy. For others, it was a decision made only after a great deal of confusion—days of thinking, vacillating, discussing, and changing one's mind.

These qualities of time and clarity are basic to our characterization of abortion passage; but so, too, is the social nature of the decision-making process. Abortion is commonly thought of as a very private and personal matter. It is not immediately recognized by many as the social process which it really is. The women involved, in addition to being in the midst of a problem pregnancy, must be viewed as participants in ongoing social relationships and occupants of socially determined status positions rather than as isolated individuals. Other persons are a key element in the decision. Sometimes these other persons shape the direction of the decision; perhaps more often they shape the interpretation given to the decision.

In the discussion which follows, we shall pursue the following questions about these "other persons": Who were the persons the women confided in? Were they told voluntarily or was the woman constrained to tell them because of

her situational circumstances? Who was not told? And why? What impact did
the reactions of these various other persons have on the decision process?

WANTING A BABY

The single issue of wanting or not wanting a baby appeared to be at the
heart of the various patterns of mood and social interaction which we will be discussing in the following sections. The issue was a central orienting point for the
woman's decision process; however, it was only one of a number of important
factors which we shall examine. The woman's initial orientation toward a baby
appeared to be a less central factor as she moved toward making a final decision and as she interacted more with others. Thus, while three-fourths of the
women who reportedly wanted to have the baby reacted emotionally at first to
their pregnancy, they constituted only a little more than half of the women who
were confused and who vacillated in making their abortion decision.

It was reported in the last chapter that two-thirds of the women were dis-
pleased upon learning they were pregnant. This does not mean that two-thirds of
the women did not want the baby. In the final analysis, only a little more than a
third explicitly stated that they did not want the child. While all of the women
studied eventually made the same decision about abortion, they did *not* all
adopt the same stance on wanting the baby.

In discussing their decision 12 women (30 percent) acknowledged that
they had wanted to have the baby:

> ⅄ . . . I debated keeping the baby because I wanted it. Yet, in my situa-
> tion . . . I didn't feel like there was really any way that I could have.
> (6)

> It's not that I didn't want it. It was my husband's child, you know.
> . . . Sure, I wanted the child. I just couldn't see it. It was just too
> much for me to handle with no help. (1)

> Well, I wanted to have it. I really did . . . I don't believe in [abor-
> tion]. I still don't. . . . I wanted to have it. (25)

It is apparent from these comments that some women wanted to have the baby
but felt that the circumstances would not allow it. It is important to note these
findings since it is commonly assumed that a woman who has an abortion does
not want the baby. Such an assumption is incorrect. The internal conflict of the
position of wanting the child and choosing abortion is evidenced in the following comment:

> He [male partner] was kind of sad about it [abortion], I think. (Do
> you mean that he wanted a baby?) Yeah. But I did, too. I had to
> keep telling myself, "This is the *right* way." I always had to keep
> telling myself that so I would go through with it. (10)

The remaining two-thirds of the women did not express any feelings of having wanted the baby. Over half (15 women or 38 percent of the study group) explicitly stated that they did *not* want a child:

> X ... I was pregnant and I didn't want the child. I didn't want the re-
> sponsibility of a child. I didn't want to bring a child into this world.
> ... (31)

> X I found out I was pregnant and I said, "Well, this isn't for me. I
> don't want to get married. I don't want the baby, or anything. ... "
> I said I didn't want it and I didn't want it. I still don't want any
> kids. (26)

> The minute I got pregnant ... I knew that I did not want another
> child. ... There wasn't a single reason I could think of that I would
> want another baby—not one. (17)

Openly stating that one does not want a child contradicts the traditional cultural equation between women and children. That may be one reason why another third of the women chose to ignore altogether the question of wanting or not wanting a child. Instead, this last group (13 women), like those who said they had wanted the baby, focused attention on the constraints of their life circumstances and talked in terms of how necessary the abortion was:

> I still to this day can't believe I actually did it, because I never
> thought I would. I was crazy about my daughter, you know, and I
> thought kids were just wonderful, and I think I always thought if
> I ever got pregnant out of marriage I would marry the father. But
> suddenly you've been divorced, you know what it's like, and it takes
> a hell of a lot of love to put up with somebody and suddenly I was
> faced with this. ... Well, I couldn't have the baby and give it away.
> In no way could I do that. For one reason, I couldn't stand to give
> away something, you know, like that. ... and I thought, "How
> could I go to work every day, facing these people that have known
> me for eight years, and suddenly I'm pregnant and not married? .. "
> And I thought, "I can't marry him because I'm not in love with
> him. ... " And when I thought about abortion and I thought, "Well,
> it seems like that's the only way. (12)

Cultural norms suggesting that women should not reject childbearing also can be offered as an explanation for interviewee 12's emphasis on how much she loved her daughter and children in general (see above). Married women were particularly careful to portray themselves as people who loved children:

> I didn't want more than two children. Financially and—well, I just
> didn't want another child. I love babies, but two is enough for us.
> (4)

If they had children, however, they tended to find it easier to state explicitly that they did not want this child.

A few of the women referred positively to having experienced feelings of being pregnant and of motherhood. These women were teenagers. In general, their comments indicated that pregnancy made them feel special or important.

> At first I wanted the abortion and then, like when I would be going to bed at night, I'd think of what it would be like to be pregnant—to have a big stomach and everything, and get married and get out of the house, away from my sister and my Mom and move in with [my boyfriend] and live with him. You know, I kind of dreamed about that, but I knew there was no way we could do it. And so, that kind of shattered that dream. (Which was it that you really wanted to do? Was it more the idea of getting married and getting out of the house or was it more the idea of having a baby?) It was all tied up together. Being big. (How did that make you feel?) I felt neat. I just—I don't know, it's kind of neat because he'd always pat me on the stomach . . . it's just a neat feeling. But I'll be able to have a baby, you know, another time. It's no big deal. (3)

One woman revealed her feelings more indirectly. She appears to have "announced" her pregnancy to her classmates by wearing symbolic clothing at a time well before her physical condition would have been likely to require it:

> It started spreading around school. Of course, I was wearing smock tops and stuff because I was about two or three months pregnant when I found out. I was at my locker talking to one of my friends in the hall and some girls went by and heard . . . so that's probably how it got started. (How did you know that it got around?) You just walk down the hall and people are staring at you. Like, if me and him was walking down the hall, one of his friends would go by and just kind of grin at us or something . . . maybe two or three said something, but the rest just kind of looked at me. They didn't look like it was, you know—they didn't look down on us. . . . It's not like that anymore. People just don't look at it that way anymore. (16)

It is possible that for high school students who are recognized by their peers as going steady, pregnancy can be a source of social status.

Enjoying some aspects of being pregnant should not be confused with wanting to have the baby. Some observers of adolescent pregnancy assume that women's reports that pregnancy "made them feel good" are proof of the intention or motivation to become pregnant in the first place and/or indicative of wanting to have the baby (see Luker 1975). This may or may not be the case. Certainly, it is not necessarily so. In this study, while some of those who reported feelings of pleasure associated with pregnancy also reported that they wanted to have the baby, others did not. Experiencing such feelings and wanting to continue the pregnancy to term were independent phenomena.

With some idea of the women's feelings about wanting a child, let us consider their interaction with others during the decision period.

INVOLVING OTHERS IN THE DECISION

Abortion was never experienced alone. All of the women studied involved at least one other person in their abortion passage. By the time they were ready for the actual abortion procedure, the majority of women had talked to from three to six other people about being pregnant and about the abortion decision (Table 6.1). Lee, in her earlier study of the illegal abortion experience, reported that the women she studied talked to approximately the same number of persons—an average of five (Lee 1969, p. 76). Her women, however, were contacting others as possible sources in a search for an illegal abortionist. The women in the present study generally knew how to go about obtaining an abortion. They did not need to contact others in order to arrange for an abortion. They did, however, have other kinds of constraints which forced them to contact people they might not have told otherwise.

TABLE 6.1

Distribution of the Study Group According to the Number of Persons Told before the Abortion Procedure

Number of Persons Told	N	Percent
1	6	(15)
2	5	(12)
3	5	(12)
4	4	(10)
5	11	(28)
6	4	(10)
7	3	(8)
8	2	(5)
Total	40	(100)

Source: Compiled by the author.

Constraints and the Need to Confide

One important source of constraint affected the 11 women who were under 18 and who, by law, needed to have the signature of one of their parents in order for the abortion to be performed. All of these women confided in at least one of their parents. It is likely, however, that many in this age group would have told their parents regardless. Five of the seven women in the next oldest age category (18-20) who were living at home also confided in their parents even though they had no such constraint.

Another source of constraint affecting a few women was transportation needed to get to the specialized clinics for the abortion procedure. Here again, a few women told people whom they had not planned to tell, in order to get a ride:

> . . . This youngest sister, she would have probably taken off work and gone with me, but she just—I just couldn't trust her to keep her mouth shut. So I said, "Well, I'd call the other sister, the next to the youngest." Very level-headed. . . . (How did you expect her to react?) To react calmly. I hated to tell her. I thought it would probably bring me down in her eyes, you know. I'm the oldest of us and they always looked up to me. . . . I called her. I said, "I'm pregnant; I have to be in the city at 7:30 in the morning for an abortion. The girl that was going to take me has done backed out on me. I'd like to have someone with me." . . . She called back and said, "I'll pick you up in the morning." (29)

It is evident that, because of fear of being stigmatized, this woman would probably not have told her sister if she had not needed someone to go with her.

If we can assume that these constraints were not as frequent nor as severe as those in the illegal abortion era, and if the women in this study, therefore, were less in need of contacting others for instrumental purposes than those in Lee's (1969) study, then we can suggest that because similar numbers of people were reportedly told in both studies, women may be more willing to tell others voluntarily today than they were in the illegal period.

On the whole, the persons contacted by the women in this study tended to be sought out for socioemotional rather than instrumental reasons. They were confided in so that the women could obtain social support:

> Well, I tried to get a lot of opinions. That's why I told my friends—so I could get their opinions, what they thought I should do. (16)

> . . . That's the reason I talked to more people than I should have about it—what I was going to do and everything—because I wanted their opinion. Like what would they do in my situation and things like that. It's not that I wanted someone to tell me, "Well, you do this and you do that." I just wanted to get their ideas. (Would you have preferred not to tell anyone?) Yes, but I felt alone as it was and I wanted to talk to somebody. I wanted to talk to people about it,

because like I say, I was going through changes anyway—financial problems and things like that. And I hadn't ever had to take all the responsibility like this before and I just didn't know what to do about it. (1)

Rather than "getting opinions," these women were actually seeking moral validation for their decisions and, beyond this, for their characters. Since choosing abortion typically was incongruent with their personal attitudes, the need for validation and social support was likely to be even greater.

Other women viewed confiding in others more in terms of tension release once the decision had been made:

I needed to talk to somebody and [my girlfriend] was away and I couldn't call her . . . you can't say things over the phone that you can say face-to-face. So I talked to Darla. She's an older woman. She's probably in her 40s, close to 40 at least. . . . She's comfortable. I feel comfortable with her. . . . (How did you feel after you talked to her?) Fine. I didn't change any of my attitudes. I felt a little more release that I had spoken out loud about it. It kind of let off some of the pressure. (5).

Well, with [my girlfriend] I talked quite a bit about it . . . and with my sister I talked to her off and on. . . . It was really a tremendous help because it relieved some of the tension and since it was on my mind so much, it was good to have somebody to talk to. (17)

Some women sought particular others because of individual, socioemotional needs. One woman, for example, was extremely apprehensive about the medical nature of the abortion procedure. She contacted a person who she thought could help with that fear:

. . . when I found out, I got in touch with that girl that had had an abortion and I told her, and I knew that I didn't have very long to decide on what I was going to do and I was really scared about—I really got scared about the abortion. (15)

In these comments, the women spoke predominantly of telling friends. As indicated in Table 6.2, next to the male involved in the pregnancy, friends were the most likely type of other person to be confided in.

Table 6.2 also shows that by the time of the abortion procedure, the percentage of women confiding in each type of other had increased dramatically when compared to the percentage told before medical confirmation. The order of preference remained the same at both stages of the experience: males involved were preferred, with friends, parents, and siblings following in that order.

TABLE 6.2

Percentage of the Women According to the Four Types of Others Confided In by Stage in Abortion Passage

Stage in Abortion Passage	Type of Others Confided In			
	Male Involved	Parent(s)	Siblings*	Friends
Just before medical confirmation of pregnancy	65	13	10	53
Just before abortion procedure	95	52	40	80

*Just before medical confirmation of pregnancy, only sisters had been confided in. By the time of the abortion procedure, a few brothers had been told. (There was less hesitation to confide in a sister.)

Source: Compiled by the author.

Thus far, we have discussed whom the woman tended to seek out to confide in and why. Now let us consider the issue of secrecy. Whom did the women want to keep their pregnancy and abortion secret from? Why? How did they manage to do this?

Secrecy

The women confided in others because they needed social support. Avoiding possible negative sanctions was the reason for secrecy. The women for the most part were aware that they were treading on thin moral ice. They were very much concerned with preserving their precarious position by avoiding all criticism and receiving as much understanding and validation as they could without risking opposition. They tended to be cautious. Frequently, there were persons they wanted to confide in, but they resisted because they could not be sure of the response or that those told would refrain from telling additional persons. One woman who seemed to find some benefits in pregnancy itself, even though she did not want a child, wanted very much to tell others. Finally, she told a child whom she was sure would keep the secret:

> I told my little niece. She's 11 years old and I always told her . . . what I was doing and she never, ever said a word. I told her that I

was pregnant, but I told her I was married because I didn't want her to get older and think she could do something like that. . . . I had to tell someone besides [my boyfriend]. I can't trust any of my friends. . . . I didn't dare tell anyone else. (Did you want to?) Sometimes I did. I wanted people to know—I really wanted to say, "I'm pregnant." But, then, I wasn't married and I thought, if my mother ever found out . . . but, really, I didn't care what anybody thought. I even wanted to tell my mother . . . she'd kill me. She would disown me. She told me she would disown me if I ever got pregnant and wasn't married . . . but I think down deep she wouldn't. She'd be hurt though, so disappointed, because nobody's better than her little girl. (30)

It is interesting that this woman's fear of moral stigma was also translated into the thought that she might be an improper example to others.

Family members were particularly avoided by many women. Among them, as indicated in the comments of the woman above, the one person whose reactions were most feared was the woman's mother:

(You said that you would never tell your parents.) No, mainly because of the religious aspect. My mother and father are Catholics and I don't need to tell you what the Catholics think of that sort of thing . . . birth control pills has been one thing . . . stopping it before it starts, but abortion is something entirely different. They are under the impression that there is nothing that you can do about it. You just make the best of it. That's the main reason I didn't tell my mom. I'd like to be able to tell her, because we've always talked about things easily. But this was one thing I couldn't talk to her about. She'd have no understanding for it at all. (5)

(If you had told your mom, did you have an expectation of how she would act?) Yeah. I was afraid that she would get mad and kick me out of the house or something. And that's what we are trying to do now is save money. I can't afford to go out and blow it. (10)

. . . but, boy, I sure didn't tell her [mother] I was having an abortion. My God, if she ever found out, I'd be dead probably. She just doesn't—she has very *firm* beliefs against this and her daughter would never do nothing like this, you know. I felt like if my mother knew, that it would be something that could possibly come between us. And, my mom and my dad are real important to me and I don't ever want something like that to come—and I didn't feel like it was going to help them any if they knew, so I just didn't bother to tell them. (Why do you think that it might have come between you? Could you make that more specific?) Well, my mom just doesn't believe in it—she thinks you just don't do that. You know, when it became a law she just wanted to go out and really raise all kind of

hell because she thinks—she just doesn't believe in it. She thinks it's
wrong—even like in a rape case or something, she thinks you should
just have the baby and if you don't want it put it up for adoption because there's so many people that do want it. I don't think she
wants to see me pregnant. . . . (35)

Having articulated her mother's beliefs, this woman continued by expressing her
fear of being stigmatized—of having her moral character lowered in the eyes of a
significant other:

. . . but I also know, I really believe, that if she had known that I
was, that my alternative to her would have just been to have it . . .
I think she would lind of look down on me or maybe that it would
be like a mark against me or something, and it would kind of cause a
little friction or something. (35)

For another woman who avoided her family, losing respect in the eyes of her
brother was stated to be of more concern than being stigmatized by her parents:

I wouldn't have gone to my parents with this for anything in the
world . . . because I love my parents more than anything in the
world and I have two little brothers and anytime that someone in
the family goes through something like this, it has an influence on
the whole family. I know it would have hurt them all terribly. I love
my little brothers and I want them to respect me, and, although
they're too young to understand it now, I think that they would
lose respect. I'm sure that they would. . . . (Do you think your
parents would have had the same reaction?) No, not really. I think
that they would have been very upset about it, but after a while they
would have gathered themselves together and they would have said,
"OK, what are we going to do about it?" But, in the sense of a 13-
year-old-boy, when they hear the word abortion in a small town . . .
I think it's still kind of, you know, a dirty thing. (31)

Actually, while the women more often reported that their mother's reaction was the first thing they worried about, siblings were the *least* preferred
group of others to confide in. Whereas the women were afraid of their parents'
anger or disappointment, they feared loss of respect on the part of siblings:

. . . I would liked to have told her [sister], but I knew that I couldn't
because I knew how she felt about it. I mean, I would have liked to
have had her with me, you know, for moral support or whatever, but
I knew that I couldn't so I just forgot about it. (How would you
have expected her to react?) She would have really been upset. I
don't know just exactly how she would have reacted, but I know
that she would have been terribly upset. . . . I think she has a pretty

high opinion of me and everything, but I thought it would lower her opinion of me if I told her about it. (11)

Not all of the women spoke of fearing harm to themselves from others who knew about the abortion. Some explained their secrecy from the standpoint of wanting to be kind and not troubling others:

> . . . they [parents] had enough problems of their own without add-ing that on to them. . . . I just didn't feel that it was something that they had to worry themselves about. . . . My mother had already helped me quite a bit with my son and I wasn't about to ask her to do it with a second one. (39)

Other women hesitated to specify that they were afraid of other people's attitudes toward them. Nevertheless, they wanted to keep the number of people they confided in to a minimum:

> There were four people that knew and that was all, and I just felt like no one else needed to know . . . not because I'm ashamed of it, but I just felt like maybe it would cause a little bit of gossip that wasn't necessary. . . . (35)

> . . . I wasn't going to tell [my girlfriends] that I was going to get an abortion because I didn't want anyone to know but the baby's father and my family. . . . I don't like my business being in the streets. . . . I don't like to be talked about—about anything, you know. An abortion or not having an abortion. I just don't like to be talked about. (26)

> If we could handle it ourselves, we wanted to. We didn't want to take any unnecessary action that would involve any other people into the situation. . . . (Was there any reason why you didn't want other people to know?) Yes, just that other people have a tendency to make things real big when they're really not that big of a deal. And to us, we just wanted to get it over with, out of the way, and move ahead . . . and like parents and things like that, I don't know how they would have reacted to it, but we didn't really care. We didn't want to have that hanging over us. (7)

Keeping secrecy was not always easy, particularly when the woman lived with those she was trying to keep the secret from. Sometimes others helped inadvertently by normalizing the woman's visible symptoms:

> . . . I got very, very sick. Extremely sick . . . and my mom fortu-nately knew of something that was going on in her office—everyone was getting sick there—so she thought I had it. (22)

Just as in the case of the women normalizing their own symptoms, others would normalize for them, but only as long as it was "logical" to do so. As we observed in the last chapter, in the cases of two women, others were the ones who actually defined pregnancy first, forcing the woman to come to terms with her condition and to have a pregnancy test.

Not only were the symptoms a problem to keep secret, but so also were the various trips to the clinic:

> (How would the people have reacted if you had told them?) Oh, they probably would have accepted it, but it would have been a hassle and I didn't want that. Do you want to hear my story—my story I made up when I came to the clinic? I had to get baby-sitters so I told them [her family] I had been "spotting" and had had my IUD taken out. Then, when I had the postsurgical checkup, I said they had put another IUD in, a size larger. Today, I said I was having it checked. It was a story I could live with. I didn't feel like a liar—just a little lie. . . . (4)

Having surmounted these obstacles, the women were still faced with the strain of their secret:

> I would get up in the morning and Mom would wonder what was going on and everything, and just the whole thing was kind of a trial to stay there the whole time. And like I was keeping this big thing from them and being around them all the time. (8)

> (You were at home?) Yeah, and that made it even harder because I couldn't show my reactions. I had to hide how I felt. Discipline. (6)

Approximately two-thirds of the women were able to protect themselves from reactions they did not want. In other words, they confided in only those people they wanted to. The remaining third did not have that control. Perhaps because they lived at home and were dependent on their parents financially and/or because of their age, those with less protection from persons whom they did not want to tell were in the younger age category.

Now we turn to the reactions of the people who were told. These persons will be considered in three groups: the male partner, parents, and friends.

THE MALE PARTNER

The male partner played a central role in the abortion experience for all but two of the 40 women studied. For one of these exceptions, pregnancy occurred as a result of a casual encounter and the male was never informed. In the second case, the woman felt she had deceived her partner about birth control. She had been taking the pill but quit without telling him. Thus, it appears, she was afraid to confront him with her pregnancy because she would also be confronting him with her deception:

> I never did tell the guy. To this very day he still doesn't know it. Because when we very first started going to bed together, he asked me if I was on the pill and I told him, "Yes." And I *was*.... And he told me, he said, "I would never want to put anyone in that situation." He said, "It would really upset me if I ever got anyone pregnant or if someone got pregnant and wanted me to marry them or something because I'm not ready to get married." And we had a real long talk about it . . . then, later on, when I thought I might have been pregnant . . . it was really weird because he brought it up and we just started talking about it. I said, "What would you do if I got pregnant and had an abortion?" And he said, "Why?" And I said, "Well, I was just wondering, you know. It doesn't really matter. I'm not going to worry about it now because I'm not." At that time that was the truth. I wasn't sure.... And so we talked about it and I said, "Well, I just don't feel that there would be any other way to go about it." I said, "I think I would just go have an abortion." And he goes, he said, "I think that would be the best thing, too, as long as that was what you wanted," . . . and we just dropped it because I had pretty much heard what I wanted to hear.... I wanted him to say he believes that abortions are OK. (31)

While this woman was afraid to discuss her abortion decision with the man openly, she did make an effort to find out his view by a hypothetical situation. Her case illustrates the fact that the women in this study felt an obligation to inform the male partners of pregnancy and to get their reaction to the resolution choice, whether abortion or not.

The majority of the male partners of the rest of the women can be fitted into one of two roles. For those women who were determined from the beginning to have an abortion, the male partners functioned as social validator, providing social support while the women finalized their decision and experienced the actual abortion procedure. In such cases, the women had taken the lead in decision making and the men concurred. Other male partners, however, performed a different role. They served to close off the alternative of marriage and/or continued partnership for women who wanted to have the baby. As is evidenced in Table 6.3, three-fourths of the men functioned in one way or the other. Still others tended to oppose women wanting abortion. Some of these men wanted to marry the woman; others simply wanted to be fathers.

The part played by the man tended to be one of making the experience easier or harder rather than changing the actual abortion decision. The only situations where the man can be suggested to have altered the abortion decision

TABLE 6.3

Frequency of the Initial Pregnancy Resolution Decision of
the Women by the Direction of the Male Partner's Reaction

Initial Pregnancy Resolution Decision	Direction of Male's Reaction					
	Agreement		Opposition		Totals*	
	N	Percent	N	Percent	N	Percent
Abortion	16	(67)	8	(33)	24	(63)
Continue pregnancy	1	(11)	8	(89)	9	(24)
Uncertain	2	(40)	3	(60)	5	(13)
Total	19	(50)	19	(50)	38	(100)

*Excludes the two cases where the men were not informed of the pregnancy.
Source: Compiled by the author.

were in the cases where the woman wanted to continue the pregnancy and have
the baby and the man opposed her. In these eight cases, the man withdrew his
support, thereby eliminating that alternative. This accounted for only 20 percent of all abortion decisions, however.

As indicated in Table 6.2, nearly two-thirds of the men were informed of
the woman's suspected pregnancy before she received medical confirmation. At
this point, most men took a "let's wait and see" attitude. They tended to doubt
the accuracy of the woman's fears and did not want to make plans about something which was not definite. For example:

> He was probably shocked to find out that I suspected that I was and
> he kept arguing that I wasn't. . . . He started to be a little bit nicer to
> me, just a little, but after the first initial shock we were both just
> kind of waiting until I found out and neither of us wanted to talk
> about it. (20)

This comment illustrates the typical pattern of male-female interaction in these
situations. While the woman may have been thinking about what she would do,
the man generally hesitated until the pregnancy was confirmed.

Male-female agreement tended to occur where abortion was the resolution
choice being considered (Table 6.3). Only one couple agreed initially on wanting
a baby. It can be assumed that if both parties agreed on having the baby, an
abortion would have been less likely to occur.

The cases of male-female agreement differed qualitatively. A few couples
apparently agreed with very little discussion:

—

> I guess it was kind of like an unspoken thing we just mutually agreed
> on. I don't know how to explain it really. (You hadn't really sat
> down and decided . . .) Well, we had—that that would be the best
> course—but we both knew before we even said anything to each
> other about it. (22)

In other cases, the woman perceived that she had to convince her partner. Sometimes this was reported to have been relatively simple:

> First, he wanted me to have it because he wanted me to have his
> baby, you know. And then I started telling him how we couldn't
> afford it and I just gave him examples and stuff like that—"What
> are we going to do for money?" you know, "I don't got a job," and
> all this stuff. So then he realized that the best thing to do was to
> get an abortion. (13)

Whether the man eventually agreed with the woman or not, the prospect
of being a father evoked a sense of pride and importance in many of the men
which caused them to hesitate, sometimes to oppose, the abortion. To such
hesitation on the man's part, the woman typically countered with an economic
issue. Suggesting the financial obligations of a child frequently secured his
agreement:

> I finally decided I'm going to have to convince him. So what I did
> was to completely drop the subject for three or four days and let
> it mull over in his mind and . . . then I finally came out and said,
> "Gee, we ought to buy ourselves a new house." . . . I said, "This
> place is crumbling down. . . . " and "How much do you think it
> would cost to get a new house?" And I said, "I could just go to
> work and it wouldn't be that bad." So I just left it at that. He
> started thinking about this, you know, and if we had a new kid
> we couldn't get a new house. . . . (What was your motive then?)
> To get him to see the economics—the limiting factor. Like if I went
> to work, it would be impossible to pay a baby-sitter for three kids
> in the summertime. The idea that our life would not get better . . .
> we would have to drop our standard of living if we had another child
> and if we would ever want anything better, it would almost be un-
> attainable. . . . Then I mentioned a few other people that had this
> done and they seemed to be walking around perfectly fine and so
> then he finally came around and he said OK. (17)

> . . . I came home pregnant . . . and I said, "I'm going to have an
> abortion," and he said, "No, I don't want an abortion," and I said,
> "OK, you want to have the baby?" and he said, "Yeah." I said,
> "Fine, we can't afford a baby the way the economy is going. We

will never be able to afford a baby because the prices are going too
high now." You know, he's not sure of his job. He could be laid off
any time. . . . I told him how I felt and I listened to how he felt and
I said, "OK, now we're both going to think about it. We won't say
any more about it." . . . And when he came home the next night he
said, "OK." . . . I gave him the alternatives . . . and I told him
exactly how it would go. I told him we can't afford one. We don't
need the added expense . . . and he aired his views on the whole
situation and then he thought about it and I thought about it and I
didn't change my mind and he did. (5)

The last two women quoted were married. By mentioning financial security and
the impact of another child upon it, they "convinced" their husbands by evok-
ing his sense of family responsibility.

The process of convincing the man produced some hesitation in one of
these two women:

(Did you ever go through any period of time when you thought you
would go ahead and have the baby?) Yes, right at the very beginning . . . because he made me feel guilty, feeling the way that I did.
I mean, what could be better than to bring a new life into the world?
(17)

The process of coming to an agreement about abortion was complicated in
another way for the many couples who were seriously involved but not committed by marriage. For them, the imputation of wanting or not wanting an
abortion and the associated symbolic meaning became a source of temporary
disruption in the decision-making process:

I didn't call him until I was pregnant and I mentioned an abortion.
. . . Then he said, "Well, God, it's going to be so hard to have a baby
for us financially. Look what it has been like already." Then I
started feeling depressed: He doesn't want to have my baby. (But he
agreed with what you were saying about an abortion?) Right . . . and
I was saying that because I knew it was a good, practical thing to
say—but I really didn't feel that way because when I found out I was
pregnant all I could think of was that it was our child I wanted. . . .
Then I wrote home and said, "You're right, this is a mistake, it's my
fault. . . . I thought it was my fault because I got off the pill. . . . I
said I would look into what they were doing about abortion. . . .
Then when he got that letter, he was with his sister; and she tells me
that he cried when he got that letter. He felt like, "Well, she doesn't
want to have my baby." So then . . . he came up to me at the air-
port and said, "I want it." And I said, "I'm glad you want it." . . .
Really, I was trying to please him and he was trying to please me.
(21)

As we shall see later in this section, the symbolic association between continuing the pregnancy and expression of love—or between terminating the pregnancy and rejection of love—was an important factor in the relationships where there was disagreement. Thus, as in the case above, the male's rejection of the pregnancy initially appeared to be viewed as a rejection of her: "He doesn't want *my* baby [italics mine]." Among those who agreed, however, the idea of trying to please the other rather than revealing true feelings was more common. A particular concern of the women was their fear that the man would later regret the abortion:

> I was most concerned about whether he would be upset later about what I was going to do . . . he said it wouldn't bother him so I guess it won't. I don't know. Later, I may find out different. . . . (28)

> . . . I was afraid he was going through with it simply to make me happy, simply to please me. And then, I was afraid that because of that, after it was all over with, he would feel robbed or cheated. (5)

Opposition by the man was disruptive for the women. As indicated in Table 6.3 approximately the same number of men opposed the woman's decision to seek abortion as opposed her decision to continue the pregnancy. According to the women, most of the men who expressed hostility toward the pregnancy being continued reacted by denying personal responsibility for it:

> When I finally did go and tell him . . . he gave me the line of, "Well, whose is it?" which upset me very badly because it wasn't like I was going to bed with every guy. . . . And when I said, "Yours," he said, "Well, what makes you think it's mine?" He was very cold. He was very rude. . . . He just didn't want to talk to me. It was just very much, "It's your problem—don't bug me because it's your problem." (6)

One woman reported that her male partner reacted in a nonsupportive manner for just the opposite reason—because he *did* take responsibility:

> He was pretty worried about what was going to happen . . . he really got hung up on himself a lot . . . (Could you explain that?) Well, I think it came out he felt guilty that he got me pregnant. (He was taking the responsibility for it?) Yes, I think so—some of it. He kind of pushed me aside and he wouldn't reach out to me because he was all hung up on, "What am I going to do?" and that really bothered me a lot. . . . I was pretty much alone as far as the whole thing was concerned. (20)

In direct contrast were the men who disagreed because they wanted the baby:

(What was his first reaction?) Well, he was happy. . . . He wanted
it . . . he wanted to marry me and everything and then I told him I
didn't want it and he was—I guess he was hurt. He said he was real
hurt and everything. . . . He acted like I had lost my mind, like I was
crazy. He seemed like, "Gee, you really are crazy not wanting our
baby. (26)

He had this great big thing about having a baby. . . . He wanted it.
(How about you?) Well, I wanted it, but then I didn't. . . That's
when me and him started fighting a lot. . . . (22)

In one case, the woman felt that beneath the surface her partner really wanted
marriage rather than a baby:

(Did he know you were planning on having the abortion if you were
pregnant?) Yes, he did . . . he didn't want me to because he figured
that if I cared for him—even though all along I told him that "I
just don't love you" . . . but he just seemed to block it out of his
mind. (Do you remember what he said when you told him you
would consider an abortion?) He . . . was real nasty about it . . . and
then, when he finally realized that whether he took me or not I was
going to go, he just relented and took me. He didn't speak to me all
the way down there hardly. . . . I think he really, down deep inside,
thought I wouldn't do it. He didn't seem to accept the fact that I
was—didn't want to have his child. (Was he happy about your being
pregnant?) No, I don't think he was . . . he just—if he could get me
to marry him by me being pregnant, he was satisfied. . . . That was
the thing in his head. That's what he wanted. He didn't care whether
I was pregnant or not. He just wants me to marry him. (12)

This last comment is quite the reverse of the stereotypic woman who gets pregnant so that the man will marry her. Here, the woman's view is that it is the man
who is using pregnancy as an excuse for marriage.

PARENTS AND SIBLINGS

The women, as reported previously, expected their parent(s) to react with
anger, disappointment, and emotional upset over their daughter's pregnancy.
For this reason, nearly half the women kept their pregnancy and abortion from
one or both parents (Table 6.2). The same fears were also present, although to a
lesser degree, in anticipating the reactions of brothers and sisters. In many cases
they, too, were not told of the pregnancy and abortion. Despite these fears, 24
(60 percent) of the 40 women confided in at least one member of their family of
origin, that is, a parent or brother or sister. On the other hand, in more than half

of these 24 cases, at least one person in the family was not told. Thus, a willingness to confide in one or two family members did not mean a willingness to tell the entire family.

Whether or not family members were told depended to a large degree on physical (and, related to that, on social) proximity. As Table 6.4 indicates, women who were living with their parents during the decision period were much more likely to confide in them than women who lived in separate households.

TABLE 6.4

Frequency with Which Parents Were Confided in by Availability and Living Arrangements of Parents, Controlling for Living Arrangements of the Women

Living Arrangements of the Woman	Which Parents Confided In									
	Mother Only		Father Only		Mother and Father		Neither		Total	
	N	Percent	N	Percent	N	Percent	N	Percent	N	Percent
Living with parents										
Both available: parents living together	2	(29)	0	(0)	9	(69)	2	(11)	13	(33)
Both available: parents not living together	0	(0)	1	(100)	3	(23)	0	(0)	4	(10)
Father unavailable: parents not living together	3	(42)	–	–	–	–	1	(5)	4	(10)
Not living with parents										
Both available: parents living together	0	(0)	0	(0)	0	(0)	11	(58)	11	(27)
Both available: parents not living together	0	(0)	0	(0)	1	(8)	1	(5)	2	(5)
Father unavailable: parents not living together	2	(29)	–	–	–	–	4	(21)	6	(15)
Total	7	(17)	1	(2)	13	(33)	19	(48)	40	(100)

Source: Compiled by the author.

The same was true in the case of siblings. One reason physical proximity made a difference was the difficulty of concealing pregnancy and abortion. As one woman put it, "They were going to find out anyway." As pointed out earlier, some of the women living at home were constrained to tell at least one parent because they needed a parent's signature for the abortion and/or for financial assistance. In addition to these "structural constraints," many of the women living at home seemed to have a greater need for their parents' support and validation:

> . . . I couldn't have done it without telling them [father and step-mother], but I really tried to do it the other way. I could have a thing from my mother, a notary public thing that she approved that I get an abortion because I was under 18, and [my boyfriend] and I could have dug up the money and . . . even if I could have gone in there and been back in time . . . I really wanted to tell them because I needed their support because I didn't have anybody else. My mother was in another state and she couldn't do anything for me—she asked me if I wanted to come out there and she could come here and all of that. My mother is very liberal as far as sex is concerned. . . . Anyway, when I finally found out I was actually pregnant, I came to the decision that I had to tell them because emotionally I knew I couldn't hack it. I couldn't go it alone and I knew [my boyfriend] couldn't give me the support I needed, so I just told my parents. (20)

The women living at home were for the most part those still in high school or those who had recently graduated. We previously characterized some of the high school students in this study as being rebellious. Nevertheless, they still eventually turned to their parent(s). To a large extent this was from a lack of any other strong supports (illustrated by the comments above and below). Young women living at home were not necessarily parent centered. Many, in fact, were boyfriend or peer centered; however, when they turned to these persons, they often did not receive the support they thought they needed. Hence, they turned eventually to their parents:

> I did tell a number of people—which was a stupid thing to do—because I was asking—like, I told the girl who was pregnant that I was pregnant, because she had confided in me, and I thought, you know, "Isn't there somebody?" So far, the people I told hadn't given any kind of sympathy. (Now, who was that?) This was just [my boyfriend]. . . . No, it was before I told my parents—I told two or three people and they just said, "Well, you're pregnant. Too bad." So I never got the sympathy I wanted. (20)

The women who did not confide in either parent, and in most cases did not confide in a sibling either, were generally those who had established their own separate households and who also tended to have strong support from another person. These other persons were either the male partner (many of the women with permanent male partners were in this group) or a very close female friend. These women were much less dependent on parents, both emotionally and materially, than the former group.

Although apprehension toward parents' reactions was expressed by almost every woman interviewed, of the 52 percent who actually told one or both parents (Table 6.4), only about one-third received the feared negative reaction:

> (When did you tell them?) It was late at night and I had just come home from work and was dead tired. It took me about ten minutes before I could even get up enough nerve. I kept sitting there wiggling in my chair and finally I said, "There is something I have to tell you," and then I couldn't say it for about five minutes. I just couldn't get the words out . . . their first reaction was calm. [My stepmother's] second reaction was—she kind of lost it. She said, "There must be something wrong with you—a girl your age having sexual relationships." . . . Dad got all upset and started crying and [my stepmother] was upset and said, "You've got to understand what you are doing to us. You may think it is all right, but this just blows our sense of morals that you'd get pregnant." You know, it just really caught them off guard. . . .. . He was too upset really and . . . she almost got nasty about how—"Look at it from our point of view" and this sort of thing; "You've got to understand what we're going through." . . . it really bothered me. (20)

Some parents' hostile reactions consisted primarily of expressing emotion. Others included instructions and action. Some parents demanded an abortion; others refused to have any part of one:

> . . . my neighbor and I were pretty close and she told me that I had better be telling Mom. . . . She came over and helped me tell my mom. (How did your mom react?) She started crying. She was very upset. She asked me how I could do such a thing to her. She didn't think I was like that. Well, at first it was just her and I talking, before I told my dad, and she thought it was all right that I didn't get an abortion and I kept it. . . . But then I told my dad. (How did he react?) Oh, he—he kind of stared at me for a few minutes like he was in shock. I was waiting for him to hit me, but he didn't. He just said, "There's only one thing to do. She's going to get an abortion." Those were the first words that came out of his mouth. (16)

> I said, "Well, I want an abortion." . . . And she goes, "I'm not signing for it. That's murder. I've always thought that was murder. Don't ask me to sign it." And that's what upset me because I didn't know what I was going to do if my dad didn't sign it. And my boyfriend got real mad at her for saying that it was murder and stuff, and

he . . . started yelling and it was just a big fight and I couldn't stay there any longer because I had been fighting with her for two hours before he came over. . . . She was just making me feel bad. . . . And she said, "No, get married. Get married and have the baby." . . . and she said, "Well, if your dad signs, that's fine. He can have it on his conscience all his life, but I'm not signing and don't even ask me to." (3)

. . . First, [the social worker] talked to me by myself and then she brought my mom in. And then me and my mom started yelling and that was the first time I had ever yelled at her. And she got mad and went out to the car and wouldn't say anything to me. (2)

The reactions of siblings, particularly sisters, were not feared as much as the reactions of parents. When sisters or brothers were told, however, the actual response was often more intensely negative than expected:

My sister, she blew up . . . and my brother's wife. They were totally against the whole idea because—well, my sister felt like it would affect me after I had done it . . . she said that I wouldn't be able to handle it . . . they both thought it was the wrong thing to do and it wouldn't really solve anything as far as financial problems or a relief for me or anything like that. I tried to explain to them the way I felt and they just couldn't understand. It kind of made me feel guilty in a way, but after I got to thinking about it, I just thought that it was the thing to do. . . . (Did anyone react differently than you had expected them to?) My sister . . . I didn't expect her to be totally against it. She called me on the telephone and she just really—she really made me feel bad. When I got through talking to her, I just had to sit down and cry, she made me feel so bad. (1)

In this case, the woman was married and so the hostility was focused on the abortion, not on the fact that the woman was pregnant. Among unmarried women, the negative reactions of siblings were aimed at the fact that their sister was pregnant and unmarried as well as toward the abortion.

The impact of family members, when negative, had a very disruptive impact on the women. On the other hand, when family members were supportive, the pregnancy and abortion were made less problematic. As pointed out before, parents tended to react more favorably than expected:

(Did anybody react differently than you expected?) Not really, except for my mom. I figured she'd sit down and cry and cry—things like this. But that night after I told her, she said, "Well, let's all go shopping," and me and her and my brother all went shopping. . . . I thought she would . . . start yelling and [say] things like this:

"I told you that's what you would do." . . . it was my Mom I was worried about. (32)

Siblings were generally less supportive than the women expected them to be; however, in general they tended to react on the supportive side rather than in a hostile way:

(You said you told your brother. When did you tell him?) About three or four days after I found out for sure. (How come you didn't tell him before that?) It was because I was scared because I really respected him, you know. I wasn't quite sure how he was going to react to it. I mean, I knew he wasn't going to disown me or nothing like that, but I was afraid maybe we wouldn't be as close anymore. He's about the only person I've got. . . . (When you finally did tell him, what happened?) He just said that I should have been using protection and I wasn't ready to get married. (16)

. . . she didn't really say that, but I kind of got the impression that [my sister] didn't think it was quite right. And I kind of think that was because of the impression that my mother had made on her. But then, I just laid out what it was and why I had made this decision and she basically went along with it. . . . I think she—in the back of her mind she thinks I did something wrong. Maybe not—I mean, I think she thinks my reasoning was right, but I still think she thinks that it is—I mean because even now, when I see her . . . she'll say, "Are you sure you did the right thing?" (35)

One reason siblings were expected to be more supportive than they actually were (and parents were not) was the women's previously noted tendency to think that younger persons accept unwanted pregnancy and abortion more readily than older persons (an incorrect assumption).

In general, it would be fair to say that "support" from family members was equivalent to a nonhostile reaction. Parents may have expressed displeasure with their daughter's pregnancy; however, they were viewed as supportive as long as they did not disrupt her further during the abortion process. For example, they were supportive if they tended to be understanding rather than angry, or if they discussed the alternatives with her rather than directly telling her what she should do. Many "supportive" family members did not remain neutral. Some, in fact, influenced the uncertain or child-oriented woman into having her abortion. These somewhat subtle attempts to sway the woman were not perceived as hostile, however. One example was seen above in the comment of interviewee 16. In another case:

. . . she [mother] started telling me all the problems there are in having one [a baby] now—that I'm going to be going to school and what am I going to do when I have it? Quit? And all this stuff. And I told her that I'd go to a mother's school. (Were you convinced that you wanted the baby at this point?) Yes. I wanted it. And so she says, "Well OK, if that's what you want," And so then we just— every once in a while for a couple of days after that we just talked about it, you know, off and on. She kept trying to convince me that I shouldn't have it. . . . I argued with her and told her I wanted it and all and . . . so then each night we would talk about it a little more and finally she goes, "You ought to get an abortion and then you can always have it when you want it." And I said, "Well, I want to get married." And she says, "Well, I'll let you get married next summer if you want." . . . so she finally convinced me that that would be the best thing. (13)

Many of those women who originally reacted to pregnancy by wanting the baby (who also tended to be younger, were living at home, and eventually confided in their parents) were influenced by this process into finally deciding to have the abortion. Frequently, a combination of parental pressure and opposition to a baby by the boyfriend resulted in the abortion decision:

Everybody was saying—like my parents and him—everybody was saying that I did it (got pregnant) on purpose and so I just decided it [abortion] would be for the best. (25)

(At some point you obviously started changing your mind . . .) Yeah. Well, my brother and his girlfriend sat me down and started talking to me. My dad was still yelling at me. . . . They just kept telling me that [abortion] was the thing to do. I stopped and thought about what my neighbor had said and so I just went with one of my friends and just thought and thought and then I went and talked to [my boyfriend] and he said he still wanted to get married, but then I decided that Mom and his mom should talk to each other, so I didn't go to school one day and his mom came up, and he started chickening out then. He wouldn't talk very much or anything. (Why do you think he didn't?) Oh, I just think he started realizing everything. I don't think he was really thinking about it that serious or something. I go, "You want me to get an abortion, don't you?" And he goes, "You don't want to." And that was another reason—I didn't want to get an abortion and he knew it. I think that's one of the reasons he said we'd get married. And so finally he admitted that it wouldn't work if we got married. And so, Mom had already made an appointment for me to get an abortion. I didn't know about it. When I got done talking to him, then she told me about it. So I just made up my mind that that was the right thing to do. (16)

Among the women who originally wanted to have the baby and whose family and lack of strong male partner support influenced them into abortion, there was a tendency *not* to view parents as having been influential in the decision:

. . . Dad said, and what he said really made sense, that it wasn't a real thing yet and I wasn't killing anything. . . . (Did your parents help you make your decision then?) No, I made it by myself. It was my decision to make and I made it . . . he said it was all up to me. He never said one way or the other. (How long did it take you to decide?) After Dad talked to me about it. . . . (18)

We now turn to the third category of others in whom the women confided: friends.

FRIENDS

In general, friends were expected to be more supportive (more understanding and more in agreement with the woman) than they actually turned out to be. Thirty-two of the women confided in a friend. Of these, while only about 15 percent received what was thought to be a blatantly opposing attitude, many others reported that their friends had reacted hesitantly, expressing more reservations than the women wanted to hear. In this sense, friends were frequently portrayed as providing less support than expected.

Being understanding and agreeing with the woman, whatever her resolution orientation, were two central components of "support" from others. While most women wanted both, friends tended to provide understanding more often than agreement. At the very least, friends provided an outlet—a means for the woman to talk openly about her experience and her feelings. Thus, even when the woman anticipated that a friend might disagree, if she was reasonably certain that there would be no overtly hostile reaction, she might very well tell this person out of her need to tell someone. An example was one woman whose closest friend had in the past herself experienced an unwanted pregnancy. The friend, however, had chosen to have the baby and at that time had expressed her opposition to abortion. Nevertheless, since she was her closest friend, the woman chose to confide in her:

I had seen how she had handled it and . . . the things that she had said then about how it was murder and all of this . . . I figured that I would tell her and she would pretty much accept what I decided to do, because this was kind of the agreement that we have, you know. I decide what I want to do and she decides what she wants to do and we more or less accept it. . . . (What did she say?) . . . she didn't act surprised. . . . (Why did you tell her?) Well, mainly because she loaned the money to me to have it done. . . . I think I would have told her anyway because I would have probably felt like I needed somebody to tell about it, to talk about it, and she would have been the logical person because she had gone through it trying to make the decision before. So I think I would have told her anyway. (11)

Perhaps reflecting this need to share the experience with another person, many of the women confided in friends who were understanding but who were not necessarily in complete agreement:

> Well, I told her at first that I was pregnant. . . . She was going to have her sister bring down her maternity clothes. She kept telling me how lucky I was that I was married, and I kept telling her underneath all of this, I said, "Doris, I'm not going to have it. I don't want another baby.". . . She didn't want to face the fact that I didn't want it and that I was thinking about having an abortion. . . . I think at first it really bothered her and I think she might have in a way held it against me a little bit, but after we started talking about it, you know, and I was very open about it—but I think it bothered her, maybe I wasn't doing the right thing. . . . She never told me, she never said, "No, you shouldn't do that" or "You are being terrible" or anything like that. She never expressed any feelings like that, but I could just tell. . . . I think it was two reasons. I think she kind of thought another baby would be nice because *she* would like to have one . . . and I think that she thought it was wrong, morally wrong. . . . She didn't think it was right to take a life and that was her feelings. (17)

> (How did your girlfriend react?) Well, she tried to—she kept asking me over and over if I was sure this was what I wanted, if I had really thought about it. I think maybe in a way she was trying to talk me out of it, but after I think I convinced her that this was what I did want, then she, you know, wanted to go with me so that I'd know that she was there and this sort of thing. She was really understanding. (How did you expect her to react?) Well, I think I was surprised because she doesn't have any kids . . . and I just thought—I was kind of expecting her to react like, "Well, it's the best thing." (35)

Some of the women wondered if they would be upsetting their friends by confiding in them:

> I wasn't really sure if I wanted to tell anybody else or if I felt like I should or could or what—I thought like maybe this was a problem that I was going to lay upon her and she was going to sit around and worry about it, you know, and I didn't know for sure if that was the best approach. . . . (35)

> I thought, "Well, I'm going to talk to her about it." And then I didn't know if I should or not because she had been through it before and I didn't—I didn't feel like I should bring it up to her or something. I felt like I didn't want to dump my problems on her, you know. We'd been pretty close and we'd done a lot of talking

about things and then I finally did tell her and I was really glad I did. She said, "Well, what do you think friends are for? To confide in and to help you with your problems." I don't know, that was a really big help. Just to know that you have a friend that's going to help you out. She said, "I'll take you down; I'll do anything for you I can." And it just made me feel real good. (31)

This last comment is illustrative of a particularly supportive other person. The friend did not question or hesitate over the woman's proposed solution. Instead she offered help. The positive impact of this type of reaction is clear in the woman's comment. A similarly positive impact is illustrated in the following case where the woman also talked about how differently she would have felt had her friend reacted in a negative way:

(How did she react?) Fine. She didn't—she wasn't shocked. She said, "Great, if that's what you have to do." You know, she wasn't down on it. I suppose if she had been down on it I would have felt worse about it maybe. If you have people browbeat you, you do feel worse about it. (How did you feel after you had talked to her?) Fine. . . . I felt a little more release that I had spoken out loud about it. It kind of let off some pressure. (5)

As has been indicated, the majority of friends the women told did not react in an overtly hostile or opposing way. Of those who did, some opposed the idea of abortion on principle:

She called me and I told her and she got rather upset at me. (What did she say?) Well, she—it's not really what she said; it's how she was acting. . . . She just was kind of very upset about it. She didn't approve of it. . . .

When asked if this reaction had bothered her, the woman replied:

Yes, it kind of did. It still does a little bit. . . . (28)

Among teenagers, opposition to the woman from friends seemed to reflect the friends' desire for her to have the baby rather than moral opposition to abortion, even though moral indictment was sometimes used:

She wanted me to have it because see, she got pregnant and got married . . . and it really made me mad because she got mad at me and hasn't spoken to me since. She hates me. She thinks I'm a murderer . . . I wasn't doing the same thing she was doing. . . . It really hurt me because when she was pregnant, I stood by her. . . . She wanted me to be just like her. In fact, she wanted me to move into the same apartment as her and raise the kid—you know, like

come over every day with our kids and play. She just had this whole
idea of what we were going to do. . . . She just wanted me to be like
her. Drop school and everything. I just didn't want to do it and she
got mad at me, calling me names and everything. (13)

This comment and the next suggest the social pressure which exists among some
groups of high school girls toward early and often unwed motherhood:

This one girl, she's really close to me, she said, "You'd better not get
no abortion." (How about the other one?) Neither one wanted me
to get an abortion. They wanted me to have it. . . . I guess they just
wanted me to have a kid. . . . (27)

In the cases of both these women, peer reaction was so severe that they eventually went to their school counselor to resolve it.

Most of the women, as we have seen, already had an idea of what they
wanted and were seeking validation. An exception was the following woman,
whose friend directly influenced the nature of her abortion decision:

She said, "Have the abortion." She said, "If I was you, I'd have the
abortion." She really kind of helped talk me into it because she said,
"You never know; you don't know if your boyfriend is going to
stay with you really for the rest of your life. If you have it [abor-
tion], you know you are not going to end up like a lot of other
women, tagging a bunch of kids around on welfare and not being
able to treat them right, or give them the things they want and
raise them to be good people." I just couldn't see doing that. My
sister, especially, I had a perfect example right there—my sister
had hers [baby] and she always had problems. . . . (15)

THE REACTIONS OF OTHERS

In the preceding three sections, the reactions of others to the women's
pregnancies and to their pregnancy resolution plans have been discussed. The
complexities of these reactions can be reduced to the following summary:

1. Nearly all the women told their male partners of the pregnancy; in fact,
for most women, this appeared to be viewed as an obligation. When telling the
man, the women generally took the position of *informing* him of her condition
and what she wished to do about it rather than *asking* him what to do. Thus, he
could either agree with her or disagree. Roughly half the men disagreed.

2. Four-fifths of the women told at least one friend of their pregnancy and
pregnancy resolution plan. As in the case of telling the male partner, the friend
was typically informed rather than asked. The women seemed to confide in

friends in order to obtain understanding and agreement, validating their condition and decision. Beyond this, however, there was also the more fundamental need simply to share the experience with another person. On the whole, the women expected more support from their friends than they actually got. While only 15 percent had friends who clearly reacted in a negative way, the majority received some questioning and hesitation rather than the unqualified agreement they appeared to have wanted.

3. Parents and siblings were the least popular group in terms of being confided in. Approximately half the women told a parent and 40 percent told a sibling. While there was more fear of a nonvalidating reaction from parents than from any other group, in actuality only a third of the parents reacted in this way. Younger women who lived at home told their parents not only because of the financial or legal requirements for abortion, but also apparently because these women wanted their parents to know. Their need to tell their parents may have been influenced by the fact that these younger women were not permanently tied to their boyfriends. When the boyfriend could not or would not support the woman, she fell back on her parents.

One of the most important qualitative features of others' reactions was their evaluative nature. This can be expressed as a dichotomy, distinguishing women who received negative reactions from those who did not. The full analytic significance of this distinction will be clear in later sections.

We have discussed the importance of abortion as a problematic situation in the lives of the women being studied. We have discussed how important validation of self is in such situations. We have also suggested that validating responses tend to smooth problematic experiences, while nonvalidating ones tend to disrupt these experiences even more. In order to explore this suggestion further, the women in the study group were dichotomized according to the evaluative nature of the responses of others.

Women who received no negative reactions from any of the three groups of others were categorized accordingly. Women who received at least one nonvalidating response, and often more, were categorized as having had "some" negative reactions from others. Eighteen women (45 percent) received no negative reactions. Twenty-two women (55 percent) received at least one.

Because of their social circumstances, certain women were more likely to receive negative reactions than others. These women could protect or insulate themselves from nonvalidating reactions better than others. Important determining social circumstances in this respect were age and whether or not the woman was living at home. Not only were these factors related to parents' reactions but to the reactions of other categories of persons as well (see Table 6.5). Of the women receiving some negative reactions very few were women 18 and over who were not living with their parents.

In the remaining sections of this chapter, we will discuss additional features of the decision-making process, examining whether or not they are related to the nature of others' responses to the women.

TABLE 6.5

Reactions of Others during the Decision Phase by Age and Living Arrangements of the Women

Reactions of Others During the Decision Phase	Age and Living Arrangements of the Women					
	Under 18 and/or Living with Parents		18 and over and Not Living with Parents		Total	
	N	Percent	N	Percent	N	Percent
No negative reactions	4	(22)	14	(78)	18	(45)
Some negative reactions	19	(86)	3	(14)	22	(55)
Total	23	(58)	17	(42)	40	(100)

Source: Compiled by the author.

MAKING THE DECISION: CIRCUMSTANCES AND ALTERNATIVES

As we have described it, the decision process began for each woman with her initial orientation either toward having the baby or toward an abortion. She talked about her pregnancy and her decision with various other persons—the male involved in the pregnancy, parents and siblings, and friends. For most of the women, these interactions were a means of sharing their experience and obtaining some degree of social support. There were two exceptions to this trend. First, parents of younger women appeared to put pressure on their daughters to have the abortion rather than the baby. Second, some of the male partners of women who wanted to have the baby closed off the path of marriage, thereby influencing them to have the abortion. Other than these two instances of others exerting pressure on the abortion decision, the reactions of others did not appreciably influence the nature of the decisions.

In previous discussion, it was pointed out that the majority of women in the study group did not explicitly state that they did not want a baby. Instead, they focused their comments on the various circumstances which necessitated the abortion. Thus far, we have not enumerated these various circumstances and the pregnancy resolution alternatives related to them. We now turn to a consideration of these.

Circumstances for Abortion

Perhaps the most frequently cited circumstance necessitating the abortion was *financial inability* to have the baby. Regardless of their current financial status, that is, whether they were dependent on parents for support or whether they supported themselves, the women commonly said they could not afford a baby. Although typically mentioned by the women, financial inability did not seem to be a critical constraint except in the case of high school students living at home. In several of these cases, parents refused to provide support and there were no other viable sources:

> (Did you think seriously about not getting married and having the baby?) No. Because my dad would have kicked me out of the house. (He said that?) Well, he said that I wouldn't be living under his roof if I kept it. (16)

For this woman and for half the study group, *marriage* was a central issue in the decision-making process. Of these 20 cases, in 13 the man was willing to marry but the woman decided against it, and in 7 cases the woman would have been willing but the man was not (see Table 6.6).

TABLE 6.6

Frequency of Various Marriage Circumstances among the Women During the Decision Phase

Marriage Circumstance During the Decision Phase	N	Percent
Decided to get married in addition to having the abortion	2	(5)
Already married	6	(15)
The man was unaware of pregnancy, so marriage was not an issue	2	(5)
Neither party was interested in marriage	10	(25)
The man offered marriage if the woman wanted to have the baby, but she refused	13	(33)
The woman would have married, but the man did not or could not offer	7	(17)
Total	40	(100)

Source: Compiled by the author.

In deciding against marriage when it was a possibility, the women's reasons varied. Some women were concerned about the potential father's ability to "settle down" and support a family. Others did not love the male enough for marriage. Some were eventually planning to marry, but felt that the "time was not right" to start a family. These women wanted a planned baby under conditions of more stability. One woman decided she was too young:

> He [the woman's boyfriend] was happy . . . because he knew Dad would never let me marry him unless I was pregnant. . . . Well, here we were practically married and I decided, "There's no way." And it just hurt him bad . . . he kept telling me that he was going to kill himself and all this stuff. . . . And he'd always talk to me and try to talk me back into going with him. . . . I didn't want to go back with him because I didn't want to get married. I was too young to get married. . . . I just started thinking—because all this time Mom had said, "You're too young," and I thought, "No." But then I I stopped and looked and thought, "I'm only 15. I can't get married at 15." I thought how rough it was—Mom got married when she was 16, she had me when she was 17, and she got divorced when she was 18. Now, that's not the ideal in life and I didn't want it to be the same way. . . . I told him why and everything, and he didn't understand it. He said it was stupid. (14)

Having the baby was included in the idea of marriage, but it seemed to be the prospect of marriage that convinced her to refuse.

Among those women who were already married, the major reason given for the abortion was *not wanting another child*. Of the six married women, one had three children and three had two children. One woman had just had her first child 4 months before. With the exception of this last woman, the women with children viewed their family as complete:

> . . . We discussed why we didn't want another baby. And I said, "You can sit down and have good reasons for it—like overpopulation, the fact that we can't afford it, adding pollution to the world—and just a lot of good reasons," I said. But the main reason, I said—we can't kid ourselves—I said, "The real reason we don't want to have one is because we are too selfish.". . . (17)

These women had their lives established and did not want to change with the addition of another child. A few indicated that they might be willing to consider an additional child at a later time but not at the moment. The remaining married woman had no children. She and her husband were embarking on a religious career program in which no children were permitted.

Almost all of the women studied, regardless of the exact configuration of circumstances, felt that *the time was not right* for a baby. Most wanted to become pregnant again in the future, but only when the circumstances were just right. Rather than deal with the problems that having the baby posed, they chose abortion. As one woman put it, "I started thinking about that and I thought, "Well, it would take care of a lot of problems."

One other reason for abortion should also be mentioned, although its role in the decision making of the women in this study is unclear. That reason is *medical indication*. Seven of the women studied mentioned a medical problem as one reason for abortion. Two cited problems associated with previous child-bearing. Another cited her own previous use of drugs as an important reason she decided to terminate her pregnancy. One woman claimed that the fact that she became pregnant while continuing to take birth control pills was a medical indication (it is not), and another cited an X ray she had after conception took place as an indication for termination. Two women offered other medical reasons—exposure to measles and a doctor's comment that a period of cramping right after she became pregnant might have been a near-miscarriage. What is interesting in these last two cases is that the medical reason was used as a successful way to legitimize the abortion in the eyes of the women's parents. Both of these women had steady boyfriends and had given very serious thought to marriage and having the baby. As soon as they had decided against this plan and had informed their parents of the abortion decision, the medical reason was mentioned:

> She thought I was going to keep it and I hadn't told her yet about the exposure to the measles. So I just came out flat, "I'm going to have an abortion, Mother." "What do you mean you are going to have an abortion?" That was the attitude. Then, when I told her about the measles, she calmed down and talked to me about what it might do. So she said she wanted me to be sure and go ask somebody else who knows about what exposure to measles could do, so I did. I went to a gynecologist and asked him and he told me. . . . She wanted to be sure that it was for a medical reason, for her own feeling of conscience and to feel good about me, too. (If it hadn't been for medical reasons, then it would have been a different story with her?) I think totally different. (21)

It should be emphasized here that this woman did not have the measles but was only reportedly "exposed." It should also be pointed out that a woman who is at risk from measles is one who is not immune. The woman did not have a test for immunity. If she had been immune, then exposure would have made no difference. We can suggest, therefore, that the remote possibility of a medical indication for abortion was used as a convenient way to legitimize and justify an abortion both to the woman herself and to her family.

Alternatives to Abortion

Besides the possibility of marrying and starting a family, or adding to a family already started, two other alternatives were open to the remaining women, all of whom were unmarried. These alternatives were to become an *unwed mother* or to have the child and then give it up for *adoption*.

Adoption was not considered seriously by any of the women studied. Their reasons were all similar:

> I couldn't ever do that. I mean, carrying it for nine months and having it—I couldn't do it. Besides that, I don't like kids being orphans and stuff. They grow up wondering why their parents didn't want them and all that. (16)

> The other alternative I could have thought of was having the baby and putting it up for adoption, but I think that's ridiculous. I mean, if you're going to go through nine months of having the baby and then putting it up and not wanting it—I mean, why didn't you just have an abortion? (3)

> I couldn't give it up for adoption. I don't think I could carry something—I'm too sensitive a person to carry something around with me for nine months, to go through all that, and then say, "Here, why doesn't somebody else just take it and raise it." I just couldn't do it. I just know I couldn't do it. (31)

> (Did you ever think about adoption?) I didn't want to do that because I figured that it was my baby and I didn't want to give it to somebody else. (14)

The emotional strain of parting with a baby they saw themselves becoming attached to was paramount in the rejection of adoption. A few women also thought the consequences for the adopted child would be undesirable.

Unwed motherhood was considered more seriously than adoption, but generally that too was rejected fairly quickly. As we have already noted, one reason for rejecting this alternative among high school women was the problem of financial support. Another fear among these women was that the child would become a burden they might begin to resent:

> (Did you ever think of having the baby and not getting married?) No. No . . . too much responsibility on myself. I'd be by myself, you know. My mom said, "I can't support another kid in the family," and it would have been just too much of a load on me to be by myself. I would have ruined my life because I couldn't go out with another guy . . . I'd have to tell him I had a baby. (3)

Another woman felt she wasn't ready personally for motherhood:

> The only way I would do it—if I had decided against the abortion, I
> would have taken the child and kept it myself. . . . And then, in the
> other sense, I couldn't—I'm not stable enough to raise a child. (31)

A final consideration given by those rejecting unwed motherhood was not
wanting to have a child without a father. One of these women was divorced and
already was raising two children without a man in the home:

> I just couldn't take another child on. I did not want another father-
> less child. (24)

Another woman had grown up herself without knowing her father:

> . . . I was thinking about it and then I just kept thinking about it and
> I decided, "No, it wouldn't be fair." . . . I was thinking what it
> would be like not to have a father at all and I just didn't think it
> would be fair. (14)

CLARITY OR CONFUSION IN DECISION MAKING

In the previous sections of this chpater, we have discussed and examined
various elements involved in the decision-making period—the woman's own desire to be a mother, her actions in telling others, the reactions of those others,
her perceptions of her own circumstances, the alternatives those circumstances
allowed and those which were closed off. Of particular importance was the distinction between women who received no negative or opposing reactions to their
pregnancy and abortion orientation and women who did. In this final section,
we attempt to characterize the entire decision-making period in terms of the
clarity or confusion which the women reportedly experienced.

Confusion

Fourteen (35 percent) of the women could be characterized as confused
during most of the decision-making period. While they were eventually able to
make a decision, they were not clear about what they would do until right before the abortion was performed. For much of the one to two weeks between
medical confirmation and the abortion, these women vacillated:

> I want back and forth an awful lot. (Between which options?) Hav-
> ing an abortion and keeping it. (Did you ever think about adoption?)

Not really, because I knew that I wouldn't want to go through a pregnancy and then give it up. (In your thinking about having the baby, was that where you would be single or were you thinking about marriage?) Single . . . he did not offer [marriage] as an option to me. . . . I really feel that for me it was only by the grace of God that I didn't go crazy. I mean literally, because it was hard . . . very difficult. (How long did it take you to decide?) . . . I think a week, because I knew the decision had to be made. (6)

First, I wanted to have the child—well, I wanted to get rid of it, and then I wanted to have it, to go through with it to see what it looked like. And then I decided if I had it, I couldn't keep it, so then I'd have it and put it up for adoption; and then, after that, I just stayed there. I decided that that would be about the best thing to do, you know, not even see it. (32)

For another woman, fear of the medical aspects of the abortion were cited as the reason for her confusion:

(When did it start becoming confusing?) Well, as soon as I started getting scared about having the abortion. . . . I had always said that that is what I would do—have an abortion. (What scared you?) Mainly what my girlfriend had told me. She made it sound kind of dirty, and, you know, like when I was real young you hear . . . all this weird stuff. . . . When it came right down to it I was scared of surgery—just having to go into surgery, it was really scary for me . . . it was the last couple of hours before the deadline that I decided to go ahead. . . . I was staying in the house and one minute I would be saying, "Well, I'll go ahead and have it [the baby]," and then the next minute I would say, "I'm going to have the abortion, that's it, final." . . . I was real confused—I kept going back and forth . . . I changed my mind three times a day. . . . So I finally said, "Well, probably, the best thing would be to go with what I had decided before I got pregnant." . . . (15)

While this woman gave being afraid of surgery as an explanation for her confusion, her account of the decision-making process revealed that her boyfriend (with whom she was living) was putting pressure on her:

As for my boyfriend,

. . . I guess he started getting scared, too, you know, thinking about how he would have to tell his mother and all of his relatives . . . that I was pregnant and we weren't married and everything . . . and he started saying, "You said you would get the abortion." He said, "You've always said that." Well, we got into a big argument one night . . . I was saying how maybe I want to keep it and maybe I should go ahead and have it [the baby], and he said, "I think you should go ahead and have the abortion," and my girlfriend said, "Well, you know, that's a pretty unwise thing to say. . . ." She told him that if her boyfriend would have said that to her, she would have gone ahead and had it [the baby] —you know, out of spite . . . but then after that he apologized and didn't say anything more about it and he said, "Whatever you decide would be fine with me." (15)

She continues, pointing out his impact on her confusion:

. . . It made it a lot easier as soon as he told me that I could do whatever I wanted . . . the more he kept saying, "Get an abortion," the more I was thinking maybe I should have it [the baby]. . . but as soon as he quit saying that, I could think a little straighter, you know, at least not bring him so much into the picture, because the more I brought him into it, the more confusing it got—you know, because I had to think about his family, too, and his mother would really be upset. (15)

Her comments suggest that a reaction from another person which questioned or contradicted the woman's own thinking was disruptive. One consequence of such disruption was confusion in decision making. Another example is even clearer in demonstrating this point. In this case, the woman was certain of her decision until just before the abortion was performed. Apparently through her mother, a group of evangelists learned of the woman's plan to get an abortion and came to her house to talk to her. They showed her slides of a nine-week-old fetus and generally tried to talk her out of the abortion:

When I went to the family guidance center, I knew that if I was pregnant I was going to have an abortion. . . . I called and made an appointment . . . and, as soon as I hung up from doing that, I called [my boyfriend] out in Oregon and told him I was pregnant and what I was going to do. . . . I just kept on telling him, "I'm going to do it; I don't care what happens," and all this. . . . (Would you say you were confused when you were making up your mind or were you always sure what you wanted to do?) No, I was kind of confused. . . . I just felt kind of bad about doing it. . . . I just felt that I was killing something. I mean, I did it, but—it's hard to explain. . . . I don't know, it really didn't start bothering [me] until these people started talking to me, from the church, telling me that I was killing somebody and all this stuff. They told me that the day before I had it done—my mom told them, I guess, and then they came the next day to my house and they were showing me all these things about how I was killing a baby. . . . But that really got to me. . . . I was thinking about calling the guy that was taking me and telling him I wasn't going to go. (Why?) From what those people had shown me. . . . (9)

In further response to questioning about the source of her confusion, she indicated that she was also thinking about the possibility of her boyfriend being able to support the baby:

> . . . I was confused because I didn't know if he really wanted me to do it [have the abortion] or not. I didn't know if he'd really settle down or not . . . I thought about that quite a bit. I thought if there was a chance he would, I'd keep it, but then I kept on thinking, "Well, no, you shouldn't think that," because I knew him. (9)

From the case of this woman, we can suggest that the questioning or opposition of others served to put abortion into doubt. Alternatives which may have previously been rejected were reconsidered. Without the validation of others, all the issues remained open to question.

Taking the insights gained from these two cases, we can ask if all the women who reported confusion during the decision-making phase received negative reactions from others. As Table 6.7 indicates, all but one did. Similarly, those women who claimed to be clear about the decision from the beginning tended to be those with *no* negative reactions from others.

TABLE 6.7

Nature of Decision Making (Clarity or Confusion) by Reactions of Others During the Decision Phase

Nature of Decision Making	Reactions of Others During the Decision Phase					
	No Negative Reactions		Some Negative Reactions		Total	
	N	Percent	N	Percent	N	Percent
Clarity	16	(62)	10	(38)	26	(65)
Confusion	1	(7)	13	(93)	14	(35)
Total	17	(42)	23	(58)	40	(100)

Source: Compiled by the author

Clarity

The majority of the women, 65 percent as Table 6.7 shows, reported they were clear from the beginning about their pregnancy resolution choice:

I would say I was clear from the beginning. I've always felt that this would be what I would do unless I was in love with the guy and we were planning on getting married. But, even then, I don't think the way to start off a marriage is with a child; but maybe if I would have been in that situation, it would have been different. Other than that—no, I was sure what I wanted to do. (31)

As soon as I suspected I was, you know—I knew that when I found out that I really was, I was going to do my very darnedest to get an abortion. . . . (You didn't have any doubts or questions afterwards?) No. (35)

Another insight as to why some women were clearer about their decision than others has to do with being well tied in to a social world. Affiliation tended to mean that a woman had a definite plan for the future. If a baby was not part of this plan, then frequently she viewed her pregnancy situation as providing no alternative to abortion:

It was like there weren't any alternatives. That's what I had to do. . . . I never had any second thoughts. (You didn't vacillate or go through confusion?) No. If I were out of school or in a different situation, I'm sure there would have been more thought, "Oh, what am I going to do?" you know, that sort of thing. . . . I had too many things to do first, and marriage was out of the question. (22)

Being affiliated—knowing who she was and where she was going—gave the women a sense of the "right time" to have a baby. Like the woman above, the following woman, too, spoke in terms of having no alternatives and wanting things to be just right before she had a baby:

(Would you say you were confused or clear about what you wanted to do all the time?) Well, it was like I knew what I had to do and I was dead set on doing it, but I didn't want to. . . . I saw how my sister was and how she was getting and I didn't want to be that way—aggravated with the baby—I didn't want to get that way. . . . Like, I'd have to have it and [my boyfriend] would still be gone . . . and I wanted to start fresh in a new place where the kid would just be with me and him. . . . (10)

PATTERNS IN ABORTION PASSAGE

The relationship between clarity or confusion during the decision-making process and the degree of social affiliation before pregnancy is only part of an entire pattern. As Figure 6.1 indicates, women who were referred to as affiliated

FIGURE 6.1

Patterns in the Women's Abortion Passages from the Discovery of Pregnancy through the Decision Phase

---

Smooth Passage

---

1. Rational reaction to pregnancy

		<u>3</u>	<u>4</u>	<u>5</u>		<u>7</u>	<u>8</u>	9	<u>10</u>
11	<u>12</u>					<u>17</u>		<u>19</u>	20
	<u>22</u>	23			<u>26</u>			<u>29</u>	
<u>31</u>			<u>34</u>	<u>35</u>	<u>36</u>			<u>39</u>	

2. One to four persons told

			<u>4</u>	<u>5</u>	6	<u>7</u>	<u>8</u>		
11	<u>12</u>			15		<u>17</u>		19	
		23			<u>26</u>				30
<u>31</u>				<u>35</u>		<u>37</u>		<u>39</u>	<u>40</u>

3. No negative reactions from others

			<u>4</u>	5		<u>7</u>	<u>8</u>		
11						<u>17</u>		<u>19</u>	
21	<u>22</u>								30
<u>31</u>			<u>34</u>	<u>35</u>	<u>36</u>	<u>37</u>		<u>39</u>	<u>40</u>

4. Clarity in decision making

1		<u>3</u>	<u>4</u>	<u>5</u>		<u>7</u>	8		<u>10</u>
11	<u>12</u>		<u>14</u>			<u>17</u>		<u>19</u>	20
	<u>22</u>	23			<u>26</u>			<u>29</u>	30
<u>31</u>		33	<u>34</u>	<u>35</u>	<u>36</u>	<u>37</u>		<u>39</u>	<u>40</u>

Disruptive Passage

Emotional reaction to pregnancy

1	2	3	4	5	6	7	8	9	10
1	2				6				
		13	<u>14</u>	15	16		18		
21			24	25		27	<u>28</u>		30
	32	33				<u>37</u>	38		<u>40</u>

Five to eight persons told

1	2	3	4	5	6	7	8	9	10
1	2	<u>3</u>						9	<u>10</u>
		13	<u>14</u>		16		18		20
21	<u>22</u>		24	25		27	<u>28</u>	<u>29</u>	
	32	33	<u>34</u>		<u>36</u>		38		

Some negative reactions from others

1	2	3	4	5	6	7	8	9	10
1	2	<u>3</u>			6			9	<u>10</u>
	<u>12</u>	13	<u>14</u>	15	16		18		20
		23	24	25	<u>26</u>	27	<u>28</u>	<u>29</u>	
	32	33					38		

Confusion in decision making

1	2	3	4	5	6	7	8	9	10
	2				6			9	
		13		15	16		18		
21			24	25		27	<u>28</u>		
	32						38		

Note: Women categorized as affiliated prior to entering their abortion passage are designated by underlining; those who were disaffiliated are not underlined.

Source: Compiled by the author.

prior to pregnancy tended to be the same women who responded rationally (pragmatically) upon learning they were pregnant. They were also the same women who tended to tell the least number of people (one to four persons) about their pregnancy and who, perhaps because of that, received no negative or opposing reactions from others. These same women spoke in terms of being clear from the beginning about their abortion decision.

In contrast to this pattern, the disaffiliated women were the same ones who tended to react emotionally upon learning they were pregnant. They were also the ones who tended to tell the most other persons (five to eight), and they tended to received at least one negative reaction from among these persons. Finally, these women spoke in terms of experiencing confusion about abortion during the decision phase.

The differences between these two groups of women become even clearer if we recall that the affiliated group tended to include women who were either entering or already well-established in an adult vocation, while the disaffiliated included more women in late childhood (teenagers living at home) or who had just become independent for the first time. Also, the affiliated women tended to have close friends or husbands as their significant other persons. Disaffiliated women, on the other hand, tended to have boyfriends or parents as theirs. This latter group of significant others, as pointed out earlier, were those most likely to be nonsupportive to a younger woman becoming pregnant. Also, the fact that the disaffiliated group was at an earlier stage in the life course meant by definition that they were not married, increasing the chances of nonvalidating reactions from others.

In the next chapter, we arrive at the abortion procedure itself. An important question is whether or not the pattern which has dichotomized the women thus far in their passage through abortion will continue.

**HAVING THE ABORTION:
"IT WAS DIFFERENT . . ."**

INTRODUCTION

This chapter brings us to the day of the abortion—the women's destination in the particular passage of experience we are studying. The central concern at this point is twofold: we are interested in the ways the women interpreted their abortions as well as in the significance these interpretations held for their immediate social worlds and for the continuing social patterns of their lives.

The women's interpretations are revealed through the themes they used in describing their abortion passages. These themes center around two important and interrelated qualities of the experience: (1) suspicions of illegitimate medical practice—the presence or absence of symbols of medical and/or moral inferiority, and (2) the perceived ease or difficulty of having the abortion—reported mental and physical discomfort as well as the medical complexity involved in the abortion procedure. Taken together, the patterning and variations in these qualities tended to produce among the women either a positive or a negative overall evaluation of their abortion experience—"positive" being indicated by an easy, pleasant, and stigma-free abortion; and "negative" being indicated by a difficult, uncomfortable, and medically questionable abortion accompanied by questions of morality.

Nearly half the women studied had an abortion that could be termed "positive" according to the definition given above. Slightly fewer than 25 percent of the women, on the other hand, had what could be called a "negative" experience. The remaining women could be categorized somewhere in between. In this chapter we will attempt to capture the qualitative aspects of the women's abortions, offering some explanations for the differences in interpretations.

The particular combination of qualities with which each woman described her abortion can be seen in part as a reflection of the particular abortion facility to which she went. Hospital abortions were generally less problematic in all respects, most likely because the setting was familiar and "legitimate." Specialized clinic abortions, on the other hand, aroused more anxiety and led the women to question medical safety and competence. The unique setting and atmosphere of each of the two specialized clinics, in turn, tended to either accentuate or diminish this questioning as the women moved through the various steps involved in the abortion procedure.

Affiliation-disaffiliation differences have been important in discriminating the qualitative aspects of abortion passage thus far. In examining the day of the abortion and the women's interpretations of it, however, the nature of the abortion facility seems to be the central discriminating factor. Turning to the impact the abortion reportedly had on the women's lives, the affiliation-disaffiliation dichotomy appears again as a major point of differentiation. Affiliated women tended to report that they were untroubled mentally after their abortions. Disaffiliated women, on the other hand, tended to report at least some mental anguish.

In this chapter we explore the above observations in greater detail, beginning with the scheduling and the waiting for the day of the abortion.

ARRANGING THE ABORTION

Once the abortion decision was made, the women scheduled their abortions almost immediately. As previously indicated, the abortions of most of the women studied (35 of 40) were performed at one of the two freestanding, specialized clinics in a neighboring city. Of the five remaining women one had her abortion done in a physician's office in another nearby town and the other four had their abortions done in the local hospital.

The clinic alternative was selected primarily because an abortion there cost approximately $400 less than the same procedure in the hospital. The women whose pregnancies had advanced beyond 13 weeks were forced to use Clinic A since none of the other facilities would perform an abortion on a woman more than 12 weeks pregnant. In addition to cost and the length of the pregnancy, some women mentioned other social and medical concerns which influenced them in their choice of facility.

One such concern was for privacy. A few of the women mentioned the "social protection" they gained by having their abortion in an out-of-town clinic:

> [The social workers at Midville Clinic] has told me I could have it here and have Doctor Doe do it, but I decided to go to the city

instead. I thought that maybe—Doctor Doe is a very good friend of [my fiance's] family, you know, and I didn't really—it wasn't that I was scared he would tell, but I didn't want to put myself in that position . . . they see him socially and we have seen him a couple of times. We have gone out to dinner with [my finance's] family, and the doctor and his family would have been there, too, and I just felt like that would be an uncomfortable position and so I just decided to go to the city. (35)

Coming to the clinic here [Midville] I thought, "Oh, I just hope there is nobody that knows my mother," you know, here that would tell her. And then I thought, if I had to go to Midville Hospital or something, I know there is someone somewhere that is going to know and is going to tell. And so, when I did get to go to the city, I was relieved by the fact that there is probably no one down there that would know me. (12)

For another woman the medical concerns of her parents led her to a hospital abortion rather than one in a specialized clinic despite the fact that her family was acquainted with the doctor who would be performing the hospital abortion:

They [parents] got all upset about the city and I'm glad I didn't go there. (Why did they get upset about that?) Because, well, it's an abortion mill. They are just making money off of people who can't go anywhere else because it's the cheapest way you can get an abortion . . . they didn't want me to go through that . . . they didn't want the risks involved. They wanted me to go to a hospital. . . . I think it was really medical reasons, because the first thing my father did was call up Dr. Doe for my abortion and he said, "What is this thing [the specialized clinic abortion]?" (What did the doctor say?) He said it was just what my dad said it was—you know, you go in, you go out, there is no guarantee that you are going to live. If anything happens, they are not responsible . . . it's just a real quickie kind of thing and it's probably safe, but it's just emotionally not a good thing and physically there are some risks involved. . . . I think it bothered my dad a little bit—he talked a long time and he said, you know, "I have a 17-year-old daughter and she's pregnant and she just came home and told us. . . . (20)

Because local doctors knew her father, this woman had initially decided to go out of town to a specialized clinic for her abortion. Her decision quickly changed once she told her parents and they characterized the clinics as "abortion mills" providing inferior care. For most women in this study, however, such medical concerns were not involved in the choice of abortion facility. Most women automatically eliminated the hospital based on cost. The out-of-town, specialized clinics were not viewed as "abortion mills" nor was the quality of the care they provided questioned. Most women knew very little about these clinics, but the fact that they were being referred there by Midville Clinic legitimized them as appropriate medical facilities.

In addition to the last woman quoted, three other women had their abortions in the local hospital. Two of these women cited as the major reason for choosing the hospital the fact that they would be able to have a general anesthetic, something not provided at the specialized clinics. Cost was not considered an important factor to any of the women using the hospital. The three mentioned thus far used their medical insurance coverage to pay for the abortion. The fourth woman using the hospital did so primarily for the convenience of staying in Midville. Her abortion was paid for by welfare.

AWAITING THE DAY

Once the location of the abortion was decided upon and the appointment made, the women began a brief period of waiting. For some, this time was as short as 24 hours. For most, it lasted three or four days. For a few, it was as long as a week or ten days.

The women's reports of this period of waiting differed greatly and not necessarily according to the length of time involved. For a few of the women it was an extremely difficult time, disrupting their normal pattern of activity:

> I thought about it all the time. . . . I'd try and get myself out of the house. I don't know. I took long walks by myself. . . . I knew I *should* do it but I didn't know if I really wanted to or not. . . . I was just really confused. . . . I was scared a lot. I kept on wanting to call and cancel it because I didn't know anything about it . . . they kind of explained it, but I didn't have anybody to talk to who had been through it. That probably would have helped. (9)

> (You waited a week?) Yes. (And that week?) All I thought about was the abortion. . . . I didn't want to talk to my parents. I just stayed in my room . . . I didn't go to school that week. . . . I was upset I guess. I didn't want to talk to nobody. (27)

For others, in contrast, the days of waiting were fairly routine:

> (Did you think about it after the appointment was made?) No. It was a relief. I didn't have to worry about it. It was a lot off my mind—I didn't have to worry about "am I?" or "am I not?" I knew that I was and I knew what I was going to do . . . I felt like someone had just taken fifteen thousand pounds off of my mind when I

found out that I was and that I could have the abortion and the date
was set for it. (31)

As soon as he had decided that we would go through with it and he
was with me on it, it didn't bother me. No, it was just like—I felt
toward it like I had decided to have surgery. (5)

The most typical characterization for the days before the abortion lies
somewhere in between. The abortion was a source of concern for most of the
women and was frequently on their minds, but it did not significantly alter their
daily activities:

. . . I just tried to go on like I wasn't pregnant and I wasn't going to
have an abortion. I just tried to put it out of my mind. (How often
would you say you thought about it?) Probably all day long. I
thought about it, like at work—I knew, "What would these people
really think if they knew I was pregnant? Here I am walking around
and they're joking and here I am pregnant and I'm going to have an
abortion in a week." I think I constantly thought about it. I was
taking classes and stuff and I'd sit there and think about it. (12)

(Was this on your mind very much?) Well, they gave me some
medication so I wouldn't feel so icky all the time and since I didn't
feel so bad I didn't think about it quite so much. . . . I mean, I did
think about it, but it wasn't something where I'd just lay awake in
bed every night wondering. (22)

THE DAY OF THE ABORTION

On the day of their abortion, the women tended to characterize themselves as "nervous" and "scared." Their descriptions suggest that a third of the
women were *very* apprehensive about the abortion. One woman, for example,
described herself as so frightened she was "shaking." A few of the women reported, on the other hand, that they were very relaxed, treating the drive to the
abortion facility just as they would any other drive. The remaining majority
were apprehensive, but moderately so.

The women interacted with others continually throughout the day of the
abortion. This began with their being accompanied to the abortion facility by
another person (in several cases, two persons). Typically, the accompanying
person was either a parent or the male involved in the pregnancy (see Table 7.1).
Only one of the women went to the abortion facility alone. She had wanted
someone to accompany her but could find no one to do so. Accompanying
persons were not allowed to be with the woman except at the very beginning of
her stay at the clinic. For most of the time, these persons remained in a separate
waiting room.

TABLE 7.1

Frequency of the Women According to the Type of Other Person Accompanying Them to the Abortion Facility

Type of Other Person	N	Percent
Parent	13*	(33)
Male partner in the pregnancy	17	(43)
Friend	7	(17)
Sister	2	(5)
None	1	(2)
Total	40	(100)

*Of these women, eight were accompanied by the mother, two by the father, and three by both parents.

Note: Eight of the women were accompanied by two persons: in three cases, these were both parents; three other women had a friend as the additional person; two others each had a sister as the additional person.

Source: Compiled by the author.

Women who were accompanied by friends or family members seldom mentioned the reactions of those persons to what was happening. Even when the women were specifically asked, they were generally vague about the other person's mood and actions. In contrast, the women who were accompanied by their male partners almost all described the man as apprehensive yet protective. In many cases, the man was perceived to be more apprehensive than the woman herself:

> He was more scared than I was. . . . He's just real sensitive, you know, He just doesn't like to see people suffer. He was afraid that I was suffering and it was really hard for me and he just didn't want to see me go through anything real traumatic. . . . He was crying while I was having it. I came down after I recovered and everything, and it was time for me to go home and he was crying like a little baby. (15)

> He was more scared than me. (3)

> He was very quiet. I'm sure he was nervous, too. Like I said, he is very sensitive to pain and afraid of my being hurt. (4)

In addition to being concerned with the woman's well-being and the medical safety of the procedure, some of the men were also perceived as feeling guilty for what their partners were having to go through:

I think he felt a little—he was worried about me. . . . He wasn't going to say anything to me. He was calm acting, but I could still feel it inside that he felt like—I don't know, it was hurting me to do something like that and I think he felt a little guilty. (30)

If he had any negative feelings, I think they would be guilt because of what I was going through. Before I went to the clinic, he thought he might be treated as a criminal. I wasn't that concerned. (36)

In most instances, the male partners who accompanied the women were perceived as sharing in the emotionality of the abortion experience. It is interesting that these same observations were made less frequently for the other types of accompanying persons. The women tended not to perceive the same level of concern and involvement in parents or friends. If the women's perceptions were accurate, then it is possible that the males' biological role in pregnancy led them to become more deeply involved than other persons. It must be pointed out, however, that over half the male partners were not present.

INITIAL PERCEPTIONS OF THE ABORTION FACILITY

The women who went to the local hospital took for granted that it was an appropriate medical setting for their abortions. They had no problem in establishing its legitimacy. That was not the case for the women who went to the freestanding clinics. While they had not questioned the clinic's appropriateness at the time of making the appointment, on the day of the abortion questions commonly arose. As mentioned previously, these questions differed according to the nature of the clinic. Although abortions were performed in both clinics in much the same way, the two freestanding clinics were very different in terms of location, physical structure of the building, and inside atmosphere (see Chapter 3). These differences appeared to influence the women to view one clinic more suspiciously than the other.

The stereotypic view of abortion held by most of the women—that abortion is something unsafe, unclean, and frightening—was introduced in our discussion of their abortion attitudes. It was suggested that these images provided a lens through which the women would perceive the events of their own abortion passage. Thus far in their passages, the stigma of abortion has indeed been in evidence. It appeared in their decision making, in their choices of confidants, and in the reactions of others to them.

The stigma associated with abortion was further illuminated when the women were confronted with having to define and interpret the clinic setting. The clinics were unfamiliar and, for many of the women, unexpected in appearance and atmosphere. Over half the women going to the freestanding clinics (19 of 35) initially perceived them in terms of illegitimacy and the deviant imagery of the abortion stereotype. Specifically, these women described the clinics in terms of two central themes: the impersonal, mass-production image associated with an "abortion mill," and the haphazard, unsanitary medical image associated with a quack abortionist.

The majority of women who perceived the abortion facility as an illegitimate or otherwise inappropriate place were clients of Clinic A rather than Clinic B (see Table 7.2).

TABLE 7.2

Frequency of Initial Perception of Abortion Facility
(Legitimate or Illegitimate) by Social Class of the
Women, Controlling for Type of Facility

| | Initial Perception of Abortion Facility | | Total |
	Legitimate	Illegitimate	
Clinic A			
Blue Collar			
N	5	13	18
Percent	(24)	(68)	(45)
White Collar			
N	3	3	6
Percent	(14)	(16)	(15)
Clinic B			
Blue Collar			
N	2	1	3
Percent	(9)	(5)	(8)
White Collar			
N	6	2	8
Percent	(29)	(11)	(20)
Hospital*			
Blue Collar			
N	1	0	1
Percent	(5)	(0)	(2)
White Collar			
N	4	0	4
Percent	(19)	(0)	(10)
Total			
N	21	19	40
Percent	(52)	(48)	(100)

*The one woman who had her abortion in a doctor's office is included here.
Source: Compiled by the author.

Perceptions of Clinic A

The descriptions of Clinic A patients often began with a description similar to the one given in Chapter 3:

> The one I went to is right down there in the middle of nowhere, down in the boonies. (Could you describe the building?) It was a big, old brown brick building setting down in among a bunch of trees right at the end of a street. It didn't even look anything like a hospital. It was just stuck down there. (39)

The meaning or interpretation underlying this description became clear when this woman was asked how she had reacted to this particular clinic setting. She said, "I thought, 'Oh, my God!' " Her exclamation is further clarified by the comments of several other clients of Clinic A:

> We was looking for this big hospital . . . when we saw it we almost fainted. . . . I said, "Wow, that looks like my junior high." It was just a little brick building and I thought, "Gosh." (What was going through your mind?) I was scared. "How could they do this to us? Send us to such a little place." . . . and then, on the way there, it was on a dirt road and . . . the houses around there were kind of povertylike, you know. I don't know, I expected a big, white hospital with all these guys walking around in white suits, white overcoats, and all. (13)

> It was such an old dilapidated building to me. I was expecting like Midville Hospital or something like that and it was just very different and I was scared. Maybe I would go in there and there would be cockroaches running around or something . . . maybe I wasn't going to have the kind of care that I had thought I was going to have . . . that's like the impression my mother had always made on me. It kind of made me think, "Well, abortions are something you just don't talk about, so maybe that's why they are sending me back here to this old, dilapidated building. Maybe just to keep hush-hush," you know, and that sort of thing. (35)

The wide discrepancy between these women's expectations and the actual appearance of the clinic not only led them to question the medical care they would receive but it also encouraged them to think in images of crime. The following comments, for example, include the words "prison" and "jail":

> (Can you remember how you reacted to the drive up there and seeing the clinic for the first time?) The drive didn't bother me but the clinic looked like a jail or something to me. It kind of scared me because it looked so—I don't know—looked so icky really. . . . You see

on all these movies about how they did it in strange ways with knives and stuff, and that's what it made me think of . . . something the law didn't know about—against the law. They did it unlawfully, you know, and you could get disease in about three seconds. That's what it reminded me of. . . . I don't know how to explain it—it just looked like not the right thing to do. (14)

To me it looked like a prison. It had bars on the windows and I didn't like it at all. I thought, "Boy, that's really a great place to go." . . . I was thinking, "I wonder what kind of medical facilities they've got," you know. "Is it such a grubby place that all it is is a doctor who isn't even qualified?" And I was thinking, "It looks like a prison." . . . it was all bricked up. It just looked terrible to me. Here I am used to Midville Hospital, a nice, clean hospital . . . and there it was run-down in one of the run-down sections of town. . . . (23)

Clinic A, as noted in an earlier description, was located in a predominantly black neighborhood. This aspect of the setting added further to many of the women's anxieties. It became even more salient to their illegitimate definition of the clinic as they entered and observed black staff members:

I tell you, when we came, all we could see outside, playing ball, everywhere, on the first floor, was just colored people. . . . It kind of scared me to think, "I'm going to go in this hospital and there's going to be all these colored people." . . . (35)

(What happened when you went in?) I almost cried. I mean, I've always been raised in small towns where there are no black people, and I walked in and all there were were black people. And I thought— you think when you see black people—to me, I saw the black people as meaning that they're doing it unlawfully. "It's going to be a black doctor." That's the first thing that I thought—that this doctor is going to be a black doctor. I kept thinking about that. . . . (14)

I thought it was some quack's place—a bunch of quacks in there. . . . Then I got in there and all I saw was colored on the first floor, and oh, boy. (39)

In summary, two-thirds (16 of 24) of the women having their abortions scheduled for Clinic A initially questioned the clinic's legitimacy (Table 7.2). They quickly associated the small size and old age of the clinic building and the low-income, black neighborhood surrounding it with the abortion stereotype left over from the illegal period—the notion of an abortion mill run by un-qualified personnel under medically dangerous conditions. These perceptions provided an extreme contrast to the women's original expectations of a large, modern hospital, similar to the one in Midville.

The women reported that their initial interpretation of their abortion facility left them extremely apprehensive. Nevertheless, they stayed. None of the women left until the abortion had been performed. One way that they have tried to justify an otherwise apparently deviant situation was to consider the fact that they had been referred by a legitimate, professional health clinic, a clinic they trusted. The comments of one woman reflect the usefulness of this notion in coping with her fear:

> I had to sit there and convince myself that I knew [that] the [social worker] —maybe not her, but that the public health department clinic was not going to send me or anybody else to a place that wasn't medically capable and OK and everything. . . . I just sat there and kept saying . . . "I just don't believe they would do that." So I felt better. (35)

While the legitimacy of Clinic A was problematic for two-thirds of the 24 women, it was unquestioned by the remaining 8 women. This latter group acknowledged that the building was older and that the neighborhood was a low-income one, but they did not connect this in their comments to illegal and inadequate medical care or to the abortion stereotype. They either ignored the clinic setting entirely or else said that it was "old but nice," that it "did not look like a hospital but was comfortable," or that it was "OK."

One explanation for the difference in perceptions of this latter group is that they had been prepared for the appearance of the clinic by the staff of Midville Clinic. Such preparation was mentioned by a few of the women. As a result of it, they reportedly were neither surprised nor frightened:

> (Was it different than you expected it to be?) No, because [the social worker] had told me the building was this really old, groaty looking thing, and it was. . . . She had already told me what it would look like and I was kind of prepared. If she hadn't told me—oh, yuk. Because it was terrible looking. (28)

> She [the social worker] had told me that it was in a *very* bad part of town. It was very depressing. It was an old hospital and she said I would get excellent care, but it might depress me. So I was all prepared for gloom and . . . really, I didn't think about it too much. (24)

These comments raise an important question but unfortunately one that cannot be answered within the framework of this research. The question is whether all of the women were prepared in the same way for Clinic A with only a few really paying attention to that warning; or whether, on the other hand, all those who reacted very strongly to the illegitimate image of Clinic A were women who had *not* received any advance preparation, and all those who reacted to Clinic A as legitimate were women who *were* prepared.

An additional explanation for the differences in interpretation of Clinic A has to do with differences among the women with respect to social class. This explanation will be discussed subsequently, after we have considered the interpretations of the women who were clients of Clinic B.

Perceptions of Clinic B

Enthusiasm was absent from even the most favorable of the initial reactions to Clinic A. First perceptions of that clinic were most frequently negative, neutral at best. Perceptions of Clinic B, on the other hand, were generally more positive. A particularly favorable comment from one Clinic B woman illustrates this point:

> It was just great. I can't say enough good things about it . . . and, you know, the building is just a beautiful, normal building. It could be anywhere. . . . The whole setting was really nice. . . . It was almost to the point of being plush. . . . (22)

The favorable reaction to Clinic B becomes clearer when directly compared to the reaction to Clinic A. As Table 7.2 shows, while only 8 of the 24 women going to Clinic A (33 percent) initially perceived it as a legitimate medical facility, 8 of the 11 women going to Clinic B (73 percent) did so. Even among those who questioned the legitimacy of Clinic B, the degree to which they considered the clinic problematic was much less than among those who questioned the legitimacy of Clinic A:

> (Was there anything about the clinic [B] that was different than you expected?) Well, the building wasn't as bad. The counselor [at Midville Clinic] said it was in the basement of the building and that sounded to me really—well, I didn't want some place raunchy. . . . And then, when we saw it, it didn't look like a medical building. (How was your husband reacting to the building?) He was very suspicious. He said if it was too bad, we'd leave. But when we went inside it was OK. (4)

> . . . the outside of the place was like a motel or an apartment and [my boyfriend] goes, "I don't think we should go in there. I don't want you hurt." And I said, "No, let's just go on down," and it was just like an office building. I mean, I thought I was in a doctor's office. . . . (3)

Both these women's adverse interpretations were immediately altered and the deviant image normalized as soon as they entered the clinic. This was not the case for women entering Clinic A.

Accounting for Differences in Perceptions

It was easier for the clients of Clinic B to define the facility as legitimate than it was for the clients of Clinic A. Why? We have suggested and have taken some effort to illustrate that the physical structure and setting, and even the skin color of some staff members, meshed with a commonly held stereotypic view of abortion as dirty and criminal in the case of Clinic A. Clinic B's physical setting, building, and staff lacked these particular characteristics. Hence, it was not associated with the abortion stereotype and tended to be seen as legitimate.

As previously mentioned, social class differences among the women going to the two clinics can also be suggested to have influenced their different perceptions. The women in this study who were scheduled for Clinic A tended to be from blue collar families. Those scheduled for abortions at Clinic B tended to be from white collar families. Medical sociologists have found that lower-income persons (including blue collar workers) tend to be more suspicious and hostile toward health care institutions and health care professionals than those in higher-income groups (Rosenblatt and Suchman 1964). Thus, we might expect that, particularly when confronted with a problematic setting such as that provided by Clinic A, blue collar women would react more negatively than white collar women. Table 7.2 confirms that this is precisely what happened.

Almost all of the blue collar women (11 of 13) who perceived Clinic A as illegitimate were 21 years old or younger. This suggests that the age of the women also may be important in the differential interpretations. Considering the factor of age (Table 7.3), only one of the seven women in the younger age group who went to Clinic B perceived it as illegitimate, whereas 12 of the 17 going to Clinic A did so. The women 21 and older, on the other hand, were just about equally divided between legitimate perceptions and illegitimate ones in both clinics.

Entering the Clinic

Entering the clinic provided the women with new observations which either confirmed or refuted their first interpretations of the clinic. Most of the women going to Clinic B had already perceived the clinic as legitimate; seeing the inside simply confirmed this interpretation. The few who had suspicions about Clinic B quickly altered their view upon entering and seeing the interior and the staff (see previous quotations). Although the legitimacy of Clinic B was quickly established, the legitimacy of Clinic A was more difficult for the women to

TABLE 7.3

Frequency of Initial Perception of Abortion Facility (Legitimate or Illegitimate) by Age of the Women, Controlling for Type of Facility

| | Initial Perception of Abortion Facility | | |
	Legitimate	Illegitimate	Total
Clinic A			
Age 14-21			
N	5	12	17
Percent	(24)	(63)	(43)
Age 22-39			
N	3	4	7
Percent	(14)	(21)	(17)
Clinic B			
Age 14-21			
N	6	1	7
Percent	(28)	(5)	(17)
Age 22-39			
N	2	2	4
Percent	(10)	(11)	(10)
Hospital*			
Age 14-21			
N	3	0	3
Percent	(14)	(0)	(8)
Age 22-39			
N	2	0	2
Percent	(10)	(0)	(5)
Total			
N	21	19	40
Percent	(52)	(48)	(100)

*The one woman who had her abortion in a doctor's office is included here.
Source: Compiled by the author.

ascertain. As we have pointed out, many of those initially interpreting Clinic A as illegitimate apparently had their perceptions validated when they entered the clinic on the first floor. Several of these women, however, altered their view when they went upstairs and began preparations for the abortion:

> . . . when I got to walking around the place and finding out that everything was all right, then I knew it *would* be all right. When they started doing actual tests on me and stuff, then I knew everything was all right. (10)

Racial stereotyping was again the basis for changing interpretations in some of these cases:

Clinic A

> The first floor scared me . . . because everybody I saw was colored. Everybody! I didn't see one white person except the girls that were waiting to go, too. And then I got upstairs and I was so relieved. I just felt so much better . . . I got upstairs and I saw some white people and it was real clean and real bright and cheerful and it really helped. It made me feel a lot better. (35)

> . . . it didn't bother me anymore after I got upstairs. I saw a bunch of white nurses and I was so happy to see them—it didn't bother me that much after I got upstairs. . . . (14)

This last woman is interesting. After she initially had interpreted the clinic's building and location as an illegitimate facility, she redefined the clinic as legitimate on the basis of the interior. She reinterpreted the building and location in terms of a small-town hospital:

> Well, it's like a small-town hospital. That's what it seems like to me. . . . It's nothing big and fancy like Midville Hospital, but it's just like a little, bitty hospital, a town hospital. . . . (14)

The same woman had referred to the clinic building previously as a "jail."

Although some women altered their interpretation of Clinic A and defined it as legitimate upon beginning their abortion procedure, others did not. For them, their initial perceptions were confirmed. Rather than the "normal" functioning of the clinic being an affirmation of legitimacy, for these women it evoked the image of the abortion mill:

Clinic B

> That's all they did there. It was like a slaughter house. (25)

> . . . I felt like I was being pushed through, you know, "Next please, next please, next please," because they asked you all these questions. . . . I felt like I was a cow getting ready to get butchered; I really did. (9)

One reason for this imagery was the fact that Clinic A, like many much larger hospitals, had the various routes the women were supposed to take mapped out along the hallways with a series of colored lines. While this practice is common, it is interesting to see how the women interpreted it in the context of an already problematic situation:

. . . they had all of these little arrows on the floor pointing which
way to go . . . and it made me think like they do this every day, you
know, and there were hundreds of girls. . . . I didn't like the arrows
on the floor. It made it seem like they were packing us all in and
standing in line and getting it done and then walking out. (15)

After you go in the admissions office, they say follow the green line
upstairs and around; and then after you pay the rest of your money,
they say follow the red line around. You are just following a bunch
of lines. . . . It was kind of like an assembly line. (39)

Summary of Initial Perceptions

To summarize the women's initial reactions to the abortion facilities, it
is important to differentiate the hospital and the two clinics. For women having
hospital abortions, there was no discrepancy between their expectations and
their perceptions of the facility. In this sense, hospital abortions were the least
problematic. Clinic abortions, on the other hand, involved discrepancies. This
was particularly true for the women who went to Clinic A where the building
and physical surroundings evoked the abortion stereotype from the illegal
period. In general, the women going to the freestanding clinics expected them to
look like the hospital in Midville. Neither clinic approximated that expectation.
Clinic B, however, was more quickly defined as a legitimate medical facility. The
women going there had their suspicions eliminated upon entering the clinic.
The women going to Clinic A, on the other hand, could not as easily legitimize
their surroundings. Many of these women passed through their entire abortion
procedure retaining suspicion.

Before continuing with the actual performance of the abortion, let us consider briefly the problem of paying for the abortion.

PAYING FOR THE ABORTION

Patterns in paying for the abortion revealed that the women, typically
with their male partners sharing half, took financial responsibility for their
abortions (Table 7.4). Most couples whose relationships had been fairly stable
agreed to share the costs:

(Did you have any problems with money for the abortion?) No, we
just figured, you know, half my fault and half his. So he paid half
and I paid half. . . . (22)

TABLE 7.4

Frequency of the Various Persons Who
Paid for the Abortion

Person Who Paid	N	Percent
Woman herself	10	(25)
Woman and male partner each sharing half	16	(40)
Male partner	1	(2)
Parents	7	(18)
Parents and woman each sharing half	1	(2)
Welfare	5*	(13)
Total	40	(100)

*In four out of the five cases, welfare assistance was only temporary. Thus, only one woman was being supported regularly by welfare at the time of this study.

Source: Compiled by the author.

Obtaining the money was generally not difficult. In some cases, the money was borrowed, but many of the women had enough of their own. The same woman continues:

. . . I had my own job at that time that paid very well. (22)

Some women (25 percent), either because they were not closely involved with the man at the time of the abortion, or because they wanted to disengage themselves from him, paid for the entire abortion themselves. In the following comment, one of these women appeared to be paying in order to assert her independence from the man:

(How was the money arranged?) I paid for it. I told him I would take care of it myself. . . . Before the time he decided to take me down there, I was talking to him on the phone and he said, "Well, I'll send you a check." I said, "No, I'll handle it myself." I didn't want to feel obligated to him for anything, whether it was financial or anything. (12)

Payment patterns also revealed two additional trends. First, although 21 of the women were living with their parents at the time they had the abortion, and most of these parents knew of the abortion, only a third of these abortions were paid for by parents. Secondly, although traditional notions of male responsibility in nonmarital pregnancy are frequently heard (for example, "he got her in trouble"), only one of the male partners from this study group paid the entire cost of the abortion. As the previous quotations indicated, in many cases the woman did not want the man to take full financial responsibility.

Most of the abortions were paid for in cash. Six women reportedly used medical insurance—in three cases the women came under their parents' coverage; in three cases the women used their own.

THE ABORTION PROCEDURE: PATIENTS' PERSPECTIVES

While the problematic or disruptive features which we will be discussing shortly were present, on the whole the women viewed the abortion procedures as "easier" than they had originally thought. For the most part, this view was a result of the simplicity of the vacuum aspiration technique:

> . . . it was a lot easier than I thought it was going to be. . . . It was easier, a lot easier. I was, you know, imagining all sorts of wild things—I thought it would take a half hour or an hour and they would have to put you out and you would be in intensive care for a couple of hours. . . . It was so easy and I was glad. (15)

> The operation itself was easier than I expected . . . because, you know, I had psyched myself up to where I thought it was going to be a major operation. They were going to cut me open and everything, but it just seemed a lot easier. (14)

> It went a lot better, I think, than I had really thought—heard—maybe expected it to go. I had expected a lot of pain. Even though the social worker here had told me, "It's not painful," I had really expected a lot. (35)

The entire abortion procedure took from five to six hours in the clinic setting and an hour or two longer for those in the hospital. Most of this time, however, was devoted to preparation and recovery. The vacuum aspiration technique itself (the same at all facilities) was done within a few minutes. As an example, the woman who had her abortion in a doctor's office reported that she was there only for an hour or so—quite a contrast to the length of time required at the other locations.

The women in the hospital setting considered the sequence of events they experienced (see Chapter 3) to be usual; it approximated a "normal" hospital routine. This was not the case for the clinic patients. As we have shown in their initial interpretations, some of these women perceived clinic activity with suspicion, describing it in terms of an assembly line or abortion mill. While the women quoted were Clinic A patients, similar although milder comments were also made by Clinic B women.

In this section, we move on to discuss the abortion procedure itself, continuing to describe and analyze the women's observations and interpretations. Attention will be focused on the women having clinic abortions since for them the problematic nature of the clinic situation as well as the problematic nature of abortion per se gives their experience particular sociological significance. As Thomas has pointed out, it is in those situations which cannot be taken for granted—and which must be newly defined—that we take stock of ourselves and devote time to reflecting on our situations (Volkhart 1951).

Reactions to the Staff

A central concern of hospital patients and clinic patients alike was that the staff members involved with their abortion procedure might react to them in a negative manner. Many women commented on how "nice" the staff members were, revealing their appreciation at the absence of the feared criticism:

> . . . the people [staff] were really understanding. They didn't make you feel like a criminal—like, you know, you got yourself in a mess and stuff like that. (22)

> They were very nice. Everyone. I thought maybe they would sort of frown at me and moralize, you know, and say, "She's the one having the abortion," but they were really very cheerful and friendly, the nurses especially. (19)

> At first I thought people would stare at you, but no one did. Everyone was nice. (2)

> I didn't feel put down. This is one thing I was wondering about— whether people at the clinic would look at you, like, "Since you're going to have this nasty thing done. . . . " I was glad it wasn't like that. That would have been hard. I felt that in a normal hospital you would get that from at least one person, whether it would be one of the nurses or technicians or whatever, at least one person would give you the attitude, "An abortion! Ugh!" (5)

Encountering negative reactions from staff members and the pain and danger associated with the medical procedure were the main sources of prior anxiety for the women. Several other aspects of the abortion procedure which they had not anticipated arose for the clinic patients. One of these concerned fellow patients.

Observing Other Patients

Almost all of the women who had clinic abortions had some observations to make about the other women there. The most common observation concerned the number of patients at the clinic:

> I don't think I really expected to see that many women there in the same situation as I was. . . . (11)

> I didn't expect that many girls to be there. I really didn't. I thought I would go in and a doctor would meet me and take me up and I would have it done and then—you know, I just thought it was me and I was the only one; and it turned out that there was a lot more girls there than I expected. . . . (15)

When asked how they reacted to the other women, responses were varied. Several women said that the other patients made them realize that they were not alone:

> . . . it made me feel a lot better because I knew I wasn't so unusual— I kind of felt like a criminal, you know, going in and having it done. (15)

> I couldn't imagine that there were going to be that many girls that were going to be there. . . . (How did that make you feel when you saw all those girls?) I wasn't alone. I didn't feel alone anymore. (1)

Some women spoke about how casual the others seemed. In most cases, they did not approve of the casual attitude they perceived:

> There were more girls there than I had expected. I didn't think there would be so many, and they were all laughing and joking. That surprised me. (4)

> There was about 40 girls there with me. Some of them were saying, "Oh, this is my third time." God, after once you'd think they'd learn. (25)

> Most of the girls seemed like it was just the normal thing to happen. . . . The girl I was with, for instance, had had it done twice before, I think, and that placed in my mind, you know, well, this must be a once a year occurrence for some girls, to have it done all the time. (7)

These perceptions of multiple abortions being common among fellow patients appear to have been quite biased. At the time of this study, personnel from both clinics estimated that 10 percent of their patients had had previous abortions. (Later estimates were as high as 15 percent, suggesting an increase in abortion repeaters.) Concerning the perceived casual demeanor of the patients, one woman had an alternate interpretation:

Well, a lot of times the casualness you observe in the other patients in an abortion clinic is quite possibly a front. I don't really feel there are very many women in the world that can really in their own mind casually have an abortion, even though they may give the appearance of being casual. (5)

Other characteristics of fellow patients were also observed and interpreted. Some women expected more blacks to be there than were there. Others commented on the fact that the presence of "older" and married women surprised them; one of these women was herself "older" and married. One of the women who expected to see more blacks was herself black. Of the other patients, another woman said:

I was surprised. Most of them looked like decent people. . . . I don't know . . . maybe something I had already preconceived in my mind . . . it was going to be a little stranger. . . . (22)

For others, typically patients at Clinic A, it *was* "stranger" because of the other women there:

They were just more freer people than me—I mean, they lived with their boyfriends and stuff like that, and the one lady was married . . . it was making me kind of feel like some dummy, you know. . . . I didn't feel that much out of place, but I did, I felt like a fool really. (28)

I know that there are people like that. That's just how they are. But that wasn't very comforting either. (Did you feel somehow that you were being placed in the same category?) Well, yes. That was the first thing when we walked in, Jeff went, "I'm her husband," because everybody else. . . . (7)

This tendency to view fellow patients as morally inferior was consistent with many of the women's preabortion attitudes. As discussed in Chapter 4, they reported having stigmatized or looked down on women having abortions. It is interesting that these women tended to continue to see themselves as "different" from the others even when they were in the very same situation.

Perhaps more important for our analysis than the perceived qualities of others was the very fact that each woman who went the specialized clinic route was very observant of other patients and actively tried to place herself with respect to them. Hospital patients did not do this. They had no opportunity; they saw only one other patient (the one sharing the room with them) at most. In the clinic patients spent a significant amount of time waiting with other patients. Characteristics of others were noted quickly—in some cases capriciously, bringing to mind Thomas' point that in an extremely problematic situation the person is ready to accept any definition that presents itself (Volkhart 1951, p. 158).

The Impact of Waiting

The questions, doubts, fears, and ambiguities of an already problematic experience were heightened by the prolonged waiting in the abortion clinics. As has been described, the women spent several hours signing forms, taking tests, and sitting in a series of waiting rooms:

> . . . I'd go from test to test, and every time I'd go to a different room or a different test I'd think, "Oh, my gosh, it's getting much closer. You've got to be strong about it." This going from room to room—. . . . It made it harder for me to tell myself that it was the right thing. I had to keep telling myself that more often. It was sad, too. It kept getting sadder and sadder. (10)

> . . . we went upstairs and we took our clothes off and got into these robes and paper shoes and then we went in a waiting room and we was watching TV and we sat there for a long time. . . . We was getting nervouser and nervouser. (13)

> I think I was in there about 30 minutes and the rest of the time we were all just sitting around waiting and waiting. . . . I was just getting more nervous as I sat there, and it bothered me to see one girl getting up and running out of the room. . . . (31)

In addition to having more time to think about herself and her abortion, this last woman was particularly upset by having to observe and be affected by the actions and reactions of the other women:

> . . . That's when I had more questions about everything than I had during the whole time before. . . . When I've made up my mind to do something, I've pretty much made it up and that's what I'm going to do and I just want to do it. The thing running through my mind was all the other girls there and the expressions on their faces. Some of them looked really young. Upstairs in the waiting room, before I ever went down with the rest of the girls, there was a woman up there just crying, just crying . . . and there was another girl sitting there, you know, with her leg over her chair, just looking into the ceiling. You could just tell she was terribly nervous. . . . Then I noticed a couple of the girls that were there were really young . . . they were just kind of clinging on to each other. It was just watching them that I got to thinking that—I don't know, it was just the more

I watched them, the more I wanted to get it over with . . . something like that is something that will really have an effect on your mind if you are not really sure of what you are doing. (31)

Some of the women talked with each other while waiting. A few became involved in the problems of the others' abortion situations to the degree that they reportedly forgot about their own. Another few women reported that they did not talk at all. As one woman said, "I was too busy fighting with myself." It would appear that most women had some conversation but that the general atmosphere of the waiting rooms was one of tension and restraint. Physical discomfort caused by the pregnancy added even more distress for some. Few women said that they enjoyed the time spent waiting. "There was such a feeling of gloom over everything," one woman observed. Thus, though many of the women felt comforted knowing there were others in the same position as they, the overall impact of the women on each other was not a calming one:

. . . and when I saw her crying, well, I felt real bad and I felt like crying, but I said, "No, I'm just going to go ahead and get it [the abortion] . . . . (26)

One woman, in recounting what a friend had told her, expressed this in a slightly different way:

My girlfriend had said, when she went down there, that there was a bunch of girls just sitting there and everybody was trying to keep calm and then one girl started crying and pretty soon everybody was in hysterics. She said if nobody would—if that one girl wouldn't have started crying, everybody would have held on, you know, and could have done it, but as soon as one person goes into hysterics, they all do. (15)

Personalizing The Abortion

The vulnerability of the women to the talk and demeanor of the other patients was exacerbated by the prolonged waiting. Another exacerbating feature was the clinic's practice of putting the women together throughout their abortion experience. This made the abortion procedure a group rather than an individual experience—in effect, a public rather than a private experience. While the vacuum aspiration was performed with only one patient in the procedure room at a time, the waiting, counseling, and recovery phases of the clinic abortions were conducted with several patients grouped together. This stood in direct contrast to the conventional medical expectations of most of the women who came to the clinics:

(Was there anything that was different than you expected?) Well, yes. I guess it was because it seemed like it was more of a group thing than an individual thing. You went into this little room and this woman—I don't know whether she was a counselor or a social worker—whatever she was, she talked to you about it, and she didn't take you individually, she took you as a group, like three or four girls at a time. That was different! I didn't expect that. Then, after the procedure, you're all sitting in this little room, you know, in little lounge chairs with heating pads on—all these women. It was just not what I expected. (Do you know what you did expect?) I think a more individual, private thing. It really didn't seem that private. Of course, they see it day in, day out. To them, it's probably nothing. I'm sure it wasn't—and maybe to some other people it wasn't either—but it just seemed kind of strange. (12)

In part, the group approach reflects a popular notion that talking together and sharing is therapeutic and relaxing. The group approach also, however, is efficient for the abortion clinic in terms of allowing the clinic to accommodate more women at less cost. In practice, the therapeutic function of the group was seldom recognized by the women. They reported that, while the counselors gave each group an opportunity to discuss their problems and feelings, most patients did not do so. There was very little reported group discussion. Instead, the counseling sessions appeared to consist primarily of a talk given by the staff member, detailing the technical aspects of the abortion and describing various contraceptive methods for the women's future use. The benefit of this latter part of counseling was commented on by nearly all the women; for example:

They sat down and told you everything they were going to do. It seemed more like you knew what was going on, so there wasn't anything to be nervous about because you knew what they were going to do and when they were going to do it and what was going on. (11)

In structuring abortions as a group phenomenon, the clinics violated the traditional medical norms of individual privacy—norms particularly salient in governing the areas of sex and reproduction, including abortion. Thus, although clinic personnel spoke in terms of trying to individualize or personalize the abortion experience (see Chapter 3), for some of the women the effect was just the reverse:

They assured me here at the clinic that the doctors . . . are real good doctors and things like that. And then, when I walked in there, there were just gobs of people there, and there was a real bad situation on one side as I walked through the door with a girl screaming and yelling and crying . . . and that kind of bothered me because I thought this whole ordeal was going to be a very structured, systematic thing and the only interruptions would be within your own self, but none of this other with all the people around and stuff. . . . (How did it make you feel?) Uneasy, just real uneasy. (7)

The only thing I really didn't like was how long and drawn out it was. I couldn't understand why, for just that simple procedure, I had to sit around that hospital [clinic] for seven hours . . . I hated it. It reminded me of the military: hurry up and wait, hurry up and wait. . . . They handled 15 abortions that morning. (Did that surprise you?) Yes, it really did. I thought it would be more of a private thing where a doctor would talk to me instead of going through all those channels. . . . (21)

Instead of a more personal experience, these women interpreted the clinic in the opposite way, once again applying the assembly line image of an abortion mill. The last woman quoted continues:

It seemed to me that they were trying to be personal by sticking me in a lounge with two people who said that they were social workers. They were trying to be, but that just turned me off. They answered a lot of questions for me but not as well as I thought a doctor could have. I just felt it was really just too much like cattle. I've had so much of that, standing in lines and getting shots in the arm and then moving on. (21)

The clinics' efforts to personalize the abortion experience raise an important and fundamental issue: the clinic view of how it should present itself versus the patient's view of how the clinic should present itself; that is, discrepancy between staff and patient definitions of an appropriate abortion facility.

In his ethnographic account of a prelegalization-period abortion clinic, Ball (1967) discussed the "rhetoric of legitimation" constructed by the clinic in order to "neutralize the context of deviance" and "generate a picture of legitimate activity." Ball defined "rhetoric" sociologically, as "a vocabulary of limited purpose; that is to say, it is a set of symbols functioning to communicate a particular set of meanings, directed and organized toward the representation of a specific image or impression" (p. 296). He went on to point out that such vocabularies include visual as well as verbal symbols. Using Goffman's (1959) notion of "fronts" (composed of an orchestrated "setting," "appearance," and "manner"), Ball described the clinic he studied in terms of how it attempted to legitimize abortion. The legitimate image offered was one of exaggerated cleanliness and competence produced by a "front" or "rhetoric" of medical professionalism in an expensive, luxurious setting. The clinic used what Ball called a "medical model" of legitimation. Unfortunately, Ball did not discuss how the audience—the women having abortions there—interpreted this "rhetoric."

What is striking in considering Ball's study is the contrast between the "rhetoric" he described and the "rhetoric" of the clinics in this study. In Ball's clinic, conventional medicine was the legitimation theme (for example, white uniformed staff with a clearly "professional" demeanor). The clinics in this study, with some important thematic variations, both adopted a "rhetoric" which *deemphasizes* the model of traditional medicine. Their focus is on deliberately avoiding rather than creating the "hospital look." Their philosophy is one of "humanizing" or "personalizing" abortion. In their view, traditional medicine is "sterile" and "cold" and "impersonal," which, as far as they are concerned, has the effect of making the patient more uneasy. Thus, personalization is seen as a way to relax the patient and make the abortion a more pleasant, comfortable experience.*

The way the clinics have tried to actualize this "rhetoric" can be viewed more systematically in terms of the Goffman distinctions among "setting," "appearance," and "manner" used by Ball.

We have already described the clinics' settings at some length—the exterior and environmental setting of both clinics as well as the interior decor. It might be mentioned here that Ball restricts "setting" to the interior. As we have shown, the broader setting provided by the building and its physical environment is extremely important in terms of clinic image. Through the reactions of clinic patients, we have learned that, largely because neither clinic resembled a hospital in the eyes of the women, the legitimacy of the clinics was thrown into question for as many as two-thirds of the women. Because of the low-income neighborhood and age and size of Clinic A's building, this clinic was viewed with particularly strong suspicion.

Once inside, Clinic B patients immediately entered a bright, modern suite. This put the women's suspicions to rest; the clinic was legitimate. Patients of Clinic A, on the other hand, entered a very plain, drab reception area. It was not until they had been admitted and paid part of their fee that they were allowed to go upstairs into a more brightly decorated area housing the actual clinic facilities. Clinic A women retained their original suspicion at least until they had gone to the upstairs area. It should also be noted that, while this area was indeed bright and newly decorated, it was also less sophisticated in style and probably less appealing to middle-class tastes than the interior decor of Clinic B. Certainly, while all the patients of Clinic B reacted favorably to the interior setting, not all of Clinic A's patients did so.

The variable interpretations of Clinic A's interior are evidenced in the following contrasting comments:

---

*Davis (1973) provides evidence to suggest that this orientation has its roots in the ideology of the abortion rights movement of the late 1960s and early 1970s.

> I figured it would be just plain old stark colors, and it's not. It's a blooming riot of color. They've got this—on the door they've got this stick-on. It looks like shelf paper. They've got that cut out in flower designs and stuff that matches the paint. It was great. The doors are all painted a different colored pastel than the walls and the woodwork's all different. It's all just—and the carpet, you know, it clashes, but it's real bright, cheery, riotous stuff. (29)

> The whole atmosphere—well, just like the curtains. They have daisy curtains. It looked like an old school building and yet they had tried to dainty it up like a little girl's room or something like that. (What did you think of that?) Oh, I would much rather it had been just white walls and white light . . . because the whole thing—I don't know, maybe some girls feel relaxed in that area, but I didn't because it just came across as phony to me. . . . I guess you'd say that it was shady, sneaky, sly. You know, dishonest. (7)

Disliking the interior and retaining their initial suspicions of Clinic A, more than one-third of the women who went there (9 of 24 or 37.5 percent, which represents almost one-fourth of *all* the clinic patients in this study), maintained a suspicious definition of Clinic A all the way through their abortion procedure.

The appearance of the staff, as we have indicated previously, was governed by the "rhetoric of personalization." White uniforms were not worn. Staff members were frequently indistinguishable from patients. This practice appears to have been viewed by the clinics as a way of fostering egalitarianism and discouraging the conventional doctor—patient/authority—submission dichotomy with the hope of relaxing and gaining the confidence of the patients. As previously quoted comments have indicated, some women questioned the absence of a white-uniformed staff. For them, seeing such attire would have been reassuring. For others, however, the desired effect was achieved:

> . . . everybody was dressed in their street clothes and you couldn't tell the—the doctor was dressed in street clothes and looked just like everybody else; and when she came in, she had to tell you that she was the doctor or you wouldn't have known. (Did you expect a more hospital type of atmosphere?) Yes, I did. I felt more comfortable, I think, because it wasn't. (11)

The manner or demeanor of the staff members was also directed toward maintaining the rhetoric of personalization. A traditional or hospitallike professional manner was deliberately avoided. As we have said, such a manner was thought to be cold and informal and upsetting for the patients. Thus, staff members emphasized a casual, friendly style of relating, with an overall orientation toward understanding and support. As with other aspects of the clinics' rhetoric, patients reacted variably. Most, however, found the manner of the staff relaxing—for example:

. . . they were really friendly. They made, I think, everybody really
feel just so much better because they were. They didn't run around
in their white nurses' uniforms. They were just real friendly. . . . It
made me feel better. (35)

This element of casualness was the essential ingredient in the women's
descriptions of the overall atmosphere of the clinics. For the majority of the
women, this atmosphere was interpreted favorably:

I didn't know what it was going to be like. I had no idea. And I was
pleasantly surprised. (What had you thought?) Just that it would be
a cold, technicallike place. And they weren't. They were just real,
warm, human people. (29)

Everything was so casual, so relaxed. That was the one thing about it
that kind of surprised me. I don't know, the hospitals here, they—
when I was there, they were kind of snotty, and there [the clinic],
they were nice. The atmosphere wasn't tense. It was relaxed. (10)

. . . the atmosphere was different. They weren't real uptight or anything like that . . . they treated you like a human being I thought.
(What had you expected?) I expected it to be very clinical, very
clinical—just a sign here, a sign there, go to this room and go in that
room. . . . I didn't expect any personalization. I didn't expect the
loose attitude about what we were doing . . . you didn't feel like you
were doing something bad or anything like that. (17)

The comments of these women suggest that the rhetoric of personalization was
"successfully" interpreted. The remark of the last woman further suggests that
the personalization of abortion, for some women, was a source of further
legitimation for their action. As the next comment shows, however, this was
not the case for all the women. For some, the personalization attempts had just
the opposite effect:

. . . it was an informal feeling. They didn't give a damn if you were
going to have an abortion. You were just a nameless person walking—well, this is number so and so. Just like a prison, more or less.
It was a cold feeling. When I had been in the hospital, the nurses
knew you and they were friendly. This place was cold and un-
feeling. . . . (23)

We have already discussed some explanations for the variation in interpretation of the clinics. As a further observation it should be pointed out that those
women who retained their early suspicions and applied the illegal abortion
stereotype throughout their abortion precedure tended to be the blue collar,

21-and-under group. These women questioned the fact that Clinic A did not exemplify the traditional medical model of health care. The remainder of the women who went the freestanding clinic route (26 of 35) resolved any suspicions they might have originally had and defined the clinics as appropriate medical facilities.

The Abortion

Let us now consider the actual moments when the abortion was performed. For the women at Clinic B, the procedure went quickly and smoothly:

> Then I went in for the abortion. It took about ten minutes. They explained to me everything they were doing as they went through the abortion. I had a hold of this lady's [counselor's] hand and I was just squeezing it as hard as I could. . . . (3)

> When you laid down for the procedure—I mean, they tried to do everything in the world to keep you from thinking about it, that it was going to hurt or anything. She [counselor] came up and took my hand, this young girl that was one of the girls I talked to and she just said, "Squeeze my hand as hard as you want to," and I said, "Well, I don't really want to do that. Just keep talking to me because if I don't think about pain then I won't have as much." (Did you?) No, not a lot. It was just a little bit. It wasn't really a pain. It was just kind of a little uncomfortable feeling. And it was a woman doctor—which was another thing which made me feel comfortable, I think. She was very nice. (31)

Several other women, like this one, commented favorably about having a woman doctor. They also, like Clinic A women, were particularly comforted by having the counselor there with them.

Clinic B women reported no disruptive elements during the performance of their abortions. The women at Clinic A, on the other hand, some of whom still questioned it as a legitimate medical facility, reported some disruption. One cause cited was the rock music which played during the procedure:

> . . . I was real quiet and real calm on the inside and then, when I went into the operating room, they had this real loud music going. . . . That automatically got me off balance because I completely had my mind geared in another direction and I never did adjust to that situation. . . . (Did you have any physical discomfort?) Umm, it seemed like there was more pressure than I had thought there would be . . . that kind of took me off guard a little. But she [counselor] stood right beside me and held my hand and she told me everything that he was going to do . . . I liked her talking to me to keep my mind off that lousy music. . . . (7)

... then they called me again and they said, "This is it." So I went
in this room and I lay down on this table. My counselor was with
me, you know, beside me, and I looked up at the walls and everything, and there was these psychedelic posters. . . . I could hear this
jazz music playing . . . you know, black music playing. . . . (How did
that make you feel?) It made me feel uncomfortable because you
don't expect to hear music playing and it's pretty loud. I was just
laying there and I was kind of tensing up . . . when you're thinking
that you're going to have an operation and all, you're thinking—well,
I do—I think of white sheets and everything and doctors and all,
like on TV. And when I saw this, it was just completely different
and I just sat there thinking, "What's going to happen next?" (13)

When the first woman later asked clinic personnel the reason for playing the
loud music, they reportedly said it was played to camouflage any screams that
might come from the procedure room. Ball (1967) also noted the playing of
music and offered the same explanation.

Another source of disruption among the still suspicious group was the
physician:

I was scared still . . . I remember what happened, but I was just kind
of in a daze. It scared me when the doctor walked in because he was
a little, short doctor and he had one of those things around his
head. . . . I don't know what you call them, but he came in there
and it reminded me of some old movie. You know, where the doctor
comes in, some quack or something. Then, I got kind of shaky. . . .
(9)

The doctor came in and he had this big thing on his head and it
make him look like a Frankenstein . . . I mean, he just looked like a
mad doctor or something. . . . (14)

As pointed out at the beginning of this section, the vacuum aspiration
procedure was generally reported to be much easier to go through than the
women had originally thought. The emotional nature of the procedure varied.
Many of the women spoke of the aspiration matter-of-factly, reporting no particular emotional reactions. Another woman's account, however, does reveal
the emotional nature of the experience:

... they prepared me, put my legs up and everything, and it was a
while before they went to work on me, but they finally started.
. . . I was kind of nervous, but I kept taking deep breaths, trying to
be calm . . . well, I was calm up to where he started dilating and that
hurt, so I was hanging on to her [counselor]. That hurt. And then,
when they started the suction bit, that's what got to me. It was kind
of sad. . . . (10)

After the abortion was completed, the women were taken to a recove_
room which was usually shared with one woman or more. They spent approximately an hour in this room. The last person quoted above continues:

> . . . then, when they got all done and everything, they took me into
> the recovery room and I felt fine. . . . (Did you still feel sad?) Oh,
> yes. I really felt sad. . . . I was laying there and there was another
> girl in there, one other girl. There were about six beds. I was facing
> her and she was having bad cramps and everything and I didn't feel
> like saying anything. I just lay there. I was sad and finally I was
> talking to her about it and asking her how she felt. And she was
> all right and everything, and I was thinking about it and I told her I
> thought it was sad and I started crying. I could have flooded out the
> place, only I kept thinking, "This is silly." (10)

The impact of being grouped together—specifically, the influence of other
patients on the woman's thinking and behavior—is further evidenced in another
account:

> I laid down and they gave me a coke and some crackers and put the
> heating pad on me and I was just sitting there looking around at the
> walls, and I looked at the girl that was supposed to go in next, and
> she just started crying her eyes out. She was crying real hard and
> that just hit me and I started crying. I cried for a little while and I
> almost fell asleep . . . then I had my hour and it was up. . . . (3)

AFTER THE ABORTION: TROUBLED OR UNTROUBLED

In the hours and first few days following the abortion, slightly more than
half the women (21) reported that they were completely untroubled by the
abortion and feeling fine:

> Oh, I felt great. . . . It didn't bother me at all. [My husband] said,
> "My God, you act like you've never been through it." No, I felt
> super. I didn't have any trouble at all.(5)

> I felt great. . . . When I come out of there, man, I was on top of the
> world. I didn't feel down. I didn't feel guilty. I didn't feel nothing.
> (29)

The women were advised to rest for several days after the abortion before
resuming their normal activities. Most reported they rested for a day or two.
Some went back to their normal routines the very next day:

> . . . I went right back to work. I was in pain while I was at work, but
> yet I didn't say anything. I'm sure I probably did things that I

shouldn't have done, but I had to because I didn't want to tell anybody. (6)

A typical comment made by these women was that their experience was something they tended to block out, something that seemed almost as though it had never happened:

> . . . it just doesn't seem like it happened. It just seems like part of my life that never did happen. I came home and lay down and went to sleep, got up and got my daughter and went to the grocery store, came home and watched TV and went to bed. . . . It seemed like those few hours I was down there never really existed, even though they did. I guess you just try and put them out of your mind. I guess that's what I did. You know, I just went about the rest of the day just like I would any other Saturday. I slept for about an hour, but I felt real good. (Did you go to work then on Monday?) Yes. (12)

> I kind of guess I blocked it out of my mind. I remembered what happened, but . . . I guess I just didn't want to think about it and I still don't, I guess, connect it—to really sit down and connect my being pregnant with what I did. In my mind, I never really connected my being pregnant with what I did. In my mind, I never really connected one with the other. (11)

While some in the untroubled group felt this sense of unreality about their abortions, others reported that they became more interested in the general topic of abortion than before. They often were more receptive to media coverage for example:

> I don't tune it out. I am usually more interested in it now. We had to do a research paper at school and I was going to do it on abortion, but I couldn't—that was kind of obvious and my boyfriend would have gotten mad at me if I would have done it. It interests me more whenever something comes up about it or I read something about it. I just see the word "abortion" and right away I read it. (3)

In contrast to those who were untroubled, the remaining 19 women reported some troubled thoughts following their abortions. The nature of these thoughts varied. One woman reported that she was very sad. Another woman reported she felt "empty":

> . . . everything was over with and I felt relieved, but then I felt— wow, I felt so empty. I just wanted to—ugh, I feel like crying thinking about it. . . . I just couldn't stand that. It still bothers me. (30)

Reflecting some of these same feelings, another woman spoke in terms of a reaction to the abortion which appears to resemble mourning:

> . . . I started crying in the wheelchair. Then the nurse bent over me and was really concerned with physical hurting, if I was all right and nothing was wrong with me physically. I said, "No, I'm sad" and "Just leave me alone," because that feeling—if the mother can't care, who can? Or if she can't—somebody has to cry. . . . I was just going through a period of, you know, decently I can show some grief just to be decent. Nobody else seemed to be decent about that at all, to me. There was just no decency. (21)

Women who reported no trouble or disruption after the abortion were nevertheless concerned about stigma and were carefully maintaining secrecy. Troubled women were even more concerned about the morality and appropriateness of what they had done. They, too, did not tell others; however, their primary orientation was toward coping with the abortion and their own doubts:

> It's not very pleasant, really . . . it's kind of something I'd just as soon forget. I mean, I'll always remember it, but I'd just as soon forget. (How was that week right after?) I had some, I don't know—I was thinking—some nights, you know how you just sit and think? You shouldn't do that sometimes, but I'd just sit and think about it and it would upset me. . . . I don't know, it was just like, "Why did I do it?" (28)

> (How did you feel afterwards?) I felt relieved. Later on in the day I had mixed feelings—by the time I got home I had mixed feelings . . . but then I got a hold of myself somewhat and I realized that this was a decision I had made and I had to learn to make decisions and stick to them. . . . It's kind of sad, but I try to think of abortion as little as possible. . . . (6)

The questioning of the abortion and the accompanying emotions had diminished somewhat by the time of the interview, six to ten weeks after the abortion. The feelings had not disappeared completely, but most women thought about it less frequently and with less intense feeling:

> It's a lot easier to discuss now than it was, but it's something that I can't put completely out of my mind and have no emotional reactions to because to me it was very important. It was something that was very hard. (6)

For the troubled group, as we have pointed out, coping was very important. These women were walking a thin moral line. With their abortions still problematic in their minds, the slightest event could further disrupt their postabortion lives. Thus, in contrast to the untroubled group, these women tried to avoid the subject of abortion as much as possible:

> . . . when I hear things, I don't know whether it's in my conscience or what, but whenever I hear things like on the news about abortion, I kind of block it out. I don't even listen to it. (And if you are reading something?) No, I don't even read anything. I just don't care to know about it. . . . (1)

> Well, I kind of avoid it just because I don't want to think about it. I know how I feel now and I don't feel guilty and I could change to think that I did the wrong thing. . . . (15)

The vulnerability of these women to information or events which would throw their past abortion into further question is well-illustrated in the following comment:

> (Have you thought about it much since you had the abortion?) Every now and then I started thinking—well, once especially when I saw—I was in a bookstore and I saw on the front of a magazine a picture of a 16-week-old fetus. It was on the cover of *Time* magazine. It was about abortion and I thought, "My God," because they told me if I was to see it right then it would look like a blood clot . . . that had really helped a lot, too, in making my decision because I couldn't think of it as a little person, you know. But then, I saw that picture and it kind of upset me for awhile, but I just said, "Don't think about it." (In what way did it upset you?) That it looked so much like a human. It looked so developed. I mean, when they had said it just looked like a blood clot, I thought it was kind of like when you break a chicken egg, you know. You can see the little white part that is supposed to be a chicken but you don't think you are killing a chicken or something. You just eat the egg. (Did it put doubts in your mind then or. . . ?) Oh, a little bit. I wondered about—since I believe in God, I wondered if it was the right thing to do. But I just said, "Well, if it was the wrong thing to do, I'll pay." But while I'm here on earth, I'd just as soon not think about it and not let it bother me. (15)

In another case, the woman's efforts to define the abortion as appropriate and to forget it, moving on to other things, were disrupted by the man involved in the pregnancy. Although they had ended their relationship, he continued to contact her:

> (In the period after the abortion, up until now, have you thought about it much?) No, I just want to block it out of my mind. (Can you always do that?) No. . . . Well, the only way it pops up, you

know, is if me and my girlfriend starts talking about it or if my ex-boyfriend calls and gives one of his prank telephone calls. (What does he do?) Oh, he'll call up and call me a murderer and things like that. (Does he still do that?) Yes, except for lately I haven't been at home when he's called—somehow, I've been dodging it. (2)

For another woman, the source of disruption was high school peers:

I've been having troubles, emotional problems . . . like when I came back to school they had stuff all over the bathroom walls like, "Jane Jones goes to bed with guys and then has abortions." And so, I was real upset . . . I was just walking down the halls real fast. I was practically crying. . . . (13)

She claimed not to have told any of these persons but speculated that perhaps her boyfriend had.

In summary, for those women already troubled by their abortion, the hostile reaction of others caused even more disruption. The woman was vulnerable to adverse reactions at the same time that she was trying to reduce the doubts and other problematic aspects of the abortion in order to achieve some degree of closure. This situation characterized most of the troubled group. Despite this, only two of the women reported that they definitely regretted the abortion. For most, rather, the issue was one of moral uncertainty—of struggling to define the abortion as a proper act. In short, the abortion remained somewhat ambiguous and unsettling for the troubled women; for those untroubled, it was a closed issue.

TROUBLED THOUGHTS AND AFFILIATION

The troubled-untroubled distinction among the study group in the days and weeks following their abortion fits into the smooth and disruptive patterns of abortion passage which were described at the end of Chapter 6. As Table 7.5 shows, those women who were affiliated at their entry into the abortion passage and whose subsequent passage could be characterized as smooth tended to be the women who reported having no troubled thoughts following the abortion. On the other hand, those women who were originally categorized as disaffiliated and whose subsequent abortion passage was characterized as disruptive also had a disruptive postabortion period. They reported having some troubled thoughts (such as sadness, emptiness, guilt, regret).

TABLE 7.5

The Presence or Absence of Troubled Thoughts Reported after Abortion, by the Configuration of the Women's Lives

| Troubled Thoughts after Abortion | Configuration of the Women's Lives | | | | | |
| | Affiliated | | Disaffiliated | | Total | |
	N	Percent	N	Percent	N	Percent
Present	5	(26)	14	(74)	19	(48)
Absent	16	(76)	5	(24)	21	(52)
Total	21	(52)	19	(48)	40	(100)

Source: Compiled by the author.

TELLING OTHERS AFTERWARD

As might be expected from the analysis just presented, very few of the women had told any additional persons about their abortion by the time of the interview. This fact simply underscores the general aura of deviance which they felt surrounded their abortion and their care to avoid being stigmatized. One woman, when asked if she were worried about anyone finding out, replied, "A little bit, because I'm afraid they would think less of me. . . . it bothers me."

Interestingly, most of the unmarried women said they would consider it important for their future husband to know that they had an abortion:

> I'd make it a point to tell him because I think it's—he's going to have to—he's going to be my husband and I think it's something he ought to know. I think that both people ought to be truthful with each other and tell each other everything. I think its only fair. (14)

When asked if they would consider ever telling their children, the women almost all replied, "No"; that is, unless one of their children got into a similar situation.

To conclude this chapter on the abortion procedure, a summary offered by one of the women interviewed seems particularly appropriate:

> (What kind of experience was it?) That's hard in a way—there were so many feelings all in this. Well, it was an *experience* I must admit. It wasn't as bad as I expected really. It was—I can't explain it. It was

weird. It was so quick. It's something that when it comes to deciding to have an abortion and you're there and you're going to do
it, OK, you get there and you do it. You know, it's got to be done,
so you go through with it. And after it's over, it's a relief, but yet
it's a feeling of emptiness. You don't want to go through it again . . .
but I do, I feel like I've learned a lot. I don't know how exactly. . . .
(30)

This woman's remark that she felt she had learned something implied some
kind of change. In the final and concluding chapters of this book we explore the
notion of change in the women's lives following the abortion.

8

MOVING ON:
RESTRUCTURING SOCIAL WORLDS
AND ESTABLISHING CLOSURE

INTRODUCTION

After the abortion, each woman's task was to reduce its problematic aspects so that she could establish a stable foundation from which to move on. For some this task was more difficult than for others, reflecting the differences between disruptive and smooth abortion passages.

In this chapter, we discuss some of the ways problematic aspects were reduced and the women's lives reorganized after abortion. First, we consider the women's social worlds, particularly their social relationships. Then we turn to their definitions of their abortion experience, directing special attention to the notion of abortion as a deviant act. Finally, we discuss the women's perceptions of how they might be different persons as a result of their abortion experience.

CHANGES IN SOCIAL RELATIONSHIPS

One way of looking at the impact of abortion on the social worlds of the women is to examine what happened to their relationships with others from the time they first suspected pregnancy to the postabortion interview. Of particular interest throughout this study has been whether or not the various phases of the abortion process were "smooth" or "disruptive"—whether or not, in other words, the abortion could be sociologically termed a "crisis." Thus, in examining any changes which might have occurred in the women's social relationships, we will focus on disruptions.

For purposes of analysis, we can separate the study group into two categories. One refers to women who experienced either no changes or who experienced only positive changes (changes which brought them closer) in their relationships with others. The second refers to women who experienced disruptions—relationships either broken off or substantially dissolved.

Disruption in Relationships

Slightly more than half of the women (22, or 55 percent) had a disruption in at least one social relationship central to their lives. For 20 of these 22 women, disruption occurred in the termination of their relationship with the man involved in the pregnancy. Some of these relationships were terminated by him, usually before the abortion. In others, the break was initiated by the woman, usually after the abortion—for example:

> I just don't want to have any more to do with him. . . . I just told him that this just wasn't going to work. . . . He really didn't know why I didn't want to see him anymore, but I just didn't want to mess with him anymore. (26)

> I'm saying I'm dating other people now, but he doesn't like to accept the fact. . . . I guess through this we got to know each other better and I realized some things that I didn't want to put up with in the future. . . . (22)

Frequently, the involvement and intimacy fostered by the pregnancy and abortion experience appeared to demand more intensity and commitment than the relationship could provide. This is illustrated by the following description of a relationship disintegrating after the abortion:

> (What happened between you two?) That's kind of—I don't really know. It got to the point where he was just—it's like he had been through all of this stuff with me and we weren't really getting along that well. He wanted me, or thought he did, but he also wanted out—he wanted his freedom now. He had had enough of close contact. He didn't want to admit it that he wanted to cut it off. He wanted to let it ride and wanted me to say, "Okay, whatever you say. If you don't want to see me tonight, fine," which I did. And then I started getting upset again, and we just had a lot of conflicts because he didn't want to see me as much and I still wanted to see him. He was starting to feel really guilty about it—about getting me pregnant—I thought maybe for a while we could both have a certain amount of freedom and still continue to date, but that didn't work either because I couldn't do it. We had to totally cut it off and be totally away from each other. So one night he called me up and . . . I said, "Well, look, just come over for an hour . . . and that will be it." And it was just like we both knew that it was going to be the end,

finish, we were going to cut it off. . . . We just couldn't do it. . . . We both felt it. There were things just beyond our control. You know, if I hadn't gotten pregnant, things might have been different; but, as far as things went, we both had so many emotional upsets, and this is all we have been thinking about for three or four weeks. So we just said, "Well, there is nothing we can do," and we never really said, you know, "Well, why don't we quit dating." I just said, "It's really tough," and he said, "Yes, I know," and I said, "I don't want to start crying," and he said, "Don't, because I will," and it was really strange. So after that, he avoided me in school. He would park on the other side of school. . . . I don't know where things are with him right now. My girlfriend says I should realize that it is over and go on, but I can't do it. There is just . . . we went through so much together. . . . (20)

The disintegration of the relationship with the man was not the only disruption. Two women reportedly each experienced a severe break with her sister as a result of the abortion:

With my sister-in-law, there is no difference in our relationship; but my sister—she doesn't call or come over or anything. She just lives across the street, but I never see her. . . . (1)

In both cases, the sisters were morally opposed to abortion.

In addition, three women experienced disintegrating relationships with friends who were opposed to the abortion and in three other cases women reported that they were no longer as close to their parents as they had been. Two of these women moved out of their parents' home after the abortion. As one woman explained, "I just don't want to stay there."

Maintaining and Cementing Relationships

While 55 percent experienced disruption in relationships, 45 percent (18 women) reported either no change or else a positive change in relationships with other persons. These other persons varied among parents, siblings, friends, and male partners. The positive change or increased closeness in the relationship was frequently attributed to "sharing" or to having confided in the other person.

Since the males involved in the pregnancy were almost always told (and told early), sharing and confiding particularly involved them. As we have illustrated, the abortion process frequently demanded too much from these relationships, resulting in their termination. In other cases, however, the relationships were already at a high level of intensity and commitment. The passage through abortion had the effect of strengthening or "cementing" them—at least, from the viewpoint of the women. For example:

I think that was the first time he ever actually has been concerned about me—*really* concerned. And I think the whole thing brought us closer because we had been through all of this soul-searching and had gone through the whole thing together. I think that it made us even closer than we were before. (17)

Only six of the women reported no change at all in their relationships. Three women, on the other hand, reported a major change. In two cases, the change was marriage, one a few days before the abortion and one soon after. The fact that the abortion precipitated the wedding was apparent:

It must have been during that week after the abortion. I decided—I was sad; and, besides that, it saddened me that my boyfriend had to leave again . . . and so I said, "This is ridiculous," and so that's when I decided I wanted to get married then. (10)

The third woman moved in with her boyfriend after her abortion and, at the same time, set a wedding date for several months ahead.

Changes in Relationships and Affiliation

As indicated in Table 8.1, whether or not the women experienced disruptive changes in relationships with others can be related to the affiliated-disaffiliated dichotomy, following the pattern established earlier. Those women who experienced no disruptive changes in their relationships tended to be the

TABLE 8.1

Frequency of Changes in Social Relationships by the Configuration of the Women's Lives

Changes in Social Relationships	Configuration of the Women's Lives				Total	
	Affiliated		Disaffiliated			
	N	Percent	N	Percent	N	Percent
Positive or no changes	14	(78)	4	(22)	18	(45)
Disruptive changes	7	(32)	15	(68)	22	(55)
Total	21	(52)	19	(48)	40	(100)

Source: Compiled by the author.

ones categorized as affiliated. Women who did report disruptions tended to be those categorized as disaffiliated.

In addition to restructuring their social relationships, the women also had to establish closure. By this, we mean that they had to make final sense, or come to an overall definition, of their abortion experience. In order to do this, they had to deal with the issue of responsibility.

DEVIANCE, RESPONSIBILITY, AND THE ABORTION

Throughout their abortion passage and into the postabortion period the women in this study were confronted with a discrepancy. Their view of themselves as "moral" persons was inconsistent with having an abortion, defined as immoral or wrong by the community (according to the women). In order to reduce this discrepancy and to establish closure on their abortion experience, the women adopted several ways of coping. As we have seen, they tended to carefully select and limit the people who knew about the abortion. After the abortion, their relationships with others were "adjusted" to eliminate persons who provided further disruption. Finally, they had to adopt a verbal stance on their abortion—a definition or interpretation of the situation. These ways of coping, if successful, would enable the women to move on into new experiences relatively free of unresolved questions about their abortion.

In this section, we consider the verbal positions taken by the women. It might be argued that, because abortion was recognized by the women as a deviant act within their community, they might have thought and spoken less highly of themselves afterward. Only one woman in the study, however, made any comment to this effect:

> . . . at first I thought, "Wow," you know, "I'm just not a good girl. I'm just another girl." I don't know. (Did you feel that it lowered you?) Yeah, it did. It still does make me feel that way. (30)

Most of the women, rather than accept the deviant implications that abortion held for them, appeared to continue to view themselves as "moral" persons, just as they were before the abortion. They were able to do this by using a particular verbal strategy when thinking and talking about their abortion.

A verbal strategy in coping with the aforementioned discrepancy could either accept or reject the committed act as deviant. The implication of deviance disappears if the act is considered to be "normal." The implications remain if the act is considered to be deviant unless the person is able to relieve herself of personal responsibility. Thus, the woman had two ways to retain her "moral" status, her self-worth: (1) she could reject the deviance of abortion, or (2) she could admit it, at the same time denying her own responsibility in having the abortion (Scott and Lyman, 1963).

Overwhelmingly, the women in this study chose the latter strategy. Two-thirds of the women made statements in which they portrayed themselves as having "no choice" in the matter of abortion, being "forced" to have the abortion:

> It was like I knew what I had to do and I was dead set on doing it, but I didn't want to. It was like I was being forced to do something, but that I didn't want to. (10)

> You know, at this point in my life and everything else, that's the only way. As far as I'm concerned, I don't see any other way—that there could be any other way. . . . I don't think it will bother me too much because it was the only way out and you have to accept that. (20)

> I was frightened of the abortion. And I was also sad as far as the child was concerned. I could feel for the part that would have been me. But, as far as circumstances go, I had no choice. (36)

Personal responsibility is the underlying theme in these comments. By portraying themselves as having no alternative other than abortion, these women guided others toward viewing them as victims rather than as perpetrators of the abortion. Responsibility for the act was abrogated.

The ultimate success of such a strategy is, of course, dependent upon the audience and the credibility of the woman's claim. Since so many of the women chose to deny personal responsibility rather than challenge the deviant definition of abortion, we can suggest that this was the approach that they perceived others could best accept. In other words, it appears that the women interpreted that it would be more effective for them to claim no responsibility—that they had no alternative in choosing abortion—than it would have been for them to claim that abortion is an acceptable act.

Two additional aspects of the women's postabortion comments support this view. First, while many women claimed to be more "understanding" as a result of their abortion experience, it can be suggested that perhaps their underlying abortion attitudes retained at least some of their earlier restrictiveness. If so, then this would certainly support the view that they did not significantly challenge or refute the notion of abortion as a deviant act. The woman quoted below became pregnant when she failed to take her birth control pills regularly. Her postabortion attitudes toward others who might be in her situation revealed that she continued to stigmatize some women having abortions:

> I think after having my abortion I can say that my views have changed some. I still don't believe in just going out and getting pregnant, having an abortion . . . just because you're too stupid or lazy to practice birth control. I think it all depends on each person's

reason. I know each person thinks they've got a good reason. Everybody's got a different reason. Some of them are a little bit stronger than others; some of them are just weak reasons, because they don't want the baby. (29)

Second, the women's comments concerning the nature of the fetus and the issue of whether or not abortion constitutes an act of killing also suggested that it was difficult for many of them to think of abortion as a nondeviant act.

Out of ethical concerns for the women and the deeply sensitive moral issues involved, the women interviewed for this study were not asked specifically about this topic. Nevertheless, only one-third of the women avoided the issue altogether. The remaining two-thirds offered their views.

While it is a central argument of many people who support abortion, and might be thought to characterize women who themselves have abortions, only 15 percent of the women interviewed made statements explicitly stating a belief that the fetus was *not* a person or human life:

I just personally don't look at a little fetus as being a person, and I don't agree with the argument that it is manslaughter. I just don't agree with that. (8)

When you are that far along, I don't really feel—I feel that it's something there, but I don't really feel that it's a life yet. . . . I don't feel that it is really a human life that early. (31)

I can't go along with the idea that from the moment of conception this is a person. (38)

On the other hand, and of central concern to the point being made, nearly one-fourth of the study group took the position in their comments that the fetus was, indeed, a life or baby or person. They also in many cases explicitly stated the related idea that abortion constitutes an act of killing that life:

I just felt like I was killing something. (9)

I thought it was terrible, taking a life. Something that is alive. You can't say that it's not because it is. No matter how small it is, it's still alive, and the thought of killing something like that just kind of makes you sick . . . you're killing something. (12)

We both realize that we've done something wrong, something immoral. It goes against our beliefs—taking a life is wrong. (19)

I didn't want to have the feeling of killing the baby and that's what I felt like. (30)

In addition, another 25 percent expressed confusion and their inability to completely come to terms with the question of the fetus:

> . . . I was brought up in the Church and I know that, as far as God and in the religious way, that it is wrong. Because that is taking a life—which I didn't really feel like—well, I don't know. I'm still kind of mixed-up about that, too—whether it was a life or whether not. (1)

> It was important in that you are making an important decision. Is this person going to live? I guess some people would say it isn't really a person—anyway, a one-day-old child that died would be much worse. (4)

What these statements reveal is that the notion of abortion as deviance was central in the women's thinking as they attempted to establish closure. Certainly, by denying full responsibility for their actions, they could protect their identity from stigma to some extent. How successful this will be in the long run is another question. Again, we conclude that many of these women were holding an acceptable definition of their abortion situation together with very fragile fabric. Of perhaps even more significance is the fact that, because of this fragility, a future disruption might throw the whole situation into question once again. The full problematic nature of the abortion would be reexposed.

In the final section of this chapter we consider another way in which the women attempted to establish closure—an additional impact the abortion experience appeared to have on their lives.

IDENTITY SHIFTS AND TURNING POINTS

For many of these women, the establishment of closure was enhanced by viewing the self as somehow "different" as a result of the abortion experience. In the majority of these cases, the changes were perceived as minor ones. Qualitatively, the women tended to look on their abortions as having taught them a lesson:

> I look back on it as a piece that taught me a lesson. . . . It was a little bit expensive lesson, but it taught me to just be a little more careful. (29)

> I think I'm going to be a more careful person than I was before; but, as far as being different, my attitudes toward abortion or anything, I really don't think I am. (12)

For some the learning experience appeared to be perceived as more significant. These women spoke in terms of maturation or the achievement of greater personal independence:

(Do you think the abortion had some effect or not?) Well . . . being independent, I think maybe I have achieved that because I was able to make the decision on my own, you know, and to go through with it. . . . I did something by myself, you know . . . without really going off the deep end. (11)

For me, it was a learning experience. I learned about myself and the emotional effects on me of a crisis situation. I felt good afterward because I think I overcame a crisis well. I feel good when I think about that. . . . (36)

I mean it made a big impact on me. I think I've grown more because of it, but I wouldn't recommend everybody to go out and do it to see how mature they can get. . . . (22)

(Do you feel like you are a different person now?) Maybe. More responsible. More able to make decisions. Like, I had to make a lot of decisions between that whole time—when to tell my mom and when to tell my dad and when to do this and when to do that. I just—I had more of a responsibility then and I've learned to take more responsibility and do what I have to do. . . . (3)

While the idea that one has changed or become a different person contributes to putting closure on past experience and helps one to move on to new situations, the notion of becoming a different person is also significant in this study because it tends to emerge from problematic situations. In the beginning chapter of this book, Thomas's observations about the passage of persons through taken-for-granted ("habitual" in his terminology) as well as "problematic" situations (Volkhart 1951) were introduced. The latter situations were described as those which necessitated persons to stop and take stock of themselves. In this sense, problematic situations provide a juncture for personal change and development.

Strauss (1959) has expanded upon Thomas's ideas and has written of such junctures as "turning points":

Some transformations of identity and perspective are planned, or at least fostered, by institutional representatives; others happen despite, rather than because of, such regulated anticipation; and yet other transformations take place outside the orbits of the more visible social structure, although not necessarily unrelated to membership within them . . . [There are] certain critical incidents that occur to force a person to recognize that "I am not the same as I was, as I used to be." These critical incidents constitute turning points in the onward movement of personal careers. . . . When the incident occurs it is likely to strike with great impact, for it tells

you: "Look! you have come way out to here! This is a milestone!"
Recognition then necessitates new stances, new alignments. . . .
(Strauss 1959, pp. 92-93).

Problematic situations or "critical incidents" require the person to reassess herself—to reflect on who she is, on priorities, commitments, and personal direction.

Abortion did not constitute a turning point in the lives of all the women
studied; in fact, it did not appear to constitute one in the fullest sense except for
a few women. These few, however, are important to note—four, in particular.

These four women were among those categorized as disaffiliated and,
hence, among those for whom the entire abortion experience was disruptive
rather than smooth. Even among the women who had a disruptive abortion passage, these women experienced particular disruption, especially in hostile reactions from others. The comments of these women illustrate the deep significance of Thomas's and Strauss's observations about the importance of extremely
problematic situations in shaping transformations of identity and in altering the
course of human careers:

> (After the abortion, would you say that your life continued pretty
> much as it was or . . .?) No, I think it really changed. I grew up very
> quick. And I learned—I had gotten very mixed up and I wasn't all
> that understanding. I had been *before* but then I had changed . . .
> and then after I was pregnant, then after I had the abortion, I be-
> came much more understanding. . . . (How important an event in
> your life was it?) Extremely. Very important. . . . This is the *biggy*.
> . . . I'm different. I look at things differently . . . just basically grow-
> ing up. . . . (6)

> . . . It [the abortion] just kind of made me change my life. I learned
> a lot from it . . . because I don't like to kid around and act like a
> little kid as much as I used to. I mean, like my friends will start
> acting a little dumb or something, you know, and I think, "Act your
> age," and they kind of get mad. But I can't help it. . . . I mean, I'm
> not trying to be that way. . . . I think I learned a lesson. . . . I just
> don't think I should have been doing it that young. . . . (16)

> I think more and more about nurses' training since I've had it [the
> abortion] done, because I got that out of the way and I've got my
> life sort of straightened out. . . . (Do you think that your abortion
> affected your life?) I think it kind of straightened me out. . . . I
> don't know. . . . I mean, now I'm not running around as much and
> everything. That's the main thing. And I feel more—oh, it's hard to
> explain. . . . (Do you like your view of the past?) No, I don't like
> it. . . . I feel a lot different, a lot better than the time before I had
> it. (9)

(How do you think that you will look back at this?) A great big mountain. It's one thing that will never come out of my life. . . . It makes me see all the things I've done wrong, and to help people out who have done the same things wrong. I don't know, it's made me grow up a lot. Really, because I can look back and see all the little dumb things I've ever done and sometimes laugh at them. . . . I quit smoking. I quit drinking. . . . It makes you think, you know, coming back here and looking at all your friends that do drink and stuff, how dumb you were. (32)

There is no way to know, from this research, where these women's paths will eventually lead. It is safe to say, however, that these four women in particular, and many of the other women studied as well, have picked up after their abortions and are moving on with a different perspective on their worlds—and, no doubt, a somewhat different identify.

9

The lengthy and detailed analysis included in the body of this book, in addition to the chapter summaries, makes repetition of all the various findings and discussion unnecessary. Thus, in this brief and final chapter, we concentrate on the two central conclusions which have emerged from this study: (1) the dual pattern of abortion exerience and the issue of crisis related to it, and (2) the fact that abortion continues to be perceived as a deviant act, even by those women who have abortions.

In this study, we have described in detail two overall patterns or ways in which the women of this study group experienced abortion. One pattern is characterized by disruption; the other is relatively smooth. After closely examining these two patterns at each of a series of stages in the abortion process, it is clear that women who began their passage well-integrated into their surrounding social worlds ("affiliated") were those who, all the way through, experienced relatively minor disruption. They reacted rationally and pragmatically to pregnancy. They received no negative or hostile reactions from others. They were clear about their abortion decisions from the beginning. After their abortions, they reported no troubled thoughts (doubts, sadness, guilt, and so on); and, in addition, they experienced only positive or, in some cases, no changes in their social relationships. Those women, on the other hand, who were "disaffiliated"— who began their passage detached, without tightly knit social bonds—experienced a relatively greater degree of disruption throughout the abortion passage. They reacted emotionally to pregnancy. They received some negative reactions from others to the pregnancy and abortion. They were confused and vacillated in making the decision. After their abortions, they were troubled about them. In addition, they experienced some disruption (either disintegration or complete breaks) in their relationships with others.

FIGURE 9.1

Relationship between Affiliation and the Two Patterns of Abortion Passage*

Smooth Passage

Rational reaction to pregnancy

1	2	3	4	5	6	7	8	9	10
		3	4	5		7	8	9	10
11	12					17		19	20
	22	23			26			29	
31			34	35	36			39	

One to four persons told

1	2	3	4	5	6	7	8	9	10
			4	5	6	7	8		
11	12			15		17		19	
		23			26				30
31				35		37		39	40

No negative reactions from others

1	2	3	4	5	6	7	8	9	10
			4	5		7	8		
11						17		19	
21	22								30
31			34	35	36	37		39	40

Clarity in decision making

1	2	3	4	5	6	7	8	9	10
1		3	4	5		7	8		10
11	12		14			17		19	20
	22	23			26			29	30
31		33	34	35	36	37		39	40

No troubled thoughts after abortion

1	2	3	4	5	6	7	8	9	10
		3	4	5		7	8		
11	12				16	17		19	20
	22	23						29	
31		33		35	36	37		39	40

Only positive/no changes in social relationships

1	2	3	4	5	6	7	8	9	10
		3	4	5		7	8		10
11				15		17		19	
21							28		30
31				34	35		37		40

Disruptive Passage

Emotional reaction to pregnancy

1	2				6				
		13	<u>14</u>	15	16		18		
21			24	25		27	<u>28</u>		30
	32	33				<u>37</u>	38		<u>40</u>

Five to eight persons told

1	2	<u>3</u>						9	<u>10</u>
		13	<u>14</u>		16		18		20
21	<u>22</u>		24	25		27	<u>28</u>	<u>29</u>	
	32	33	<u>34</u>		<u>36</u>		38		

Some negative reactions from others

1	2	<u>3</u>			6			9	<u>10</u>
	<u>12</u>	13	<u>14</u>	15	16		18		20
		23	24	25	<u>26</u>	27	<u>28</u>	<u>29</u>	
	32	33					38		

Confusion in decision making

	2				6			9	
		13		15	16		18		
21			24	25		27	<u>28</u>		
	32						38		

Some troubled thoughts after abortion

1	2				6			9	<u>10</u>
		13	<u>14</u>	15			18		
21			24	25	<u>26</u>	27	<u>28</u>		30
	32		<u>34</u>				38		

Disruptive changes in social relationships

1	2				6			9	
	<u>12</u>	13	<u>14</u>		16		18		20
	<u>22</u>	23	24	25	<u>26</u>	27		<u>29</u>	
	32	33			<u>36</u>		38	<u>39</u>	

Note: Women categorized as affiliated prior to entering their abortion passage are designated by underlining; those who were disaffiliated are not underlined.

Source: Compiled by the author.

The pattern and the differences just enumerated are clearly shown in Figure 9.1. It is the affiliation-disaffiliation dichotomy which distinguishes the women falling into one pattern from the women falling into the other at each juncture in the abortion process.

These two patterns of abortion experience provide insights bearing on the argument of whether abortion is a crisis or whether it is a medical procedure like any other. Abortion can be a crisis. On the other hand, it does not have to be. The way abortion is experienced depends largely on the woman's particular roles in her social world, the way she is tied to a social position. It also depends on the reactions of others to her abortion, on the type of medical facility where she has the abortion performed, and on her perceptions of that facility.

In other words, the way abortion is experienced is very much a product of the situational circumstances of abortion passage. These circumstances mediate previously socialized attitudes and established behavior patterns; and, in the long run, they appear to be more important. It should be pointed out that these findings stand in contrast to much of what has been previously concluded about women experiencing abortion. As we have discussed, past work has tended to focus on personality features typically viewed as permanent or constant or on attitudes of a particular type of upbringing, determined sociodemographically, as explanations for how a woman might experience abortion. The findings of this study support the view, stated at the outset, that human action largely reflects the situational demands and constraints of the present.

In demonstrating the importance of the women's relationships to society in influencing how abortion is experienced, we have given further support to Durkheim's notion of integration and the insulating power of socially cohesive groups (Durkheim 1951, pp. 210, 214). The sense of identity and purpose and social support provided by social groups can be viewed as having encouraged affiliated women to act decisively. These social bonds allowed an otherwise problematic situation to be enacted and made sense of with relative ease.

The second set of findings or conclusions in this study has to do with abortion as deviant behavior. Abortion, as we said at the beginning, is legal but, from the standpoint of public acceptance, it is not moral. Our study has verified this, at least in one Midwestern community. The women we studied tended to approve abortion only under very restrictive circumstances. Even when they themselves became pregnant, often under the very conditions for which they disapproved of abortion, their attitudes did not appear to change much.

That abortion is deviance was evident also in the women's constant concern about being stigmatized for their abortion. Afraid of negative reaction, of being viewed as immoral, they kept their abortion from as many people as they possibly could. They worried about other people finding out. They lied on the day of their abortions in order to keep their activities secret. Some went back to work before it was advisable, taking a medical risk, in order to keep the secret.

CONCLUSIONS

The abortions evoked the deviant, illegal abortion stereoty[.]
This became particularly clear in the women's observations upon fin[.]
abortion facility. The clinics' exteriors were unexpected and, therefore,
atic, throwing their appropriateness and legitimacy as medical facilit[.]
question.

Having an abortion put women who were not committed to a caree[.]
deviance in the position, nevertheless, of doing something, albeit briefly, which
was generally disapproved by the people around them—in many cases, by their
own families. The discrepancy between the women's views of themselves as
moral persons and the fact of having the abortion was a central problem which
they had to resolve in order to establish closure and move on to new situations.
As has been shown, the moral basis for abortion being viewed as deviance (abortion as the killing of a life) was denied explicitly by only 15 percent of the
women studied. Thus, the women appeared to retain the idea that they had committed an immoral act. In order to resolve the inconsistency between this and
their moral character, they attempted to deny responsibility for the abortion.
They talked in terms of being forced to have an abortion, of not having had a
choice. They did not, as they could have, talk in terms of themselves as lesser
persons as a result of the abortion, even though they knew that many persons
would consider them so.

To conclude the findings that abortion constituted deviance and to summarize the final position of the women, the act of abortion appears to have put
them in a fragile position as far as their worth as persons was concerned. The
women were balancing precariously. Even for those with a smooth abortion passage, one wonders whether, if in the future they were suddenly challenged about
the abortion, they would not find their experience, in retrospect, becoming
problematic. Perhaps to avoid such a possibility and to protect themselves, many
of the women tended to demarcate their abortion as a learning experience. They
cut themselves off from future negative implications by viewing themselves as
having changed. They took the position of being a different person now from
when they had the abortion. For most, this change was viewed as relatively
minor; that is, it did not drastically change them as persons. For others, however, the abortion was viewed as a major turning point in their lives.

TABLE A.1

Frequency of Pattern of Birth Control Use among the Women by Age

Pattern of Birth Control Use	Age					
	14-21		22-39		Total	
	N	Percent	N	Percent	N	Percent
Conscientious	0	(0)	3	(100)	3	(7)
Abandoned reliable method	9	(53)	8	(47)	17	(43)
Sporadic use	13	(87)	2	(13)	15	(38)
No use	5	(100)	0	(0)	5	(12)
Total	27	(68)	13	(32)	40	(100)

Source: Compiled by the author.

TABLE A.2

Frequency of Pattern of Birth Control Use among the Women by Marital Status

Pattern of Birth Control Use	Marital Status					
	Never Married		Ever Married		Total	
	N	Percent	N	Percent	N	Percent
Conscientious	1	(33)	2	(67)	3	(7)
Abandoned reliable method	7	(41)	10	(59)	17	(43)
Sporadic use	11	(73)	4	(27)	15	(38)
No use	5	(100)	0	(0)	5	(12)
Total	24	(60)	16	(40)	40	(100)

Source: Compiled by the author.

TABLE A.3

Frequency of Pattern of Birth Control Use among the Women by Education Level Achieved

Pattern of Birth Control Use	Education Level Achieved							
	Some High School		High School Graduate		Some College		Total	
	N	Percent	N	Percent	N	Percent	N	Percent
Conscientious	0	(0)	2	(67)	1	(33)	3	(7)
Abandoned reliable method	5	(29)	9	(53)	3	(18)	17	(43)
Sporadic use	4	(27)	5	(33)	6	(40)	15	(38)
No Use	4	(80)	1	(20)	0	(0)	5	(12)
Total	13	(32)	17	(43)	10	(25)	40	(100)

Source: Compiled by the author.

TABLE A.4

Frequency of Pattern of Birth Control Use among the Women by Social Class

Pattern of Birth Control Use	Social Class					
	Blue Collar		White Collar		Total	
	N	Percent	N	Percent	N	Percent
Conscientious	1	(33)	2	(67)	3	(7)
Abandoned reliable method	12	(71)	5	(29)	17	(43)
Sporadic use	6	(40)	9	(60)	15	(38)
No use	3	(60)	2	(40)	5	(12)
Total	22	(55)	18	(45)	40	(100)

Source: Compiled by the author.

TABLE A.5

Frequency of Pattern of Birth Control Use among the Women by Religious Affiliation

| Pattern of Birth Control Use | Religious Affiliation | | | | | | | |
| | Protestant | | Catholic | | Other | | Total | |
	N	Percent	N	Percent	N	Percent	N	Percent
Conscientious	2	(67)	1	(33)	0	(0)	3	(7)
Abandoned reliable method	10	(59)	6	(35)	1	(6)	17	(43)
Sporadic use	11	(73)	3	(20)	1	(7)	15	(38)
No Use	4	(80)	1	(20)	0	(0)	5	(12)
Total	27	(68)	11	(27)	2	(5)	40	(100)

Source: Compiled by the author.

TABLE A.6

Frequency of Pattern of Birth Control Use among the Women by Configuration of Social Life

| Pattern of Birth Control Use | Configuration of Social Life | | | | | |
| | Disaffiliated | | Affiliated | | Total | |
	N	Percent	N	Percent	N	Percent
Conscientious	1	(33)	2	(67)	3	(7)
Abandoned reliable method	9	(53)	8	(47)	17	(43)
Sporadic use	5	(33)	10	(67)	15	(38)
No use	4	(80)	1	(20)	5	(12)
Total	19	(48)	21	(52)	40	(100)

Source: Compiled by the author.

TABLE A.7

Frequency of Pattern of Birth Control Use among the Women Ages 14-21 by Social Class

| Pattern of Birth Control Use | Social Class | | | | Total | |
| | Blue Collar | | White Collar | | | |
	N	Percent	N	Percent	N	Percent
Conscientious	0	(0)	0	(0)	0	(0)
Abandoned reliable method	7	(78)	2	(22)	9	(13)
Sporadic use	5	(38)	8	(62)	13	(48)
No use	3	(60)	2	(40)	5	(19)
Total	15	(56)	12	(44)	27	(100)

Source: Compiled by the author.

METHODOLOGICAL NOTES

A description of the research setting and a systematic account of the method by which data for this study were collected have already been given. The purpose of this appendix is to fill in some of the gaps—particularly those of a behind-the-scenes nature. Included here, then, is a brief outline of the natural history of the study and some of the important decisions that were made. Also included are some personal observations about intensive interviewing and the relationship between researcher and interviewee. Finally, a description is given of the procedures used in organizing and analyzing the data.

THE DEVELOPMENT OF THE STUDY

This research took approximately three and a half years from its earliest inception to its completion. For the first year, I knew that I wanted to study abortion and that I wanted to study it from the standpoint of the lives of the women involved; but beyond that, in terms of specific research questions and design, I was uncertain. My first decision was to begin to find out more about abortion by reviewing the research literature and observing and talking with both patients and the providers of abortion services in the community where I lived. This meant visiting clinics and, at one point, doing participant observation as a pregnancy counselor trainee. During this period I took notes, jotting down all my ideas, observations, and preliminary research questions.

By the end of the first year, I had collected a volume of these notes and "insights." I had also received an encouraging boost from the University of Minnesota Graduate School in the form of a modest research grant. By that time, too, two major problems had been solved. First, I had developed a clear picture of the theoretical perspective with which I would enter the field and which would underpin the direction of my interviews. Secondly, the obvious had finally occurred to me: by trying to specify variables and further limit the scope of the study, I had been spending time trying to do ahead of time exactly what the study should be designed to tell me. In other words, my study was going to be exploratory.

With the realization that what I really needed were data and not a study designed so that all the variables and relationships were planned in advance, the project crystallized in my mind. I went back to all my notes and jottings from the preceding 18 months and started to make an outline that eventually became my interview guide.

The next problem was finding subjects. That took about three months. Of central importance was obtaining as systematic a sample as possible in order to be able to assess representativeness. I finally concluded that a good way to obtain a sample would be to use the clients of an abortion clinic or hospital as a sampling frame. The women would be contacted at the facility and interviewed about a month later. I contacted four different facilities. All expressed interest in the project, but none was willing to give me access to clients. One of my disadvantages, in failing to secure cooperation, was not having a sponsor, someone to help establish my legitimacy. Another disadvantage was that the facilities themselves had little to gain from cooperating, at least in their view. Three were private facilities and were essentially businesses. In the last analysis, they didn't want to do anything that might harass their clients and thereby jeopardize their business.

Finally, I contacted a fifth facility, the public health clinic referred to as Midville Clinic. This clinic provided family-planning services, offering abortion referrals rather than actually performing abortions. At Midville Clinic, apparently out of interest in the topic (I still had no sponsor), staff members were extremely enthusiastic and volunteered to do all they could to help me. What emerged were the beginnings of a plan to select interviewees. To repeat, if a researcher must work with an agency or organization while collecting data, then having a sponsor is extremely important. At Midville Clinic, one particular staff member became my *de facto* sponsor. This person served to further legitimize my presence to other staff members and was an intermediary through whom I could pass along information to others of the staff who were helping me secure volunteers. Having an in-house sponsor as a liaison was particularly important when problems arose.

Having finally established a way to select subjects, I began to contact the women. It took another six weeks, however, before the interviews could begin and another five months before the interviewing was completed. Nearly two and a half years had elapsed.

SOME PERSONAL OBSERVATIONS ON INTENSIVE INTERVIEWING

Much has been written about how to and how not to interview. My purpose here is not to rehash what can be found in any number of sources on interviewing but, rather, to add a few observations about my own work.

Because of the particularly sensitive subject matter of abortion, I defined my role to be as nonjudgmental, supportive, and understanding as possible. I gave the women facial and verbal signs of encouragement as they went along. One technique I found very useful was to repeat back to the woman part of what she had just said. Frequently, I would do this to stimulate her to continue, so I would end in an open-ended way—for example, "So, you have said that you told your brother. . . ?" By leaving the statement hanging, the interviewee was encouraged to finish it herself, continuing the story. Repeating back in this way also appeared to please the women in that it showed them that the interviewer was listening. Only when this open-ended technique failed did I explicitly ask probing questions.

Another technique I found helpful when asking questions about possibly threatening topics (for example, what birth control practices had been followed) was to repeat the questioning at several different points during an interview. This technique was used for key questions as well as for sensitive ones. In the case of threatening topics, the woman might initially be prone to give a socially acceptable answer. Reintroducing the topic later allowed her either to confirm or to clarify earlier statements and, often, to add more detailed information.

People like to talk about themselves as long as they feel comfortable doing so. The women in this study were no exception. One point, however, must be elaborated. I have emphasized the fact that most of the women in this study were concerned with keeping their abortion secret. At least half were also troubled after their abortion and were trying to forget about it. Why, then, would they volunteer to be interviewed and readily offer such open and detailed information?

First, it must be pointed out that wanting to keep the abortion secret and not wanting to talk about it are two different things. As long as the women felt they would not be stigmatized and as long as they felt the person confided in would not tell others, the women appeared quite willing (even anxious at times) to talk. For many, talking about the abortion appeared to be therapeutic. A woman may previously have felt the need to talk to someone but may not have been willing to seek out a listener, particularly a professional, because that would have involved admitting "needing help." This study provided a channel for the woman to talk, without its being defined as a therapeutic session.

Secondly, the interviewer was a stranger—not a part of the woman's world and someone she would be likely not to see again. The interviewer was also a professional who would not discuss the interview with anyone else. For these reasons, the women may have felt they could talk about their most private lives and feelings relatively freely.

Finally, the study was presented to the women in terms of offering them a chance to help others. Thus, for those who really wanted to help, it gave them a vehicle. For those who wanted to talk for therapeutic reasons, it gave them a "cover"—that is, they could think of it in terms of helping others.

For most women, all these reasons were probably important in explaining their willingness to talk openly.

Just how the women actually perceived the interview situation is impossible to know. Some insight into this question, as well as into the motivations of the women volunteering, is provided by the following comment from one of the interviewees:

> ... I told my roommate that I was going to come here and talk to you about this and that I wanted to be sure and be here. . . . And she said, "I wouldn't want to talk to anybody about it." And I just thought that was kind of interesting and I said, "Well, why not? This lady is trying to do—well, that's what sociology is all about, you know. Sociologists all do research." And I said, "That's what they do; they write, they gather up all this information, and they do it to help people." And I said, "I feel that my opinion, although it's maybe not all that good or that bad, if I can help I will. . . . " (31)

ANALYZING THE INTERVIEW DATA

After the interviews were completed, another key decision involved whether to take (or "code") only certain material off the tapes or whether to transcribe all the material into written form, doing the coding later. In order not to miss important insights, to get the full significance of the women's own words (in context), and to be sure to capture the continuity of abortion passage (which events led to which others), I decided in favor of verbatim transcriptions. This was a costly decision in terms of time. Working full time, it still took several months to transcribe all the material. (The project was now in its third year.) Another advantage of transcribing, however, is that, if the researcher does it, it provides an opportunity to hear all the interviews another time. Thus, while transcribing, I reaffirmed and modified old hunches about the data as well as developing new ones.

Perhaps the most crucial part of a qualitative, analytical study such as this one is organizing and making sense out of the masses of data which one produces (approximately 800 pages of single-spaced typewritten material was generated from the 40 interviews). How did I go about organizing all this material? The first step was to make two copies of the original set of transcribed interviews. One copy was to be used for reading and making notations during the analysis; the other copy was to be cut up into the quotations which eventually would be incorporated into the manuscript. The original copy was left intact and unmarked. The original had been typed for easier reading using both red and black—red for the interviewer's remarks; black for the respondents'.

The analysis copy of each interview was separated into two parts, one dealing with the time period before each woman started suspecting pregnancy and the other dealing with the time after. The second part was marked at the point where the day of the abortion was discussed. These divisions were made for purposes of quick identification—to avoid having to read the entire interview in order to find a particular stage of abortion passage.

The data were analyzed and written up chapter by chapter—in effect, by stages in the passage. Taking as an example the chapter on decision making, I will attempt to explain the procedures followed. First, taking the interview guide, I made an initial outline of all the questions which pertained to this particular stage of abortion passage. Then I read all the material in each interview relevant to that stage, writing down topics, possible category systems, and any observations as I went along. Then I reorganized my outline, modifying it accordingly. With this tentative chapter outline, I went back through all the interviews a second time, this time tabulating frequencies of certain events and noting the page and interview numbers of all quotations pertaining to each topic. This was done on a master chart. Each woman was listed by her identification number, the numbers running along one side, and all the various things I wanted to record were listed across the top, for example, number of persons told, content of interaction with the male, and so on.

At this point, I turned to the second copy of the data set. I went through each interview again, cutting out the quotations I had noted on my chart and pasting them on individual sheets of paper, noting the topic each pertained to and the identification number of the woman. Eventually, I had several hundred sheets which I could organize into piles by topic and category. For example, I had a pile of quotations describing what the decision-making period was like. Reading the quotations in this pile, I was able to categorize them eventually into one group expressing "confusion" and another group expressing "clarity."

A chart was made and piles of quotations accumulated for each chapter. Using the outline, I wrote the chapter, taking into account the frequencies of events, qualitative categories and quotations, and additional observations, all of which were noted on the chart.

By using separate copies, one for reading the interviews and another for the actual cutting up of the interviews, I did not lose track of whether I had already used a particular quotation or not. As soon as one comment was cut out of an interview, I stapled to a clean sheet of paper the section preceding the comment and the section following it, with a space where the missing quotation had been. Thus, each interview was kept in sequence and it was easy to tell which parts had already been used.

The process of analyzing, writing, and rewriting took approximately another year—an exhausting yet exhilarating period of time.

Aarons, Z. A. 1967. "Therapeutic Abortion and the Psychiatrist." *American Journal of Psychiatry* 124 (December): 745-54.

Adler, N. 1975. "Emotional Response Following Therapeutic Abortion." *American Journal of Orthopsychiatry* 45: 3 (April): 446-54.

Aitken-Swan, J. 1971. "Some Social Characteristics of Women Seeking Abortion." *Journal of Biosocial Sciences* 3 (January): 96-100.

Alan Guttmacher Institute, The. 1975. "The Unmet Need for Legal Abortion Services in the U.S." *Family Planning Perspectives* 7 (5) (September/October): 224-30.

American Law Institute. July 30, 1962. *Model Penal Code*. Changes and Editorial Corrections in May 4, 1962. *Proposed Official Draft*. Philadelphia: American Law Institute.

Aptekar, H. 1931. *Anjea: Infanticide, Abortion and Contraception in Savage Society*. New York: Wm. Godwin.

Arney, W. R. and W. H. Trescher. 1976. "Trends in Attitudes Toward Abortion, 1972-1975." *Family Planning Perspectives* 8 (May/June): 117-24.

Athanasiou, R. et al. 1973. "Psychiatric Sequelae to Term Birth and Induced Early and Late Abortion: A Longitudinal Study." *Family Planning Perspectives* 5 (Fall): 227-31.

Ball, D. 1967. "Abortion Clinic Ethnography." *Social Problems* 14 (Winter): 293-301.

Bates, J. 1954. "The Abortion Mill: An Institutional Analysis." *Journal of Criminal Law, Criminology, and Police Science* 45: 157-69.

Bates, J. and E. Zawadski, 1964. *Criminal Abortion*. Springfield, Illinois: Charles Thomas.

Beck, M. B. 1971. "Abortion: The Mental Health Consequences of Unwantedness." in R. B. Sloane, ed. *Abortion: Changing Views and Practices*. New York: Grune and Stratton.

Becker, H. S. et al. 1961. *Boys in White: Student Culture in Medical School*. Chicago: University of Chicago Press.

Blake, J. 1971. "Abortion and Public Opinion: The 1960-1970 Decade." *Science* 175 (February 12): 540-49.

———. 1973. "Elective Abortion and Our Reluctant Citizenry: Research on Public Opinion in the United States.", in H. Osofsky and J. Osofsky, eds. *The Abortion Experience: Psychological and Medical Impact*. New York: Harper and Row.

Blumberg, B. and M. Golbus. 1975. "Psychological Sequelae of Elective Abortion." *Western Journal of Medicine*, 123: 3 (September): 188-93.

Blumer, H. 1969. *Symbolic Interactionism*. Englewood Cliffs: Prentice-Hall.

Bolter, S. 1962. "The Psychiatrist's Role in Therapeutic Abortion: The Unwitting Accomplice." *American Journal of Psychiatry* 119 (October): 312-16.

Bourne, J. P. 1972. "Abortion: Influences on Health Professionals' Attitudes." *Journal of the American Hospital Association* 46 (July 16): 80-83.

Bureau of the Census. 1973. *1970 Census of Population: Volume I. Characteristics of the Population*. Washington: Government Printing Office.

Calderone, M., ed. 1958. *Abortion in the United States*. New York: Hoeber-Harper.

Cates, W. and R. Rochat. 1976. "Illegal Abortions in the United States, 1972-1974." *Family Planning Perspectives* 8 (March/April): 86-92.

Center for Disease Control. 1977. "Abortion Surveillance 1975." Washington, D.C.: Department of Health, Education, and Welfare, April.

Char, W. and J. McDermott. 1972. "Abortions and Acute Identity Crisis in Nurses." *American Journal of Psychiatry* 128: 8 (February): 66-71.

Cobliner, W. G. 1974. "Evaluating Teenage Abortion Requests." *Orthopanel* 19, Raritan, New Jersey: Ortho Pharmaceutical Corp. 2-5.

Cutright, P. 1971. "Illegitimacy: Myths, Causes, and Cures." *Family Planning Perspectives* 3:2 (January): 25-48.

David, H. P. 1972. "Abortion in Psychological Perspective." *American Journal of Orthopsychiatry*, 42 (January): 61-68.

Davis, N. J. 1973. "The Abortion Market: Transactions in a Risk Commodity." Ph.D. dissertation, Michigan State University.

Deutsch, H. 1945. *Psychology of Women*. vol. 2. New York: Grune and Stratton.

Devereux. 1955. *A Study of Abortion in Primitive Societies*. New York: Julian Press.

Diamond, M. et al. 1973. "Sexuality, Birth Control and Abortion: A Decision-Making Sequence." *Journal of Biosocial Science* 5: 347-61.

Dobrofsky, L. 1974. "Female Role Perceptions Which Influence Decisions about Pregnancy." Paper presented at the Midwest Sociological Society Meetings, April, Omaha.

Dunbar, F. 1954. "A Psychosomatic Approach to Abortion and the Abortion Habit." in H. Rosen, ed. *Therapeutic Abortion*. New York: Julian Press (re-released in 1967 as *Abortion in America*).

Durkheim, E. 1951. *Suicide*. New York: The Free Press.

Duster, T. 1970. *The Legislation of Morality*. New York: The Free Press.

Festinger, L. 1954. "A Theory of Social Comparison Processes." *Human Relations* 7: 117-40.

Finkbine, S. 1967. "The Lesser of Two Evils." in A. Guttmacher, ed. *The Case for Legalized Abortion Now*, Berkeley: Diablo Press. 15-25.

Fleck, S. 1970. "Some Psychiatric Aspects of Abortion." *Journal of Nervous and Mental Disease* 151 (July): 42-50.

Ford, C., P. Castelnuovo-Tedesco, and K. D. Long. 1972. "Women Who Seek Therapeutic Abortion: A Comparison with Women Who Complete Their Pregnancies." *American Journal of Psychiatry* 129 (November): 546-52.

Foote, N. 1951. "Identification as the Basis for a Theory of Motivation." *American Sociological Review* 16 (February): 14-21.

Friedman, C. M., R. Greenspan, and F. Mittleman. 1974. "The Decision-Making Process and the Outcome of Therapeutic Abortion." *American Journal of Psychiatry* 131: 12 (December): 1332-37.

Galdston, I. 1958. "Other Aspects of the Abortion Problem: Psychiatric Aspects." in M. Calderone, ed. *Abortion in the United States*. New York: Hoeber-Harper.

Gebhard, P. et al. 1958. *Pregnancy, Birth, and Abortion*. New York: Harper Brothers.

Goffman, E. 1959. *The Presentation of Self in Everyday Life*. Garden City: Doubleday, Anchor.

Gusfield, J. R. 1967. "Moral Passage: The Symbolic Process in Public Designations of Deviance." *Social Problems* 15 (Fall).

Hall, C. S. and G. Lindzey. 1957. *Theories of Personality*. New York: John Wiley.

Harper, M. W., B. R. Marcom, and V. D. Wall. 1972. "Do Attitudes of Nursing Personnel Affect the Patient's Perception of Care?" *Nursing Research* 21: 4 (July-August): 327-31.

Henslin, J. 1971. "Criminal Abortion: Making the Decision and Neutralizing the Act." in J. Henslin, ed. *Studies in the Sociology of Sex*. New York: Appleton-Century-Crofts.

Himes, N. E. 1963. *Medical History of Contraception*. New York: Gamut Press (first ed. 1936).

Johnson, D., et al. 1974. *Churches and Church Membership in the United States: 1971*. Washington: Glenmary Research Center.

Jones, E. F. and C. F. Westoff. 1973. "Changes in Attitudes Toward Abortion: With Emphasis Upon the National Fertility Study Data." in H. Osofsky and J. Osofsky, eds. *The Abortion Experience: Psychological and Medical Impact*. New York: Harper and Row.

Kane, F. J. et al. 1973a. "Emotional Reactions in Abortion Services Personnel." *Archives of General Psychiatry* 28 (March): 409-11.

——. 1973b. "Motivational Factors in Abortion Patients." *American Journal of Psychiatry* 130 (March): 290-93.

Kimmey, J. 1973. "How Abortion Laws Happened." *Ms.* (April): 48-49.

Lader, L. 1973. *Abortion II: Making the Revolution*. Boston: Beacon.

Lee, N. H. 1969. *The Search for an Abortionist*. Chicago: University of Chicago Press.

Lessard, S. 1973. "Aborting a Fetus: The Legal Right, The Personal Choice." in E. Morrison and V. Borosage, eds. *Human Sexuality: Contemporary Perspectives*. Palo Alto: National Press Books.

Lidz, T. 1954. "Reflections of a Psychiatrist." in H. Rosen, ed. *Therapeutic Abortion*. New York: Julian Press (re-released in 1967 as *Abortion in America*).

Lofland, J. 1966. *Doomsday Cult: A Study of Conversion, Proselytization, and Maintenance of Faith*. Englewood Cliffs: Prentice-Hall.

——. 1971. *Analyzing Social Settings*. Belmont, California: Wadsworth.

Luker, K. 1976. *Taking Chances: Abortion and the Decision Not to Contracept*. Berkeley: University of California Press.

Manning, P. 1971. "Fixing What You Feared: Notes on the Campus Abortion Search." in J. Henslin, ed. *Studies in the Sociology of Sex*. New York: Appleton-Century-Crofts.

Marder, L. 1970. "Psychiatric Experience with a Liberalized Therapeutic Abortion Law." *American Journal of Psychiatry* 126 (March): 1230-36.

Margolis, A. et al. 1971. "Therapeutic Abortion Follow-Up Study." *American Journal of Obstetrics and Gynecology* 110: 243-49.

Mascovich, P. R. et al. 1973. "Attitudes of Obstetric and Gynecologic Residents Toward Abortion." *California Medicine* 119 (August): 29-34.

Maxwell, J. W. 1970. "College Students' Attitudes Toward Abortion." *The Family Coordinator* 19 (July): 247-52.

McCormick, E. P. 1975. *Attitudes Toward Abortion*. Lexington, Mass.: Lexington Books.

Mead, G. H. 1934. *Mind, Self and Society*. Chicago: University of Chicago Press.

Merton, R. 1957. *Social Theory and Social Structure*. Glencoe: The Free Press.

Miller, R. S. 1975. "The Social Construction and Reconstruction of Physiological Events: Acquiring the Pregnancy Identity." Paper presented at the Midwest Sociological Society Meetings, April, Chicago.

Miller, W. B. 1973. "Psychological Vulnerability to Unwanted Pregnancy." *Family Planning Perspectives* 5: 4 (Fall): 199-201.

Mills, C. W. 1959. *The Sociological Imagination*. New York: Oxford University Press.

Moore, E. C. 1973. "Abortion: Ambiguity and Ambivalence." Paper presented at the American Sociological Association Meetings, August, New York.

Niswander, K. R. and R. Patterson. 1967. "Psychologic Reaction to Therapeutic Abortion I: Subjective Patient Response." *Obstetrics and Gynecology* 29 (May): 702–06.

Notman, M. T. 1973. "Pregnancy and Abortion: Implications for Career Development of Professional Women." *Annals of the New York Academy of Science* 208 (March): 205–09.

Osofsky, H. and J. Osofsky, eds. 1973. *The Abortion Experience: Psychological and Medical Impact.* New York: Harper and Row.

Osofsky, J. and H. Osofsky. 1972. "The Psychological Reaction of Patients to Legalized Abortion." *American Journal of Orthopsychiatry* 42 (January): 48-60.

Patt, S., R. Rappaport, and P. Barglow. 1969. "Follow-Up of Therapeutic Abortion." *Archives of General Psychiatry* 20 (April): 408-14.

Payne, E. et al. 1973. "Methodological Issues in Therapeutic Abortion Research." in H. Osofsky and J. Osofsky, eds. *The Abortion Experience: Psychological and Medical Impact.* New York: Harper and Row.

Pearson, J. F. 1973. "Social and Psychological Aspects of Extra-Marital First Conceptions." *Journal of Biosocial Science* 5: 453-96.

Peck, A. and H. Marcus. 1966. "Psychiatric Sequelae of Therapeutic Interruption of Pregnancy." *Journal of Nervous and Mental Disease* 143 (July-December): 417-25.

Peyton, F, A. Starry, and T. Leidy. 1969. "Women's Attitudes Concerning Abortion." *Obstetrics and Gynecology* 34 (August): 182-88.

Pohlman, E. 1969. *The Psychology of Birth Planning.* Cambridge: Schenkman.

——. 1971. "Abortion Dogmas Needing Research Scrutiny." in R. B. Sloane, ed. *Abortion: Changing Views and Practices.* New York: Grune and Stratton (originally in *Seminars in Psychiatry*, August, 1970).

Pomeroy, R. and L. Landman. 1973. "American Public Opinion and Abortion in the Early Seventies." in H. Osofsky and J. Osofsky, eds. *The Abortion Experience: Psychological and Medical Impact.* New York: Harper and Row.

Presser, H. 1974. "Early Motherhood: Ignorance or Bliss?" *Family Planning Perspectives* 6 (Winter): 8-14.

Reichelt, P. and H. Werley. 1975. "Contraception, Abortion and Veneral Disease: Teenagers' Knowledge and the Effect of Education." *Family Planning Perspectives* 7 (March-April): 83-88.

Rosen, R. A. H. and L. J. Martindale. 1975. "Abortion as Deviance: Traditional Female Roles vs. The Feminist Perspective." Paper presented at the American Sociological Association Meetings, August, San Francisco.

Rosen, R. A. et al. 1974. "Some Organizational Correlates of Nursing Students' Attitudes Toward Abortion." *Nursing Research* 23 (May-June): 253-59.

Rosenblatt, D. and E. Suchman. 1964. "Blue-Collar Attitudes and Information toward Health and Illness," in A. Shostak and W. Gomberg, eds. *Blue Collar World: Studies of the American Worker*. Englewood Cliffs: Prentice-Hall.

Rossi, A. 1966. "Abortion Laws and Their Victims." *Trans-Action* (September): 7-12.

———. 1967. "Attitudes on Abortion." in A. Guttmacher, ed. *The Case of Legalized Abortion Now*. Berkeley: Diablo Press.

Roth, J. 1963. *Timetables: Structuring the Passage of Time in Hospital Treatment and Other Careers*. Indianapolis: Bobbs-Merrill.

———. 1972. "Some Contingencies of the Moral Evaluation and Control of Cleintele: The Case of the Hospital Emergency Service." *American Journal of Sociology* 77: 5 (March): 839-56.

Russell, K. and E. Jackson. 1973. "Therapeutic Abortion—The California Experience." in H. Osofsky and J. Osofsky, eds. *The Abortion Experience: Psychological and Medical Impact*. New York: Harper and Row.

Sandberg, E. and R. Jacobs. 1971. "Psychology of the Misuse and Rejection of Contraception." *American Journal of Obstetrics and Gynecology* 110 (May 15): 227-42.

Sarvis, B. and H. Rodman. 1973. *The Abortion Controversy*. New York: Columbia University Press.

Schwartz, R. H. 1968. *Septic Abortion*. Philadelphia: Lippincott.

Scott, M. and S. Lyman. 1963. "Accounts." *American Sociological Review* 33 (February): 46-62.

Selltiz, C. et al. 1959. *Research Methods in Social Relations*. New York: Holt, Rinehart and Winston.

Shah, F., M. Zelnik, and J. F. Kantner. 1975. "Unprotected Intercourse among Unwed Teenagers." *Family Planning Perspectives* 7 (February): 39-44.

Shelton, J., E. Brann, and K. Schultz. 1976. "Abortion Utilization: Does Travel Distance Matter?" *Family Planning Perspectives* 8 (November/December): 260-62.

Sherman, J. 1971. *On the Psychology of Women*. Springfield, Illinois: Charles Thomas.

Sherwin, L. and E. W. Overstreet. 1966. "Therapeutic Abortion Attitudes and Practices in California Physicians." *California Medicine* 105: 337-39.

Simon, N. et al. 1967. "Psychiatric Illness Following Therapeutic Abortion." *American Journal of Psychiatry* 124 (July): 59-65.

Simon, N. and A. G. Senturia. 1966. "Psychiatric Sequelae of Abortion: Review of the Literature." *Archives of General Psychiatry* 15 (October): 378-89.

Smith, J. C., R. Kahan, and W. Burr. 1974. "Abortions in the United States: Before and After the Supreme Court Decisions." Paper presented at the American Association of Planned Parenthood Physicians, April, Memphis.

Sorensen, R. 1973. *Adolescent Sexuality in Contemporary America*. New York: World Publishing.

Spengler, J. J. 1931. "The Decline in Birth-Rate of the Foreign Born." *Scientific Monthly* XXXII (January): 57.

Steinhoff, P. G. 1973. "Background Characteristics of Abortion Patients." in H. Osofsky and J. Osofsky, eds. *The Abortion Experience: Psychological and Medical Impact.* New York: Harper and Row.

Strauss, A. 1959. *Mirrors and Masks: The Search for Identity*. Glencoe, Illinois: The Free Press.

Taussig, F. J. 1910. *The Prevention and Treatment of Abortion*. St. Louis: C. V. Mosby Co.

———. 1942. "Effects of Abortion on the General Health and Reproductive Functions of the Individual." in H. Taylor, ed. *The Abortion Problem*. Baltimore: Williams-Wilkins.

Tietze, C. 1974. "Experience with Legal Abortion in the United States." Paper presented at the International Congress of Medical Sexology, August, Paris.

Tietze, C. and S. Lewit. 1973. "A National Medical Experience: The Joint Program for the Study of Abortion (JPSA)." in H. Osofsky and J. Osofsky, eds. *The Abortion Experience: Psychological and Medical Impact*. New York: Harper and Row.

———. 1969. "Abortion." *Scientific American* 220 (January): 21-27.

Villard, H. 1926. "Legalized Elimination of the Unborn in Soviet Russia." *Journal of Social Hygiene* (May).

Volkhart, E., ed. 1951. *Social Behavior and Personality: Contributions of W. I. Thomas to Theory and Social Research*. New York: Social Science Research Council.

Walter, G. S. 1970. "Psychologic and Emotional Consequences of Elective Abortion." *Obstetrics and Gynecology* 36 (September): 482-91.

Weinstock, E. et al. 1975. "Legal Abortions in the United States since the 1973 Supreme Court Decisions." *Family Planning Perspectives* 7 (1) (January-February): 23-31.

Westoff, C., E. C. Moore, and N. B. Ryder. 1969. "The Structure of Attitudes Toward Abortion." *Milbank Memorial Fund Quarterly* XLVII (January): 11-37.

Wilson, D. C. 1954. "The Abortion Problem in the General Hospital," in H. Rosen, ed. *Therapeutic Abortion*. New York: Julian Press (re-released in 1967 as *Abortion in America*).

Wiseman, J. P. 1970. *Stations of the Lost: The Treatment of Skid Row Alcoholics.* Englewood Cliffs: Prentice-Hall.

Wolf, S. R., T. T. Sasaki, and I. M. Cushner. 1971. "Assumption of Attitudes Toward Abortion During Physician Education." *Obstetrics and Gynecology* 37: 141-47.

Zahourek, R. 1971. "Therapeutic Abortion and Cultural Shock." *Nursing Forum* 10: 1: 8-17.

Zelnik, M. and J. F. Kantner. 1975. "Attitudes of American Teenagers Toward Abortion." *Family Planning Perpsectives* 7 (2) (March-April): 89-91.

MARY K. ZIMMERMAN is an NIH Research Fellow and Adjunct Instructor in the Department of Community Health at the University of Kansas Medical School. From 1972 to 1974 she was instructor of Sociology at the University of Wisconsin, River Falls.

Dr. Zimmerman has published articles and reviews appearing in *Sociology of Languages of American Women* and *Teaching Sociology*. Reflecting her interest in women and health, she is currently studying hypertension and job pressures among employed women.

Dr. Zimmerman holds aa B.A. from the University of Michigan, Ann Arbor, and an M.A. and Ph.D. from the University of Minnesota, Minneapolis.

THE FERTILITY OF WORKING WOMEN:
A Synthesis of International Research

edited by Stanley Kupinsky

IMPACT OF FAMILY PLANNING PROGRAMS
ON FERTILITY: The U.S. Experience

Phillips Cutright and
Frederick S. Jaffe

SEX AND CLASS IN LATIN AMERICA

edited by June Nash
and Helen Icken Safa

WOMEN AND MEN: Changing Roles, Relationships,
and Perceptions

Libby A. Cater and
Anne Firor Scott with
Wendy Marfyna

WOMEN AND WORLD DEVELOPMENT: With
an Annotated Bibliography

edited by Irene Tinker,
Michele BoBramsen, and
Mayra Buvinic

WOMEN'S INFERIOR EDUCATION: An Economic
Analysis

Blanche Fitzpatrick

WOMEN'S RIGHTS AND THE LAW: The Impact of
the ERA on State Laws

Barbara A. Brown, Ann E. Freedman,
Harriet N. Katz, and Alice M. Price